BOSWELL'S

ENLIGHTENMENT

BOSWELL'S
Enlightenment

Robert Zaretsky

THE BELKNAP PRESS OF
HARVARD UNIVERSITY PRESS

Cambridge, Massachusetts
London, England
2015

Library of Congress Cataloging-in-Publication Data

Zaretsky, Robert, 1955–

Boswell's enlightenment / Robert Zaretsky.

pages cm

Includes bibliographical references and index.

ISBN 978-0-674-36823-1 (cloth : alkaline paper)

1. Enlightenment—Scotland. 2. Philosophy and religion—Scotland—History—18th century.

3. Boswell, James, 1740–1795—Travel—Europe.

4. Authors, Scottish—18th century—Biography.

5. Scots—Europe—History—18th century.

6. Travelers—Europe—History—18th century.

7. Europe—Description and travel. I. Title.

B1302.E65Z37   2015

828'.609—dc23

[B]   2014037309

To my father, Max Zaretsky, and stepmother, Adele Zaretsky,

for their support and love over the years

CONTENTS

BOSWELL'S
ENLIGHTENMENT

THE VIEW FROM
ARTHUR'S SEAT

Voltaire, Rousseau, immortal names!

IN 1756, JAMES BOSWELL and William Temple, their friendship recently formed at the University of Edinburgh, strode down the city's broad High Street, which stretched eastward from the great castle that glowered over the city to the Canongate and Holyrood Abbey, the city's ancient seat of religious authority. Past the Luckenbooths, a dark mass of wooden commercial stalls lining the street; past the knots of pedestrians and stands of itinerant salt and peat sellers, fishwives and scissors-grinders, balladeers and soliloquists, water porters hunched under great barrels of fresh water, women pushing low carts filled with yellow sand, shouting "Ye-sa" and doling out their goods to servants and wives to clean their stone floors; past carriages splashing through the puddles reflecting the dull sky; past the occasional squealing pig or stray chicken darting in front of the narrow and severe faces of gray stone residences: the boys were too immersed in elevated thoughts to pay much heed to what Daniel Defoe had declared the "largest, longest and finest Street for Buildings and Numbers of Inhabitants, not in Britain only, but in the World."[1]

Longest and largest, perhaps, but not always the finest. The young friends more than once leaped across the gutters that served as the town's sewer system. Until very recently, to the rolling of drums and chorus of voices bellowing "Gardyloo"—a phrase thought to be of French origin, warning pedestrians "Prenez garde de l'eau"— buckets of slop were tossed from windows at 10:00 p.m., their foul contents splattering onto the street where they remained until the arrival of scavengers. Even then, enough remained "to offend the eyes, as well as the other organs of those whom use has not hardened against all delicacy of sensation."[2] The two friends hardly noticed the "Wha wants me?" Man, walking along High Street with a chaise percée for needy passers-by. The floppy overcoat he wore, though not fashionable, was practical, providing a modicum of privacy to his clients.[3]

Nor did they pay any more heed to the High Kirk of St Giles, the great Gothic church whose nave scarcely two centuries before had echoed to the fierce sermons of John Knox. Founder of the Scottish Reformation, Knox and his followers overthrew the "synagogue of Satan," better known as the Catholic Church. In the rubble of shattered stained glass and splintered crosses, Knox laid the foundations of the Church of Scotland, known as the Kirk, and its severe worldview that made no room for theater and dancing, gambling and music. For those residents unwilling to surrender such pastimes, the Kirk used pillories, scourges, and ducking stools as means of persuasion. When these tools failed, there were always public executions to focus, if not the mind of the heretic, at least the minds of those gathered to watch.

Yet, Knox's declaration "All worldlie strength, yea even in things spiritual, decays, and yet shall never the work of God decay" was borne out by the two young men who continued to converse with great animation, Temple with an English accent, Boswell with a

Lowlands lilt, about literature and theater and art—the very pastimes Knox had vainly tried to expunge.[4] They reached the end of High Street and descended along increasingly narrow streets, past low doorways of tenements piled high with several floors of "flets"—the local word for flats—against the walls of which an occasional denizen might prop himself to sleep off a binge at one of the city's many taverns.

They descended into Holyrood Park, where the pile of Holyrood Palace stood, half-submerged in a mossy bottom, and headed for the foot of Arthur's Seat, the hill bulging nearly a thousand feet above the city. The view from the summit was breathtaking. The eye easily glimpsed the great flat expanse of the Firth of Forth to the north of the city, beyond the densely packed maze of buildings, veined by wynds and narrow streets. One's breath could also be taken away, quite literally, by the bristling skyline of funnels belching hundreds of tons of coal smoke into the air, earning the city the moniker "Auld Reekie," Middle Scots for "Old Smokey."

The city slowly receded below as the friends clambered along the path traversing the ancient volcano, passing herds of sheep grazing on the moist turf. For Temple, the son of an English merchant just south of the border in Berwick, this was the first ascent. But not so for Boswell, whose ruddy complexion had, through exertion, turned bright crimson. Upon reaching the rocky summit, he put his arm through Temple's as they walked past the ruins of a small and ancient chapel. As if they had long rehearsed this moment, they fixed their eyes on the eastern horizon and shouted with all the abandon of their sixteen years: "Voltaire, Rousseau, immortal names!"

————————

With the European continent to one side, Edinburgh to the other, James Boswell stood above what seemed the one and same phenomenon: the Enlightenment. But neither the view nor viewer is straightforward. James Boswell and Enlightenment are as complex as the coils of wynds and streets forming the old town of Edinburgh below. A few preliminary words, then, are called for on both the man and his times.

Until recently, the Enlightenment was one, not many. It was a single event that spanned eighteenth-century Europe; a single event that ranged far and wide, but whose language was French and capital was Paris.[5] In its salons and academies thrived, as the historian Peter Gay noted, the "party of humanity." There were, he announced, "many *philosophes* in the eighteenth century, but there was only one Enlightenment."[6] These philosophes broadcast the good news of modernity: the rightness of reason, the possibility of progress, and the existence of a set of laws governing all societies. These men and women did not deny that reason and social laws might be variously expressed according to place and time, or that progress would be a slow and uneven process. But they did believe that beneath the welter of linguistic and geographical differences, behind the chaos of historical events, below the heavy sands of tradition and superstition, there abided a single and unchanging set of values.

Two hundred and fifty years later, the simplicity of this view has given way to a more complex picture. Indeed, in just the fifty years since Gay's book, our understanding of the era has dramatically changed. In a sense, historians have retraced Boswell's climb of Arthur's Seat and, upon reaching the summit, are less dazzled than dizzy. The passing centuries have made our perspective richer and denser; the accumulated weight of historical research has collapsed the standard model of a single Enlightenment. In his insistence on a "unified field theory" for the Enlightenment, Gay is the historical profession's Einstein. Time has taken its toll on Gay's various metaphors—"party," "family," and "flock"—that imposed a kind of unity on the conflicting and contradictory characteristics of the Enlightenment. Like physicists working in the shadow of Heisenberg and Bohr, historians have since resigned themselves to a phenomenon that refuses to obey any single set of laws.

But beyond this negative consensus—that the Enlightenment was not what we once thought it was—there is little agreement as to what it was, when it was, and where it was. In regard to its geographical contours, the Enlightenment has long since surged beyond the walls of Paris. Historians have underscored, for instance, the importance of Holland in the early phase of the Enlightenment. The religious tolerance and proto-republicanism of the United Provinces provided a kind of intellectual hothouse in the last decades of the seventeenth century, allowing radical thinkers like Benedict Spinoza and Pierre Bayle to flourish.[7] Much has been written on Great Britain, a nation once thought immune to the Enlightenment, if only because it was empty of French philosophes. More recently, though, historians like J. G. A. Pocock and Roy Porter have argued that the British Enlightenment did not parallel the French experience for the simple reason that the British had already freed themselves of the oppressive political institutions found across the Channel.[8]

These recent works on the Enlightenment, which range across the Western hemisphere, reflect an emphasis on national contexts.[9] But for some historians, geographical borders are misleading; for them, it is less "each country had the Enlightenment it deserved," as Gay remarked, than "each *county* within each country had the Enlightenment it deserved."[10] As Charles Withers argues, not only were national identities problematic in the eighteenth century, but so too was the linguistic, economic, and cultural stew of communities found within a single national border. Thus, "what was once taken as the Scottish Enlightenment differed in fact within and among the towns of Aberdeen, Edinburgh, Glasgow and even smaller centers."[11]

A similar flux also afflicts the Enlightenment's chronology. When confined to France's borders, the Enlightenment stretched no further back than early eighteenth-century thinkers like the Baron de Montesquieu, author of *The Spirit of the Laws* and *Persian Letters*. Of course, historians readily acknowledged the impact of Francis Bacon, Isaac Newton, and John Locke on France: How could they not when the French themselves praised this trio of Englishmen? But they tended to focus on Locke's work, thus locating the beginnings of the Enlightenment at the end of the seventeenth century. More recently, historians like Jonathan Israel have argued for a longer eighteenth century—or depending on one's preference, a shorter seventeenth century. Until 1650 or thereabouts, Israel claims, European civilization shared the same religious, political, and philosophical beliefs. After the century's midpoint, however, that same civilization began to fissure. "Everything, no matter how fundamental or deeply rooted, was questioned in the light of philosophical reason and frequently challenged or replaced by startlingly different concepts generated by the New Philosophy and what may still usefully be termed the Scientific Revolution."[12]

Israel's work also reflects our abiding uncertainty over the conceptual and social contours of the Enlightenment. Earlier scholars like Gay located the revolutionary spirit of the Enlightenment in the work of the eighteenth century's usual suspects: the flock who built, volume by volume in the mid-eighteenth century, the monumental nest of the *Encyclopedia*. But Israel and others have taken issue with this interpretation. The standard bearers of the radical Enlightenment, they argue, are Baruch Spinoza and Pierre Bayle, not Voltaire and d'Alembert. What other historians take to be the high noon of the Enlightenment in the mid-eighteenth century was in fact its dusk. For Israel, the Enlightenment's "most crucial developments were already over by the mid-eighteenth century."[13]

In a similar fashion, cultural historians like Robert Darnton question the traditional focus on a "High Enlightenment" that starred celebrated philosophes who, when not writing great works, were busy exchanging bons mots in the literary salons of Paris. Such a focus, Darnton warns, ignores the subversive work of the "Low Enlightenment." This Parisian Grub Street was a mirror universe to polite society and literary salons, a collection of embittered wannabes who, enamored by the prospect of joining forces with the philosophes, had quit their provincial homes and moved to Paris. But rather than finding a welcome mat, they instead bumped into closed doors. Once a movement dedicated to liberating humankind from the shackles of tradition and superstition, the Enlightenment had become an institution no less exclusive and conservative than the ones it replaced. These young men, spurned by their erstwhile heroes, turned their pens against them. In the shadowy world of clandestine publishing, these disappointed suitors denounced not only the claims of Church and state, but also mocked the pretensions of the Enlightenment.[14]

Roy Porter, in his seminal *Flesh in the Age of the Enlightenment,* reminds us that keeping body and soul together—or, indeed, keeping them apart—was not just a metaphor for life on Grub Street, but also one of the most compelling issues of the age. The great advances made in the physical sciences during the eighteenth century inevitably came at the expense of traditional religious beliefs. What were the ties, if any, between body and soul? Was there even a place for the soul if man was, as Locke declared, a blank slate or, as the French philosophe La Mettrie later affirmed, a machine? Were the soul and self one and the same? Was the self yoked to the body?

Or, as Locke suggested, was it the sum total of an individual's experiences—that which "has reason and reflection, and can consider it self as it self"? At the same time, the imperative to know oneself came to mean also knowing one's body. As the wildly influential early eighteenth-century journal the *Spectator* declared, even the pagan Galen "could not but own a Supreme Being upon a Survey of this his Handywork."[15] As for the passions that drove and disturbed this "Handywork," could they be mastered by reason? Was the self in control, or instead did deeper and greater forces control the self?

Running through the Enlightenment, be it High or Low, Radical or Moderate, is the common cause on behalf of "philosophical reason." But philosophical reasoning turned out to be reasoning without end: once launched, the Enlightenment had no final port or destination. It is this endless voyage that defines the nature of the Enlightenment. If it were a ship, the Enlightenment's name could well be *Sapere Aude:* "Dare to Know." Toward the end of the eighteenth century, Immanuel Kant used this phrase in his well-known essay, one written long after the movement's heyday: "What is Enlightenment?" The phrase has panache but is also problematic, for it implicitly denies the possibility or desirability of an ending. By its very nature, the pursuit of knowledge will never reach a climax or resolution. The grand questions asked by the men and women of the Enlightenment remain with us today. How can we best define human liberty? On what basis do we proclaim human equality? What are the rights and duties of the citizen? How do we determine the limits of the state? What constitutes the good life?

These questions all presuppose the centrality of the individual. Debate over the individual's place in society and his role in the world goes back as far as Socrates, just as explorations of the inner self are as old as Augustine. Early modern thinkers like Montaigne posed the great question "What do I know?" But it was only in the late seventeenth and eighteenth centuries that such questioning became widespread and systematic. The Enlightenment's emphasis on individual autonomy and individual rights, private goods and private lives, differed from the understanding non-Western cultures held of the relationship between the individual and his world. More significantly, if only for Europeans, it also differed from the way in which their ancestors had understood this same relationship. From an earlier world that subordinated the individual to collective identities, a world which itself was subordinated to the designs of a supreme maker, the Enlightenment turned the relationship on its head: the world was now subordinated to the wills and desires of autonomous human beings. The proper study of humankind was no longer the hereafter, but the here and now; no longer the ways of God, but the ways of man and woman.

It is here that the *Sapere Aude* collided against the great reefs of faith and religion—a collision that the philosopher Charles Taylor has called "The Great Disembedding." This "disembedding" was, in part, social. As Taylor notes, the sort of self-questioning we now take for granted had no place in this earlier world.[16] It was, he asserts, as inconceivable for medieval or early modern men and women to ask themselves "What would it be like if I were someone else?" as it is for us *not* to ask ourselves this same question. Life then was collective, not discrete; its "purpose" fixed by tradition and religion, not individual aspirations or efforts. That we now not only ask such questions about our lives, but that the question of identity has become so central to our lives is, for Taylor, "the measure of our disembedding."[17]

This led to a more radical, though more elusive, kind of disembedding, marking our banishment not just from a coherent and cohesive society, but also from a meaningful and purposeful cosmos. In Max Weber's celebrated distinction, the "enchantment" of our ancestral world evaporated, leaving behind the dust-dry landscape of "disenchantment." The causes of this spiritual drought were many, but the relentless sun of philosophical reason is chief among them. Once it was enlightened, the world banned the supernatural; it was seen as a machine, liable to scientific explanation, just as it became a vast material depot, condemned to commercial exploitation. Reason not only threatened to consume a world that had been transformed into an object, but also to consume itself. As Friedrich Nietzsche scribbled in his notebook more than a century ago, the "nihilistic consequences of our natural sciences—from its pursuits there follows a self-decomposition, a turning against itself."[18]

The legacy of the Enlightenment has been, in so many respects, a good and great thing. A world without the values of freedom, equality, and justice; denied the claims of reason, tolerance, and dialogue; stripped of individual action and achievement would be inconceivable. But at the same time, these benefits have come at tremendous cost. Far-sighted critics who lived during the first great waves of the Enlightenment were already tabulating this grim balance sheet. Jean-Jacques Rousseau and Joseph de Maistre, J. G. von Herder and Giambattista Vico, Edmund Burke and J. G. Hamann disputed the reigning orthodoxies of the age. Their insights have since been adopted by critics of the Enlightenment hailing from all points of the ideological compass, from traditional conservatives and progressive communitarians to Marxist and postmodern theorists. At the very least, what all of these camps hold in common is Marx's diagnosis that, with the ascendancy of Western reason, "all that is solid melts into air." As Taylor notes, we are "now in an age in which a publicly accessible cosmic order of meanings is an impossibility."[19] A merely secular outlook "involves stifling the response in us to some of the deepest and most powerful spiritual aspirations that human beings have conceived."[20] In the end, it is not the rightness of the Enlightenment's methodology we question, but instead the rightness of the world it has given us.

Few places offer a better view of the *Sapere Aude*'s voyage than Arthur's Seat in the mid-eighteenth century. While the *Sapere Aude* was launched in seventeenth-century Great Britain and built by the likes of Newton and Locke—or, perhaps, in Holland where it was designed by Spinoza—and made Paris one its first ports of call, the ship was captained —or, perhaps, *commandeered*—by Scottish thinkers.

Yet, the nationality of the ship's crew has not always been recognized as Scottish. The term "Scottish Enlightenment" was coined scarcely more than a century ago and its meaning, and at times even validity, have been debated ever since.[21] A prominent historian of the era, Richard Sher, asserts that the Scottish Enlightenment remains an "enigma."[22] The enigmatic character is due not just to the intellectual contents of this particular enlightenment, but how these contents spilled into and affected the world. While it is "true that Scottish philosophy made an impact," another historian of the era, Michel Malherbe, notes, "it is also true that it meant different things at different times and in different places."[23]

Historians will never agree whether, as the title to a recent history of the Scottish Enlightenment claims, the Scots "invented the modern world."[24] But they would certainly agree that the Scots have lent themselves to an academic cottage industry. Dozens of scholarly monographs and popular histories dedicated to capturing this elusive phenomenon have been published ever since Hugh Trevor-Roper declared open season on the Scottish Enlightenment in a

celebrated address in 1967. The distinguished historian, who subsequently expounded on the self-invention of Scotland, defined
this historical period as "that efflorescence of intellectual vitality
that became obvious after the defeat of the last Jacobite rebellion
in 1745."[25]

Of course, it is in the self-interest of historians to declare their
particular subject as one shrouded in confusion—hence the great
need for their own books. But there decidedly is something odd to
this "efflorescence of intellectual vitality." Contemporaries were already aware of this quality to Scottish intellectual life. David Hume
spoke for his generation when he wondered how it was that a nation like Scotland, struggling under great political, economic, and
linguistic handicaps, had nevertheless become the center of such
remarkable intellectual activity. "Really it is admirable how many
Men of Genius this Country produces at present," Hume wrote to
a friend in 1757. "Is it not strange that, at a time when we have lost
our Princes, our Parliaments, our independent Government, even
the presence of our chief Nobility, are unhappy in our Accent &
Pronounciation, speak a very corrupt Dialect of the Tongue which
we make use of; is it not strange, I say, that, in these Circumstances,
we shou'd really be the People most distinguish'd for Literature in
Europe?"[26] Across the Channel, the high priest of the French Enlightenment, Voltaire, agreed. With his tongue only partly in cheek,
he declared "today it is from Scotland that we get rules of taste in
all the arts, from epic poetry to gardening."[27]

As their remarks suggest, Scotland's native son seemed as surprised as his celebrated French contemporary that so unlikely a
place as Scotland had become the capital of enlightened thought.
It happens that both men also knew one of this capital's most remarkable, yet representative figures—the very same youth who had

shouted Voltaire's name from the heights of Arthur's Seat and who would soon lay siege to that venerable Frenchman at his Swiss estate of Ferney. And it was less than two years after he scaled Arthur's Seat that he sallied to Hume's Edinburgh residence where, having gained admittance to the house, engaged the notorious philosopher in a long and wide-ranging chat on subjects of genius, style, and history. As he reported in a letter to Temple, Boswell was not only "entertained" in Hume's company, but he also reaped a "great deal of usefull instruction."[28]

Boswell has himself entertained readers of his journals, but the journals also provide a great deal of useful instruction. Few individuals reported in so sustained and thorough a manner as did Boswell from the front lines of the Enlightenment. He was a child of his era's embrace of reason, its quest for material and intellectual improvement, and its devotion to progress. As a student at university in Edinburgh, Boswell plunged into the intellectual revolution of his time and rode the great swells of the Scottish Enlightenment. He read widely (if not always deeply) and conversed excitedly (if not always wisely) with the greatest thinkers of his age, revealing a genius for friendship that won over the likes of Adam Smith, Lord Kames, and Adam Ferguson, as well as Hume. In London, Boswell attached himself most famously to Samuel Johnson, but also befriended David Garrick and Oliver Goldsmith, John Wilkes, and Joshua Reynolds. On the European continent, when not barging into the lives of Rousseau and Voltaire, he swerved wildly off the beaten track, risking life and limb by sailing to Corsica to meet the revolutionary leader Pasquale Paoli.

In many ways, Boswell's continental tour in the mid-1760s maps the complex nature of the Enlightenment. Consider his simple joining of Voltaire's and Rousseau's names at the top of Arthur's

Seat. Though both thinkers are central figures in the Enlightenment, their profound differences were already clear to a perceptive observer like Boswell. Voltaire and Rousseau disagreed mightily on the nature and place of culture and civilization, theater and literature, politics and education. But their different attitudes toward faith and God made for an even starker contrast, particularly in the wake of yet another event that occurred shortly before Boswell's yelp from Arthur's Seat: the Lisbon earthquake of 1755. Between the poles of Voltaire's skepticism and despair and Rousseau's faith and acceptance swung the feelings and thoughts of Boswell, as well as many of his contemporaries.

Popular historical accounts tend to see the shifts from one historical era to another in simple and straightforward fashion, one where the Age of Faith neatly folded up shop and gave the keys to the Age of Reason. But the view from Arthur's Seat in 1756 reveals a very different process, one that witnessed a slow and uneven retreat of traditional religious belief. If the Enlightenment was the West's great intellectual turning point, it is clear that many "enlightened" Europeans failed to fully turn with it. The conflicting credos of reason and faith, progress and tradition pulled these eighteenth-century Europeans in opposing directions. Caught betwixt and between, unable to fully embrace either future or past, these men and women reflect not only the perplexities of their epoch, but also anticipate the clashes between the secular and religious worldviews of our era. We are mesmerized, of course, by the story of how our ancestors straddled these divergent worldviews. But their experiences also enable us to better understand our own predicament in our own century, where faith remains tenacious and reason at times seems impotent.

Our own predicament makes Boswell so compelling a figure: few contemporaries straddled these two worlds with the same degree of absorption and acuity, wonder and wit, verve and volubility. Many scholars have noted Boswell's ability to re-create conversations and characters in his journals—an ability that makes him a remarkable witness to his age. He spoke in his journal about his gift at adapting himself "to the tone of any bearable man I am with [so] that he is as much at freedom as with another self." But this gift also makes us privileged witnesses to Boswell's own inner world. In his pursuit of Voltaire and Rousseau, Hume and Johnson, Paoli and Wilkes, Boswell was not merely a celebrity seeker—although he was that—but, for want of a better term, a truth seeker. Boswell's problem was his inability to reconcile the truths of his era with the truths with which his religious upbringing marked him. A rational worldview may well be liberating for others, but did little to ease Boswell's fears concerning death. The metaphors used by his enlightened contemporaries were worse than useless to him: "If my mind is a collection of springs, these springs are all unhinged, and the Machine is all destroyed; or if my mind is a waxen table, the wax is melted by the furnace of sorrow, and all my ideas and principles are dissolved. Good GOD, what horrid chimeras!"[29] Pursued by the shadows of his Calvinist upbringing, Boswell never escaped his past; obsessed with the ultimate disposition of his soul, he was tormented by his future.

In an age where death was a constant and dire presence, Boswell nevertheless stands out for his preoccupation, if not obsession, with his mortal end. He had a lifelong attraction to public executions, attending dozens of them, transfixed by the ways in which the victims approached their last moments. More important, Boswell's chronic "hypochondria"—the contemporary term for depression—was closely tied to his preoccupation with his mortality. When afflicted by this "foul fiend," he wrote, "all the doubts which have ever disturbed thinking men come upon me. I awake at night dreading annihilation, or being thrown into some horrible state of being." Most important, Boswell strove to rid himself of this dread by questioning others on the topics of faith and reason, death and immortality. His brash interviews of Hume, Voltaire, and Rousseau; his incessant grilling of Johnson; his long conversations with friends, wife, and children were often fueled by this morbid preoccupation.

Of course, Boswell never found lasting respite from these preoccupations and fears. He was unable to square his deep needs against the skeptical assault of Enlightenment reason, and he struggled through his life to fashion a consistent self amidst his contradictory impulses. In the end, he was a patchwork product, the result of the countervailing forces of his time. Likening his friend to a moth drawn inexorably to a candle, Johnson captured this tragic tension: "That creature was its own tormentor, and I believe its name was BOSWELL."[30]

Few periods in Boswell's life better crystalize this tension than 1763–1765, the years of his Grand Tour. From the moment he sailed for Holland from the port of Harwich, leaving behind on the beach his newly made friend Samuel Johnson, to his return to Dover from Calais a year and one half later, when he helped onto the dock his newly met travel companion (and bedmate) Thérèse Levasseur, the common-law wife of Jean-Jacques Rousseau, this remarkable Scot toured not just the Continent, but also the ideas and ideals, hopes and fears of his era. Other biographers have narrated Boswell's Grand Tour, most notably Frederick Pottle, in his massive and essential *James Boswell: The Earlier Years 1740–1769*, and more recently Peter Martin, in his graceful and deft *A Life of James Boswell*. My book does not pretend to compete with the fullness or detail of these works, both of which were invaluable in my own writing. Instead, my goal is more modest: to place Boswell's tour of the Continent, and situate the churn of his mind, against the intellectual and political backdrop of the Enlightenment.

Like Pottle and Martin, I discovered in Boswell's journals a life so much more complex and compelling than suggested by tags like "Corsica Boswell" or "Johnson's biographer." But I have chosen to trace one particular aspect to the Scot's life: his struggle with the great questions dealing with the sense and ends of life, brought into being by the Enlightenment. The intellectual tension that marked, even motivated, the young Scot's Grand Tour remains very much with us today. No less important, Boswell's particular understanding of philosophy, its purpose and power, also echoes in recent literature. Much has been written of late about taking philosophy out of the academy and returning it to common life. The historian of philosophy Pierre Hadot long argued that the ancient schools of philosophy, far from serving "academic" aims, served as *manières de vivre,* or guides to how best to live one's life. In their various ways, Epicureans and Stoics, Platonists and Cynics sought to form rather than merely inform their students: to transform their approach to life rather than transform them into scholars.[31] Similarly, in his book *The Art of Living,* Alexander Nehemas returns to the Socratic dialogues in an effort to resurrect an understanding of philosophy as a worldly activity and not a mere academic pursuit. Surveying the state of modern philosophy, and its divorce from our everyday lives, Nehemas observes—rightly, I believe—that "there is a lingering sense in most people as well as a few philosophers that somehow that is not how matters should be, a sense of puzzlement and even of disappointment that the lives of philosophers do not reflect their convictions."[32]

For James Boswell, this sense was not lingering, but present and powerful. His attraction to philosophy and philosophers was not simply intellectual, but deeply personal, perhaps even existential.

His expectations of philosophy were both more modest and more ambitious than our own: he was uninterested in mastering the writings of a single thinker or the intricacies of a specific field, but was deeply interested in trying to master his life. Boswell matters not because his mind was as original or creative as the men and women he pursued, but because his struggle to make sense of his life, to bend his person to certain philosophical ends, appeals to our own needs and sensibilities. He was, to be sure, the moth portrayed by Johnson—but many of us flutter around that same flame, both drawn to and dreading its light.

— 1 —

IN THE KIRK'S SHADOW

Unhappy me, who, in the bloom
Of youth, must bear the heavy gloom
Of a grief-clouded mind.

JAMES BOSWELL WAS BORN in Edinburgh on October 29, 1740, on the eve of All Saints' Day. The date was propitious. An amalgam of Christian and pagan traditions, All Saints commemorates the deaths of Christian martyrs. At the same time, the Scots celebrated the pagan equivalent, called Samhain, or "Summer's End." On this night, legions of dead souls quit the underworld and come to roost in our own world. Who can say which aspect, the sacred specter of Calvinism or profane superstitions of Gaelic Scotland, left a greater mark on young Boswell's mind? Perhaps the question itself would have made little sense to Boswell, for whom the two worlds seemed to merge effortlessly.

The West Bow in Edinburgh's Old City—the street where Boswell's first school was located—was a very narrow passage endowed with sharp bends and sudden slopes. As any schoolboy in the 1740s would attest, ghosts and witches inhabited its dark corners and leaning tenements. The most fearsome spirits were Major Weir and his sister

Jane, both of whom were charged in 1670—the height of the so-called Burning Times—with practicing witchcraft. Three-quarters of a century after they were found guilty and burned at the stake, the Weirs still occupied, if not the actual street, certainly the imagination of young Boswell. Even as he aged, Boswell sloughed off these fears with great difficulty. Up to the age of eighteen, he confessed, he knew moments when his "spirit was crushed," when he was "terribly afraid of ghosts," and "could not be alone at night." He did finally get over it, Boswell claimed, by "a habit of not thinking, not by reasoning about it."[1] Yet long after he turned eighteen, Boswell would still occasionally creep into the beds of male friends in order to ward off these figments of his feverish imagination.

Had he lived long enough to read Walter Scott, Boswell might have credited the novelist's explanation for the persistence of such fears. In his account of witchcraft trials and popular superstition in Scotland, Scott blamed the rigors of the Calvinist faith. It was as if "human credulity, no longer amused by the miracles of Rome, had sought for food in the traditionary records of popular superstition."[2] Against this background, Boswell's fears were hardly exceptional: "The eternity of punishment was the first great idea I ever formed. How it made me shudder! . . . I imagined that the saints passed the whole of eternity in the state of mind of people recently saved from a conflagration, who congratulate themselves on being in safety while they listen to the mournful shrieks of the damned."[3]

As Boswell explained many years later in an autobiographical sketch he wrote for the benefit of Jean-Jacques Rousseau, these crippling fears were partly the work of the family servants, who entertained the child "with an infinity of stories about robbers, murderers, witches, and ghosts." No less important, they were also the legacy of Boswell's mother, Euphemia Erskine. She came from a family with distant ties to the Scottish crown—a genealogy that

Boswell would later use to impress others as well as himself—but little more of certainty can be said about Euphemia: she is virtually absent from Boswell's journals. In one of his rare allusions to his mother, however, Boswell strongly hints at the emotional weight she exercised on his young imagination: "My mother was extremely pious. She inspired me with devotion. But unfortunately she taught me Calvinism."[4]

By his mother's Calvinism, Boswell meant the doctrine of salvation uniquely through grace. More broadly, though, by "Calvinism" he understood the stern worldview associated with the Protestant revolutionary John Knox. Over the course of the mid-sixteenth century, Knox not only helped undo the rule of Queen Mary, but also undermined the "papist" or Catholic tendencies of her institutions. With the establishment of the Church of Scotland, known as the Kirk, the practices and traditions of everyday life were transformed. From the late sixteenth to early eighteenth centuries, the eyes of a dour and demanding God—or, at least, the eyes of those who pretended to be his earthly representatives—were fixed on his creatures. Inevitably, many of his creatures fell short of the Kirk's expectations. As late as the first decades of the eighteenth century, the Kirk still meted out a variety of punishments, ranging from the accused wearing sackcloth at the church door and hearing the public rebuke of the local minister to bearing the weight of excommunication. Indeed, as late as 1696, local authorities in Edinburgh executed a student named Thomas Aikenhead for the crime of uttering blasphemous notions about Christian theology.

Depending on one's perspective, the summit or cellar of religious practice occurred on Sundays. The streets of Edinburgh emptied and pews of churches filled. It could hardly be otherwise as church attendance was obligatory and public spaces were policed by groups of elders "perlustrating" the streets, trawling for malingerers and deserters. In 1709, the Edinburgh Kirk declared: "Take into consideration that the Lord's Day is profaned by people standing in the streets, vaguing [strolling] in the fields and gardens, as also by idly gazing out windows and children and apprentices playing in the streets." As a result, the Kirk commanded each Session "to take its turn in watching the streets on Sabbath." So powerful was the Calvinist imperative to dwell on one's inner rather than outer appearance that barbers were even forbidden to deliver wigs to their clients.[5]

Sundays tested a young Scot's endurance and strength. Sermons stretched through the day and spilled into evenings when fathers quizzed their children on the contents of the sermons and assigned works of religious devotion like *The Fourfold State of Man,* reviewing man's history from his predetermined fall to his possible redemption, and the *Theatre of God's Judgments,* whose edifying tales included that of a nobleman whose divine reward for hunting on the Sabbath was a child born with a dog's head.[6] Having distributed these educational works to his children, the father then retired to his "praying apartment"—a miniscule closet carved from the dining area where he would wrestle with his soul. Indeed, "wrestling" was the common phrase for such activity: ministers exhorted their flocks to "wrestle" against their desires—to "come over the belly of felt wants"—and prepare themselves to meet their Maker so that they "may expire without the shruggs of death."[7] Such a peaceful exit from this world seemed unlikely, though: the doctrine of original sin dictated that the men, women, and children wedged into the pews were little more than "guilty lumps of hell."[8]

Small wonder, then, that Sundays promised the "dreary terrors of hell" for Boswell.[9] Soon after turning forty, Boswell revisited the church he attended as a child with his family. He had hardly settled himself in the family pew when he was swept by memories of his "pious mother" and the "inwardly dark and cold" fears she had kneaded so deeply into his being. Euphemia, Boswell wrote to Rousseau, "was of that sect which believes that to be saved, each individual must experience a strong conversion. She therefore put in my hands a little book in which I read of the conversion of very young children. I remember that one of these children was only three years old." Raised in Calvinist Geneva, Rousseau would not have been surprised. But what would he have made of another passage that Boswell cut from the final draft? His mother, he wrote, "was a very delicate young lady who was very melancholy and who had been raised completely away from the world with scrupulous, pious and visionary notions."[10] It is not clear whether Boswell attributes his mother's melancholy to her upbringing or to being thrust into the real world when she married his father. In either case, the melancholy—what Boswell calls "hypochondria" in his sketch—suffered by his mother left a profound mark on her son.

It also left a lasting impression on his health. He was, as he later confided to Rousseau, a "very delicate child." When he appeared ill, Boswell's mother would overreact, keeping her son home and spoiling him with sweets. As a result, he came to prefer being weak rather than strong, because when well he would then be returned to his hated school.[11] At the age of twelve, Boswell suffered from scurvy, but his physical health thereafter flourished—with the important exception of his nineteen or so bouts of gonorrhea. The disease, along with his excessive drinking, would eventually take its toll on even Boswell's robust constitution, as well as on his pleasant, if unexceptional, features.

Boswell's father viewed his own eternal state with greater equanimity than did his wife. While no stranger to Calvin's *Institutes of the Christian Religion,* he was better versed, and surely more at home, in works of jurisprudence like the *Institutes of the Law of*

Scotland. Trained as a lawyer, the elder Boswell eventually rose to Scotland's highest civil and criminal courts, earning him the title Lord Auchinleck. Tellingly, at the end of his letter to Rousseau, Boswell boasts to the theorist of republicanism and author of *The Social Contract* and *Discourse on the Inequality of Men* that he is the proud son of a Scottish laird. It is no less telling, perhaps, that Boswell commonly fudged the actual nature of the title, which laid no claims to peerage or aristocratic ancestry. Along with his mother's world of the saved and damned, Boswell also was steeped in his father's world of titles and duties.

Lord Auchinleck's title was based on the family estate of Auchinleck, a vast expanse of land in southwestern Scotland. From its highest points, Boswell could see the Firth of Clyde; but from just about any point, the child found inspiration for his fertile imagination. There was, he told his friend John Johnston, "a vast deal of Wood and Water, fine retired shady walks, and every thing that can render the Country agreeable to contemplative minds."[12] Boswell later shared these same sentiments with Rousseau: at Auchinleck he "felt a classic enthusiasm in the romantic shades of our family's seat in the country."[13] The estate fired Boswell's ancestral pride as well as his "classic" longings. The "romantic shades" he so loved radiated from the decaying and mossy walls of the old and uninhabited castle at Auchinleck. It was to these massive ruins that Boswell would wander or lead visitors. As for the neoclassical pile built by his father, it was little more than a severe emblem of the responsibilities he was expected to assume. The Horatian motto that the elder Boswell had inscribed over the front entrance spoke to the ambivalence toward his father that Boswell would feel his entire life: "All you seek is in this remote place—if you have fitted yourself with a good steady mind."

Steadiness of mind was one of the last qualities to come to Alexander Boswell's mind when he thought of his son; while "remoteness" entered James Boswell's thoughts when he considered his father. The great expectations father and son held of one another were never met. Lord Auchinleck meant his son to follow in his footsteps, just as he had followed his own father in the study and practice of law. And it went without saying that, while pursuing this ambition, James would exhibit the sober and steady qualities that Lord Auchinleck himself embodied. Auchinleck's expectations were not unusual for a man of his time and place. As Boswell himself recognized, his father only wished him "to pursue the law and be in the style of his eldest son."[14]

Embarking on a legal career in Scotland meant embarking on a packet ship destined for Holland. Unlike the system of common law prevailing in England, Scottish jurisprudence was based on Roman civil law. Though there was a law faculty in Edinburgh, many Scottish law students voyaged to the mecca for Roman law, Holland, for a year's study. Alexander Boswell had himself studied at Leyden, while many of his contemporaries went to Groningen or Utrecht. This study-abroad program was embraced by the law faculty at Edinburgh, convinced that the influence of studying in Holland was "felt in molding the character and bearing of men [and] communicated the light of a good example, and gave the tone of a high principle to the profession."[15]

For Lord Auchinleck's son, though, the molding of character was tantamount to being buried alive. Boswell wilted when confronted by the respectable and dull prospects held out by his father. "I am a good deal uneasy at hearing that Utrecht is a stiff dull place," he moaned to Johnston. "Alas my friend! I fear I am born to misery."[16] In his journal, Boswell described his father as a "worthy" man who wanted only the best for him. He repeated this estimation more than once to William Temple and Johnston, telling the latter that Lord Auchinleck "is truly a worthy man. I assure you he is."[17] Clearly, Boswell was not entirely persuaded by his own protestations. Though "worthy," Boswell himself quickly added, Lord Auchinleck was also "somewhat narrow in his notions."[18] All of his "little mistakes," Boswell assured Johnston, "are owing to a confined and narrow Education."[19] Given his fears, which soon were shown to be well founded, that his father might read his journal, Boswell's use of "narrow" was diplomatic.[20] In private, he raged to his friends about his father's severe and distant ways, rebelling repeatedly against the great weight of paternal expectations and fear of emotional and financial punishment. (More than once, Auchinleck threatened either to cut his son's allowance, or cut him altogether from his will).

The first armfuls of tinder for Boswell's rebellion were gathered at the University of Edinburgh, which he first entered at the age of thirteen. In fact, the university itself had also established its own intellectual independence. Once a bastion of scholastic and Cartesian teaching, the university had, by the end of the seventeenth century, been pried open through the introduction of an entirely new style of thought. The writings of John Locke pushed aside those of Aristotle, though not without friction. It was only in 1730 that a declared Lockean, John Stevenson, a professor of logic at the university, began to lecture on the *Essay Concerning Human Understanding*.[21] More important, Stevenson spirited a great deal of literature and literary criticism into his lectures. He shared with his students his love of ancients like Homer and Cicero, but also near-contemporaries like John Dryden and Alexander Pope. By adding Joseph Addison to this list of great writers, Stevenson acknowledged the tremendous impact that Addison's magazines the *Tatler* and

Spectator had on popular taste. Stevenson's range and eloquence turned the eyes of young Scots to a world far wider and deeper than their ancestors had known. One of his students, Alexander Carlyle, recalled that in Stevenson's class "our minds were more enlarged, and that we received greater benefit from that class than any other."[22]

Boswell and Temple attended Stevenson's class in 1756–1757; their "worthy, red-nosed" teacher inspired them to read widely on their own.[23] Together in Edinburgh, Boswell and Temple would "talk over our several studies." Temple dreamt of spending his life with Boswell, in "philosophick retirement, amids rocks and falling waters, in the grove sacred to friendship and love [and] converse with a Socrates, Plato or a Tully!"[24] When they were apart later in life, the two friends continued their exchanges in letters, which also sharpened their pens in a manner that, they hoped, would earn Addison's, if not Socrates', approbation.[25] When not excitedly sharing views on theatrical productions, or bemoaning long hours spent over law books, Boswell in particular would cast himself as a character in his letters, entertaining Temple with accounts of social gatherings and his meetings with great men.

In this vein, Boswell related to Temple his visit to the lodgings of David Hume, the notorious freethinker, which he undertook with neither an invitation nor letter of introduction in hand. Boswell was surprised, it seems, that philosophical skepticism and personal warmth could coexist in the same man: "He is a most discreet, affable man as ever I met with and has really a great deal of learning." Attempting to reassure either himself or his friend, Boswell declared that Hume "is a very proper person for a Young Man to cultivate an acquaintance with."[26] Ultimately, though, Boswell never could reconcile Hume's attractive character with his alarming works. As we will see, what Boswell cultivated over the next two decades was less an acquaintance with Hume than a familiarity with a world-view that, in its thoroughgoing skepticism and systematic doubt, was made of the very stuff that tested Boswell's religious convictions and emotional needs.

By 1759, Boswell was no longer the "grave, sedate, philosophic" fellow who, just two years earlier risked becoming, in Temple's estimation, an "Old Man too soon."[27] Instead, he now was more likely to become an immediate embarrassment to his family. Bored with his law studies, Boswell grew increasingly fascinated by the theater and enthralled by the prospect of romantic encounters. Given the dubious sexual mores of actors and actresses, Boswell's new-found interests were often one and the same. To the staid Temple, Boswell sent a letter, written in verse, in which he tried to reassure his friend. "You tell me / and I thank you for't / That you have heard an odd report that your old Friend's strange alteration / Is now at deeds of Fornication / Just as expert as formerly / At grave sedate Philosophy / An actress too (You know her name) / Is said to be his fav'rite Flame."[28]

Inevitably, Boswell's parents were horrified by reports that their son was frequenting such dubious company. Boswell was certainly aware of his mother's attitude toward the theater: as he nearly told Rousseau (himself no friend of theater), but then refrained, his pious mother wept when she had been forced to attend the theater. For a pious woman like Euphemia, as with the old guard of the Kirk, the theater was little more than the devil's work. Lord Auchinleck was no less hostile, though for different reasons. His concerns were more practical: while only the good Lord knew if theater would nudge young Boswell's soul toward hell's fire, the Lord of Auchinleck knew it would stand in the way of a gainful profession. More than once

Lord Auchinleck muttered to friends in his broad Scots accent: "There's nae hope for Jamie, mon . . . Jamie is gane clean gyte."[29]

In the end, it was the elder Auchinleck who had nae hope: the theater virus had lodged itself in his son at a very early age. In his journal Boswell recalled "my boyish days when I used to walk down the Canongate [where stood Edinburgh's one theater] and think of players with a mixture of narrow-minded horror and lively-minded pleasure; and used to wonder at painted equipages and powdered ladies."[30] Obviously, the charms of the actresses he met in Edinburgh—who frequently acted offstage as courtesans—played no small role in Boswell's infatuation.

But something more deep was at work as well. The great arbiters of social mores in early eighteenth-century England, Addison and Richard Steele, insisted in the pages of the *Tatler* and *Spectator* that the world was a stage. But they carried this metaphor so far that the distinction between actors and audience, scripted and sincere language, more or less disappeared. Polite society was, as Addison held, a "Fraternity of Spectators" consisting of "every one that considers the World as a Theatre, and desires to form a right Judgment of those who are the Actors on it."

To a degree extreme even in this age of self-fashioning, Boswell threw himself into this hall of mirrors. In his journal and letters, with his friends and teachers, he gazed at himself, seeking to achieve the right tone, right gesture, right sentiment. The rule, Steele reminded Boswell, was to keep "your Desires, your Words, your Actions, within the Regard your Friends have for you." While the longing for admiration might strike some observers as vanity, Boswell no doubt recalled Addison's tut-tutting: don't pay them heed. Such a passion, according to Mr. Spectator, "is not wholly to be discouraged, since it often produces very good Effects."[31] The "commerce of discourse," in Steele and Addison's eyes, was designed both to impress others and impress ourselves; by acting well, we pleased others and thus pleased ourselves.

Living on his own in Edinburgh and freed from his father's dour gaze, Boswell thus pursued his education with actors and actresses in the city's taverns and inns. That there existed a close bond between the taverns and university provided small solace for Lord Auchinleck. Nevertheless, the many taverns, or howffs, of the Old Town were often little more than extensions of the university classrooms. It was there that students and professors, writers and artists, merchants and professionals gathered to discuss literature and politics over tables littered with bottles of claret, port, ale, and whisky. This was due as much to the lack of adequate housing as to the love of alcohol: cramped personal lodging encouraged the growth of clubs and societies that met in public inns.

Indeed, the densely packed character of the city cultivated close ties among the local literati. Visitors to Edinburgh marveled at the open and convivial character of the intellectual scene. According to William Smellie, a local publisher, most European cities, though they "contain many literary men, the access to them is difficult; and even after that is obtained, the conversation, for some time, is shy and constrained." How different, though, was his native Edinburgh: "the access to men of parts is not only easy, but their conversation and the communication of their knowledge are at once imparted to intelligent strangers with the utmost liberality."[32]

That young Boswell blossomed in this liberal atmosphere was, for his father, a matter of concern, not contentment. Finally, weary of his son's hobnobbing with actors and lax attitude toward studying, Auchinleck packed his son off to the University of Glasgow. For the laird, that city's greatest attraction was the absence of theaters. Whether the presence of Adam Smith, who had just published his *Theory of Moral Sentiments* and held the university's chair of Moral

Philosophy at the university, was also a boon, Auchinleck never said. What mattered was that, when it came to the seductions of the theater, Glasgow might just as well have been the furthermost of the Outer Hebrides.

———————

When Daniel Defoe visited Glasgow in the early 1720s, he liked what he saw. Glasgow, he wrote, was "a very fine city." The principal streets, he declared, were "the fairest for breadth, and the finest build that I have ever seen in one city together." Stone houses were lined along these noble thoroughfares, "generally equal and uniform in height, as well as in front; the lower story generally stands on vast square dorick columns, not round pillars, and arches between give passage into the shops, adding to the strength as well as beauty of the building." Defoe was smitten: Glasgow, he marveled, was "one of the cleanest, most beautiful, and best built Cities in Great Britain."[33]

There was little mystery behind the reason for this granite-like solidity: as Defoe noted, one met in Glasgow "the face of trade, as well foreign as home trade; and, I may say, 'tis the only city in Scotland, at this time, that apparently increases and improves in both." Defoe neglected to specify that King Tobacco ruled Glasgow's ports. Prior to the Act of Union, England had kept a closely guarded monopoly on the tobacco trade. Perhaps inevitably, this monopoly spawned in Glasgow a bustling, if illegal, traffic in tobacco. Once the Act of Union legalized the trade, Glasgow's smugglers became respectable—and astonishingly wealthy—merchants. By 1751, this small city of 30,000 inhabitants was importing more tobacco than London and the rest of England combined.[34]

When the Edinburgh–Glasgow coach deposited Boswell, weary from more than twelve jolting hours on the rutted and poorly kept road between the two cities, in this small and thriving city in 1759, he was less struck by the city's bourgeois solidity than its dour religiosity. All the fine buildings and Doric columns in the world could not make up for the absence of theater. For the elders of the local Kirk, or Church of Scotland, popery and theater were all of a piece. The Scottish reformer James Burgh lambasted "the Lewdness or Impiety of most of the Plays themselves, or the infamous Characters of the Actors and Actresses."[35] Not surprisingly, in 1754 the building turned into a temporary theater for Boswell's friend West Digges, an actor famed for his portrayal of Macheath in John Gay's *The Beggar's Opera,* was razed to the ground by an enraged Presbyterian mob. (Just a few years after Boswell's stay in Glasgow, the locals reaffirmed their distaste for the stage when they burnt down yet another building where the actress George Anne Bellamy had been slated to appear.[36])

What was a young man to do? Especially one like Boswell, no less attracted to dissipation than to the stage? Not only was the theater banned from the city, but the commerce of discourse also had a spectral existence. Literary clubs were few and the arts scene was marginal. To his despair, Boswell discovered an often-overlooked facet to this corner of Scotland: the persistence of religious piety. In 1742, the Great Awakening, which had already touched parts of England and the North American colonies, had reached southwest Scotland. The immediate spark was the report of parishioners in the town of Cambuslang, just south of Glasgow, fainting or falling into convulsions during the sermons of their minister, William M'Culloch. The minister had for many years failed to keep his flock awake on Sundays, so the fact that they were quite suddenly speaking in tongues caught the attention of "wounded souls" throughout the region. A long series of open-air meetings stretched across the summer, drawing ever-greater numbers of men and women eager to hear the gospel preached by local and visiting evangelical preachers. The movement climaxed with the arrival of the charismatic preacher George Whitefield, welcomed by a crowd of more than 30,000.

It is impossible to know how many accepted Whitefield's invitation to "come, just as you are, to Christ." But there was clearly a large pool of candidates for such a choice: at the end of the eighteenth century, various Dissenters still represented more than 40 percent of Glasgow's population. The presence of this community of Covenanters weighed heavily on local culture. Even at the midpoint of the Age of Enlightenment, Glasgow's streets remained dark at night: as a local historian noted, "it was presumed that no one would be out of his own house after sunset; the indulgence, and the innocent amusements of life were either unknown or were little practiced."[37]

And yet, it was here, in Glasgow, that one of the age's most original thinkers, Adam Smith, wove a theory and defense of the very world that created Boswell and dismayed Glasgow. When Boswell in early autumn 1759 enrolled in Smith's class in rhetoric at the University of Glasgow, Smith had just published his *Theory of Moral Sentiments*. If it had happened on stage, both men would have dismissed it as contrived. But as it happened in life, their meeting is a happy coincidence for historians.

In a letter to Johnston, the exiled Boswell dwells on the theatrical world from which his father had just yanked him. With masterful understatement, he tells Johnston that the sudden and forced departure from Edinburgh "made me not a little uneasy at first." Though "resolved to bring my mind to be contented with the Situation which was thought proper for me," Boswell nevertheless begged Johnston to send him news of "theatrical passions" that were running so high in Edinburgh: such crumbs, at least, "will afford me some entertainment, when deprived of the exalted pleasures of the Stage." Boswell concluded the letter with a poem whose last stanza carried the lament "Unhappy me, who, in the bloom / Of youth, must bear the heavy gloom / Of a grief-clouded mind."[38]

Yet there was one ray of light that pierced Boswell's overcast thoughts. Every weekday morning, after a breakfast of herring, porridge, and ale, Boswell crossed the Trongate toward the university, a massive freestone pile whose clock tower dominated the cityscape. As the clock reached 7:30 a.m., Boswell quickly made his way to the large room where nearly a hundred students were preparing for the arrival of their professor, Adam Smith.

Since 1752, when he assumed the chair of Moral Philosophy at Glasgow, Smith had been a celebrity. It was less his flair than lack of it that attracted his students. He would begin his class by reading from a set of prepared notes, but gradually, as one student noted, the subject matter "seemed to crowd upon Mr. Smith [and] his manner became warm and animated, and his expression easy and fluent." As he followed his thoughts, Smith seemed to forget his students; instead, having "conceived an opposition to his opinions," he argued as with himself.[39]

But appearances were just that, appearances: Smith was acutely aware of his audience. Like Boswell, most of the students were still in their teens. Rather than offering dry commentary on ancient texts, Smith instead rummaged about in the contemporary world to illustrate his arguments. The manners, and customs, social ideals and foibles of his students and of himself were all for the taking. An accomplished storyteller, he insisted that his students attend to his performance, shouting at those busy taking notes that he hated "scribblers." He was equally alive to the bored and listless—when he saw a student whose eyes were closing, he "felt at once that all was wrong" and that he "must change either the subject or the style of [his] address."[40]

An encore would take place in the early afternoon when a few of the most promising students called on Smith at his manse on Professors' Court. The setting was less formal: Smith's mother, who kept house for her bachelor son, often greeted the students at the door. (It was common knowledge among his students that the best way favorably to impress their professor was through his philosophy or his mother.) While these sessions were not, like his lectures, staged, Smith nevertheless remained attentive to his audience. One former student recalled that Smith would, based on the direction of the conversation with a student, "discover the bents and extent of their faculties[,] adapting his hints to their plans of life."[41]

One of Smith's fiercest fans, Boswell quickly became a regular at the afternoon sessions. In a letter to Johnston, he declared that Smith was a truly amiable sort, treating his students "with all the easiness and affability imaginable." His review grows even more emphatic: the sentiments Smith expressed at these gatherings "are striking, profound and beautiful, the method in which they are arranged clear, accurate and orderly, his language correct, perspicuous and elegantly phrased."[42] Though far from Mrs. Cowper at the Canongate, Boswell at least had a box seat for Mr. Smith at the Professors' Court.

But Mr. Smith understood that he too had a box seat for the performances of his impressionable student. Author of *The Theory of Moral Sentiments*, which he had published shortly before Boswell's arrival in Glasgow, Smith must have marveled at how this young man channeled his book chapter and verse. If life is a stage, and Boswell one of its apprentice actors, Smith was its greatest theorist. With him, we move from the fraternity of spectators to the impartial spectator.

––––––––––

The Theory of Moral Sentiments, based on Smith's lectures, quickly became a best seller. "The Public seems disposed to applaud it extremely," David Hume wrote from London, and "the Mob of Literati are beginning already to be very loud in its praises."[43] No less enthused was Edmund Burke, who described the book as ingenious, elegant, lively, and, yes, sublime. The philosophes in Paris were enthusing over it at the cafés and salons, while in sleepy Cambridge Boswell's friend Temple, who had not even read it, nevertheless reported that the book had won "immortal honor."[44]

If Boswell had asked Smith how it felt to be famous, the older man would have directed him to the opening lines of the book: "As we have no immediate experience of what other men feel, we can form no idea of the manner in which they are affected, but by conceiving what we ourselves should feel in a like situation."[45] In a word, as a spectator to Smith's situation, all Boswell needed to do was exercise his imagination in order to know the answer.

In effect, *The Theory of Moral Sentiments* is an ingenious theory of spectatorship. In his effort to answer the perennial question what makes human beings good, Smith replied: others do. Others make us good not by threatening punishment or pain, but instead by promising applause. This is the source of the human faculty of sympathy, or what Smith called "fellow feeling." Sympathy, for Smith, is the work of our imagination: we flex our intellectual muscles in order to re-create and react to another's situation. The other is me—or, more precisely, what I would be were I in the other's situation.

Look around, Smith asked his students: Could anything please you more than to see in your classmates the same fellow feeling swelling in our own breast? Of course not. We place our own self in that situation and respond accordingly. Just as Hamlet is the creation not just of Shakespeare, but of each and every one who has seen a performance of the play, so too is the other the creation of our own imagination.

Yet Hamlet is not alone in his dark rumination—or, rather, he is alone, but *we* are not. We are watching him, but we also are watching one another as each of us responds to that tragic figure. We rejoice, Smith insists, whenever we observe that others adopt our own passions; the others rejoice, in turn, upon seeing our own response of joy. We long for that relief, Smith writes, which nothing can give us but "the entire concord of the affections of the spectators with [our] own." As a result, when we find ourselves at the theater, our eyes are not just on the stage, but also on our fellow spectators. Of course, we do our best to contain our sympathetic sorrow as the staged tragedy unfolds. But when the events finally overtake us and our eyes fill with tears, "we carefully conceal them, and are afraid, lest the spectators, not entering into this excessive tenderness, should regard it as effeminacy and weakness."[46]

Since nature, Smith observes, makes us so that we are repulsed by excess and attracted to restraint, we spend our lives "tuning up" or "tuning down" our expressions and emotions so as better to win the world's applause. What happens, though, if we are alone? Can one be good, Smith wondered, "in a solitary place"? The answer is yes—at least if we have spent enough time in the world in order to internalize it. We take the world—or, rather, its audience—with us by means of the "impartial spectator."

What is it, Smith wonders, that moves each and every one of us—whose passive feelings are usually sordid and selfish—to sacrifice our own interests for the sake of our fellow beings? Can the distant call of benevolence ever overcome the din of our self-seeking desires? Do the abstract lessons we learned as children—what Smith calls the "abstruse syllogisms of a quibbling dialectic"—tame our deepest impulses?

Hardly, Smith replies. Instead, there is a far more powerful agent on which we, and society, depend: it is, he declares, "the inhabitant of the breast, the man within, the great judge and arbiter of our conduct." The inevitably distorted view we have of ourselves, according to Smith, "can be corrected only by the eye of this impartial spectator." The good man is the man forever aware that he is on stage, forever alive to the eyes fixed on his actions, forever seeking the approbation and applause of others. This man "has never dared to suffer the man within his breast to be absent one moment from his attention. With the eyes of this great inmate he has always been accustomed to regard whatever relates to himself."[47]

Yet even Smith feared that prolonged isolation would weaken the voice of our "great inmate." In solitude, he warned, "we are apt to feel too strongly whatever relates to ourselves." We will exaggerate the good acts we have done others as well as the unjust acts others have done to us; we will too quickly be buoyed by our good fortune, just as we will be sunk by our bad luck. As a result, to maintain our self-command, the impartial spectator "requires often to be awakened and put in mind of his duty by the presence of a real spectator."[48]

Far from his friends and family, living in a city empty of Edinburgh's intimacy and sociability, Boswell had few real spectators to call upon. It was a propitious time for the Catholic faith to call upon him.

———————

In the wake of the Reformation and the English Civil War, Roman Catholicism in Scotland was mostly the affair of a few Highland clans. Elsewhere in Scotland, the observation made by an English visitor—"To be opposite to the Pope is to be presently with God"— held true through the mid-eighteenth century.[49] By then, though, Roman Catholicism was well on the way to becoming just one more of the many Christian sects in Scotland whose presence, if not welcomed, was mostly tolerated.[50] Nevertheless, the spread of toleration was sluggish and uneven. Just a few years before Boswell entered university, a minister in nearby Aberdeen was charged with the crime of being a "trafficking Papist." Found guilty, he was banished from the country and warned that, should he return, he would be hanged.[51] Three decades later, in 1779, the government's effort to end civil disabilities on Roman Catholics sparked riots in Edinburgh—a rehearsal of sorts for the Gordon Riots in London in 1780.[52] In short, the Catholic Church's presence in Edinburgh was no less marginal than was the theater's. As one historian has noted, "For many Protestants, especially clerics, it was a cardinal principle that play-going and going to mass were both forms of idolatry."[53]

This made both of them equally attractive for the increasingly restless and rebellious Boswell. That both institutions specialized in the staging of spectacle further eased their merging into a single goal in Boswell's imagination. But something more, something deeper may have been at play, too. In Glasgow, a city barren of friends and distractions, Boswell was forced back upon himself. His attention inevitably drifted from his dry legal texts to a small pile of Catholic works given to him in Edinburgh by a Jesuit, Père Duchat. The good father had been introduced to Boswell by Mrs. Cowper, the same actress about whom Boswell versified in his letter to Temple and with whom, it appears, he had his first affair. Cowper, ten years older than Boswell, not only initiated him into the mysteries of the boudoir and stage, but also, as a practicing Catholic, introduced Boswell to the mysteries of the Roman Catholic Church.

Among the books Boswell carted with him to Glasgow was Bishop Bossuet's *An Exposition of the Doctrine of the Catholic Church*. While it is easy to make both too much and too little of what Boswell read, it is telling that Bossuet's writings had helped engineer a far more famous conversion just a few years earlier. Upon reading the Frenchman's *Exposition* while at Oxford in 1753, Edward Gibbon fell victim (in his words) "to the noble hand" of the author and became, though only for a short while, a Roman Catholic. Boswell, too, had begun to fall to that same noble hand even before he returned to Glasgow in 1760. During his son's stay at Auchinleck during winter break, Lord Auchinleck found him reading deeply in the *Exposition*—so much so that he began to worry in earnest.[54]

But what weapon, precisely, did Bossuet's hand carry in Boswell's case? The seventeenth-century cleric had written the *Exposition* in order to win back those who had strayed from the true Church. As with Bossuet's celebrated sermons, the book's prose is powerful and clear. While the second half deals largely with the intricacies of the Eucharist, the first half addresses issues that were surely of greater concern to the young Boswell. On the question of justification, so close to Boswell's heart, Bossuet agrees with his Protestant controversialists on the primordial roles divine grace and charity play in our salvation. Yet Bossuet, unlike his Protestant challengers, does not stop with this severe and bleak assessment: "It is but too true," he continues, "that 'the flesh lusteth against the spirit, and the spirit against the flesh,' and that 'in many things we all offend': so that though our justice be real, it is not perfect justice on account of the assaults of concupiscence. Wherefore the constant sighs of a soul afflicted at its faults are the most essential duty which Christian justice can discharge."[55]

The subtle and humane middle ground that Bossuet stakes out—namely, awareness of our inevitable imperfections itself represents the individual's effort to work with God for his salvation—deeply appealed to Boswell, torn between his desire for spiritual reassurance and his love of earthly delights. On the one hand, Bossuet wrote, we can do nothing of merit without the sanctifying grace of God. But on the other hand, just as the precepts and exhortations of the gospel attest, "we must work our salvation by the movement of our will, aided by the grace of God."[56] It was this "other hand" that meant so much to a young man for whom the Church of Scotland seemed to have just one hand to offer.

Ultimately, Bossuet's message offered at least as much to Boswell as did the spectacular medium of Catholic pomp and ritual. Why else would he risk as much as he did by his decision to convert? The unhappy consequences of joining the Roman Catholic Church by the mid-eighteenth century were severe and several. While Boswell no longer risked his life or freedom by converting—the formal punishment of being hanged, drawn, and quartered for converting to Roman Catholicism had fallen out of use—he would pay a staggering number of social and professional costs. Not only would he be immediately removed from his father's will, he would also certainly have been banned from the bar, from the military and, worst of all, from polite society in both London and Edinburgh. In effect, Boswell threatened to create for himself an existence that was as marginal as the actor's—and without the compensatory joys, if he joined the priesthood, he had come to associate with inns and bedrooms.

In any case, Boswell held firm to his plan—or, at least, held firm to the impression that he was holding firm. In early March 1760, upon sending to his father a letter detailing his treasonous intentions, Boswell bolted from Glasgow. Scarcely three days later, he arrived in London and, most probably through the medium of one or more Catholic booksellers, made contact with the city's small Roman Catholic community. He lived incognito at the ramshackle residence of a Catholic wigmaker, where he was visited by "Romanish clergy [who] filled me with solemn ideas."[57] Boswell also attended his first mass, which filled him with "wonderful enthusiasm."[58]

But Boswell was either incapable or unwilling to cover his tracks and was soon found by a fellow Scot and associate of Lord Auchinleck, the earl of Eglinton. Auchinleck, who had asked Eglinton to find his son, may have been a severe man, but he was not foolish: rather than having Eglinton bundle up Boswell and return him to Scotland, he instead asked the nobleman to keep an eye on him. The strategy worked: within days, Boswell had moved into Eglinton's elegant quarters and dropped his plans for conversion. A libertine, Eglinton made certain that Boswell would not again venture down the path marked by Bossuet. As Boswell himself noted a few years later, he could not gainsay the success of Eglinton's method for "freeing me from the gloom of superstition." After a pause, he added: "Although it led me to the other extreme."[59]

— 2 —

AT HOME WITH HOME

I was sure I had genius, and was not
deficient in easiness of expression, but
was at a loss for something to say.

SOON AFTER HE WAS PULLED from the folds of the Roman
Catholic Church and returned to Scotland, Boswell fell into the
wide orbit of Henry Home, Lord Kames, a central figure in Scottish thought and politics. Seduction is, in effect, a form of gravity:
the two men, though separated in age by nearly a half century and
in society by wildly different prospects, were attracted to one another for reasons that were no less intellectual than psychological.
Oddly, the same could be said of the mutual attraction exercised
at the same time between Boswell and Home's daughter, Jean, who
fell into bed together for reasons not all that different from those
that led Boswell to fall into the same carriage carrying Home on a
tour of the Scottish Lowlands.

———

Henry Home, who acquired the title Lord Kames upon being named
to Scotland's powerful Court of Sessions in 1752, was not just a formidable legal scholar; along with Frances Hutcheson he laid the
philosophical foundations for the Scottish Enlightenment. Equally

important, he was a powerful patron and administrator; when not writing works of legal or aesthetic theory, he was balancing the books and directing the resources of the many governmental boards on which he sat. The author of *Elements of Criticism* and *Essays on the Principles of Morality and Natural Religion,* Kames also busied himself with works like *The Gentleman Farmer* and *Progress of Flax-Husbandry in Scotland.* Here, as elsewhere, Kames's views were, in the words of one contemporary, "exceeding crusty."[1] This was equally true of his administrative activity, particularly as member of the Board of Trustees for Arts, Fisheries and Manufactures, where Kames happily delved in the minutiae of landholding practices, bleaching, and flax farming.

Kames's writings on agricultural and mercantile affairs have long since fallen outside the pale of the liberal arts. In his time, though, the liberal and practical arts were one and the same. As his distant kinsman David Hume observed, among the advantages of industry is that it "commonly produces some refinement in the liberal [arts]; nor can one be carried to perfection, without being accompanied, in some degree, with the other . . . The spirit of the age affects all the arts; and the minds of men, being once roused from their lethargy, and put into fermentation, turn themselves on all sides, and carry improvements into every art and science."[2]

The theme of "improvement," regardless of the subject, runs through Kames's writings. One of the country's most powerful barristers, Kames believed that the law is not unchanging and hidebound strictures, but instead adaptive and malleable. Law, he argued, is an evolving expression of the dynamic between politics and society. As he declared, the "law of that country is wrong which does not accommodate itself to the fluctuating manners of the people."[3] By "accommodate" Kames did not at all mean "subordinate"—on the contrary. Law is ultimately grounded in universal principles, he believed, common to all men. There exists, Kames insisted, a kind of natural law. But in order to pull societies toward the great and common goal, legal codes must adapt themselves to the time and place peculiar to each generation and people.

———

When Kames turned his reflections from law to morality, he did so under the influence of his contemporary Francis Hutcheson. Born in Belfast and a professor at Glasgow, Hutcheson was indebted to John Locke's work—but in his influential *Inquiry into the Original of our Ideas of Beauty and Virtue,* he repaid the debt in a currency of his own stamp. The son of a Presbyterian minister, Hutcheson refused to cast original man, as did Locke and Thomas Hobbes, in a state of absolute solitude. Human beings, by their very nature, have always been social beings. More important, the origins of "natural law" lay not in reason, as Locke claimed, but instead in our sentiments. Hutcheson agreed with Locke's portrayal of man as a "blank slate" who derives knowledge from his external senses. But, he argued, this was little more than a profile of humankind. A full portrait would reveal that along with the external senses we are endowed with an internal sense that governs our moral sense.

Benevolence, for Hutcheson, is instinctual: an internal reflex "antecedent to all reason from interest."[4] Quite independent of our will, we find pleasure in the good done not just to ourselves, but also to others. The whole system of the mind, in particular our moral faculty, "shows that we are all under natural bonds of beneficence and humanity toward all." We have no need of other proof, he concludes, that "this first state founded by nature is so far from being that of war and enmity, that it is a state where we are all obliged by the natural feelings of our hearts, and by many tender affections, to innocence and beneficence towards all."[5]

Hutcheson's scheme was the fruit of a careful negotiation between reason and religion, and it appealed deeply to his contemporaries. It put not just a human, but a smiling, face on the stern and forbidding Calvinism that had been hurled from Scottish pulpits by John Knox and his followers. A world pocked by human greed, violence, and fear—a fallen and sinful world—gave way to a good world presided over by a God who had equipped us to recognize, and distinguish between, right and wrong, just as we do with sweetness and bitterness. In fact, Hutcheson had neatly turned the tables on both Knox and Hobbes. Both of these men, though one was deeply religious and the other deeply skeptical, shared a similar disdain for humankind, believing we can be saved only by authoritarian rule. The only difference, really, was that Knox placed that rule in the hands of the Church, while Hobbes handed it to the state.[6]

Not only did Hutcheson seek a third way between the equally bleak prospects offered by Hobbes and Calvin, but he also expressed it in language aimed at the general reader. Famed for his lectures at Glasgow, Hutcheson brought the same clarity and immediacy to his writings. Gently sticking his elbow in the ribs of other theologians and philosophers, he noted, "we have made Philosophy, as well as Religion . . . so austere and ungainly a Form, that a Gentleman cannot easily bring himself to like it."[7] His politics and philosophy, like his prose, reflected his personality: convivial and refined, moderate and, most important, hopeful. Hutcheson believed that man, thanks to his inner faculty of moral reason, ineluctably chooses what is best both for him and his fellow human beings. "As nature has implanted in every man a desire of his own happiness, and many tender affections towards others . . . and granted to each one some understanding and active powers, with a natural impulse to exercise them for the purposes of these affections; 'tis plain each one has a natural right to exert his power, according to his own judgment and inclination, for these purposes, in all such industry, labor, or amusements, as are not hurtful to others in their purposes or goods."[8]

Kames, in contrast, tended to inspire fear, not the reverence and love felt by Hutcheson's followers. It is no accident that Boswell, who would later try to capture the latter's notion of benevolence in his series of essays titled *The Hypochondriack,* described Hutcheson as "able and benignant."[9] Yet both men agreed that morality had to be grounded in something steadier than the sands of history and social custom. As Kames wrote near the beginning of his *Essays on the Principles of Morality and Natural Religion,* he wanted to "restore morality to its original simplicity and authority."[10] But Kames dug more deeply into Hutcheson's notion of man's moral faculty. No "clear notion of morality," Kames observed, can "rest upon simple approbation." Instead, instances of moral beauty or moral deformity arise from the ends toward which such acts aim. "Thus we find the nature of man so constituted, as to approve certain actions, and to disapprove others; to consider some actions as fit and meet to be done, and others unfit and unmeet."[11] We do the right thing, Kames believed, not simply because it *feels* good, but because it *is* good.

The different shades to Hutcheson's and Kames's characters reflected their differing analyses of morality. For the former, man tends toward the good from a sense of well-being, whereas for the latter he obeys it from a sense of duty. But while severe, Kames's perspective is optimistic: paving the path of duty are the stones of culture and civilization. Education refines our moral faculty, exercising our sense of obligation "till it comes to be productive of the strongest as well as the most delicate feelings."[12] But, crucially, education and experience properly understood serve these ends not by burnishing our faculty of reason, but our faculty of knowing right from wrong, fitness from unfitness. As Kames warns, "The Author of nature has not left our actions to be directed by so weak a principle as reason."[13]

Perhaps only a man convinced, like Kames, that we do the right thing because it is good could be oblivious to the antics committed under his own roof by James Boswell. This is not to say that the older man was blind to Boswell's unpredictable character. After beginning a letter to Boswell in 1761, Kames blurted out: "How many qualities good and bad does that name bundle up together!"[14] During his youth Home was himself notorious for his riotous, at times rebellious behavior. Like many of his fellow Scottish law students, he loved claret. With tongue partly in cheek, Home justified his bouts of claret-soaked conviviality on the grounds of social tradition. As he told Boswell, Home was periodically invited, when still a young lawyer, by a powerful judge to dine at his house. He could not, of course, "refuse when invited." And so, resolved "not to do things by halves," Home would cancel all of his appointments and go to dinner, where he would imbibe "bumpers" and make a "drinking afternoon of it" before going home to sleep it off in bed. Being Kames, he then drew a universal and historical lesson for Boswell: "Drinking takes its turns in all countries, like the smallpox, and then ran itself out. The Romans drank hard. Now the Italians did not."[15]

By 1761, when Kames entered Boswell's life, the former's love of claret had given way to port, and his independent mind was hardening into an increasingly intolerant one. Nevertheless, as one of Scotland's most celebrated figures, Kames drew to himself a number of young men with intellectual ambitions. Adam Smith and his distant kinsman David Hume numbered among his so-called *élèves*, and Kames, who recognized Boswell's literary talents and sheer energy, wished to add the young man to the list. In 1762, soon after they met, the two men conversed at length on what had quickly become their favorite subject: Boswell. With his usual candor, Boswell told Kames about his literary ambition: "I told him that I should like much to be distinguished in that way: that I was sure I had genius, and was not deficient in easiness of expression, but was at a loss for something to say, and, when I set myself seriously to think of writing, that I wanted a subject."[16]

Most telling was Boswell's reason for seeking to distinguish himself through writing: "It is making another self which can be present in many places and is not subject to the inconstancies of passion, which the man himself is." Kames's reply—that Boswell should write "lively periodical papers"[17]—at least credited Boswell's ambition to write. But it failed to do true justice to the young man's motivations. While Kames was practical and sharp eyed, he was not particularly reflective or empathetic. "Business," he reminded Boswell, "is the chief purpose of life, and imagination is given us for recreation only."[18] As for the "lively" sketches he suggested to Boswell, Kames considered them little more than a pastime: "Man was intended for more important occupations than to pass his time merely in amusement, which ought to be subservient to business and never encroach upon it."[19] Kames's advice was thoroughly Scottish: hard-nosed and commonsensical. Yet, as we shall see, Boswell's reasons for writing were no less Scottish. In effect, he transformed the Calvinist command to read one's soul into the Enlightenment imperative to know oneself—or, perhaps more accurately, the Romantic imperative to *write* one's self.

Boswell would act on Home's suggestion that he turn to writing, but not before he acted on a very different suggestion made to him by Home's only daughter Jean. At the age of seventeen, Jean had married a Scottish landowner named Patrick Heron. From all accounts, Heron was a kind-hearted but bland man. As strong-willed and independent as her father, Jean quickly tired of her domestic situation. Though married scarcely a month, Jean threw herself into an affair with Boswell when he visited the Homes in December 1761. Boswell later told Rousseau that Jean Heron "let me see that she loved me more than she did her husband. She made no difficulty of granting me all." Not only was she decisive, but she was also "a subtle philosopher." In Boswell's re-creation of the affair, Heron tells him: "I love my husband as a husband, and you as a lover, each in his own sphere. I perform for him all the duties of a good wife. With you I give myself up to delicious pleasures. We keep our secret. Nature has made me so I shall never bear children. No one suffers because of our loves. My conscience does not reproach me, and I am sure that God cannot be offended by them."[20]

Jean spoke for God and herself, perhaps, but not entirely for her lover: the affair, which continued at the Heron estate, made Boswell increasingly uneasy. While he found Jean's casuistry appealing, Boswell was not entirely feckless. As he tells Rousseau, the woman's father—Boswell does not identify by name either Jean or Lord Kames in his letter—"had heaped kindnesses on me." As a result, he was "seized by the bitterest remorse. I was unhappy." But not so unhappy that he ended the liaison; instead, in an equally subtle piece of philosophizing on his part, he confessed that he continued his "criminal amour, and the pleasures I tasted formed a counterpoise to my remorse."[21]

It was thus with more than his usual baggage that Boswell joined Kames for a tour of the lowlands in the fall of 1762. Keen on the young man's irrepressible company, and paradoxically acting on his friend Lord Auchinleck's request to try and repress his son's behavior, Kames had already suggested the idea for the "jaunt." Boswell accepted with alacrity and, from mid-September to mid-November, traveled across the southern counties of Scotland in Kames's company, periodically breaking free and visiting friends and associates on his own. His goal, however, was not simply to pass the time. It was, instead, to re-create the passage of time in a journal. In a letter to his friend John Johnston, Boswell reveals his plan: "I intend to keep a journal in order to acquire a method, for doing it, when I launch into the Ocean of high life."[22] In other words, Boswell was decided upon rehearsing for an even grander project come the end of that year when he would move to London.

But more immediately, Boswell seemed also aware that he was rehearsing for the role of James Boswell. The idea for the journal was hatched in conversations between Boswell and Johnston and another friend, William McQuhae. The plan was for Boswell to mail installments to the two young men; Johnston and McQuhae expected to be entertained while, most certainly, Boswell expected to entertain. And this he did—perhaps too well.[23] Self-conscious and self-congratulatory, the journal struggles under the weight of the many picturesque flourishes and literary allusions Boswell lards into the narrative for the benefit of his friends. Yet there are frequent and stunning moments when Boswell catches life on the fly, achieving the literary equivalent of looking over his shoulder at a moment he has just lived and fixing it in his memory. The journal, which begins in self-deprecation—Boswell's horse vaulted him into a pile of muck—weaves across the lowlands, from a cake-eating contest in Cumberland to clan politics in Wigtown, from a hunt in Kirroughtrie to family gatherings at the Kames estate. There are, as well, accounts of Boswell's forays into theatrical productions— playing the role of Macheath in John Gay's *The Beggar's Opera*—and musical evenings, when he tried his hand at playing the flute. In these scenes, Boswell observes—and, with growing confidence, *choreographs*—moments of everyday life with great verve. At the same time, he fashions nuggets of conversation that often move the reader to laughter or tears—or both, as in a conversation with Hume. When he called on the great philosopher, Hume did not limit himself to erudite subjects, but also related a story about his great nemesis, Samuel Johnson, and David Garrick, the celebrated Shakespearean actor and director of the Drury Lane Theatre. When invited by Garrick to visit him backstage at the theatre, Johnson abruptly refused: "I will never come back," he said, "for the white bubbies and silk stockings of your actresses excite my genitals."

As we will next see, the journal was also the means by which Boswell served his apprenticeship not just as a writer, but also a spelunker of the self. In the life and lives he re-creates in his Harvest Jaunt journal, however, Boswell remained mostly on the surface of things. Perhaps in this respect, as in so many others, Kames provided an important model. While Kames was not a superficial thinker, he also was not particularly reflective. His prolific career as a writer and jurist shielded him from inner doubts and hesitations; his incapacity for introspection translated into unfortunate personal traits. He betrayed, as a result, a kind of violent arrogance in personal dealings. There was, for example, his habit of greeting friends and associates with "Well, ye brute, how are ye today, brute?"[24]

More serious was the way in which Kames's callousness leeched into his legal rulings. His great and unswerving attachment to whipping, transportation, and hanging, particularly in cases involving property, unsettled many of his contemporaries, including Boswell. Kames, though, was untroubled: "The objects of the penal laws," he declared with perfect equanimity, "are to be found among that abandoned and most abject class of men, who are the disgrace of the species."[25] Only the presence of the hangman, he concluded, could deter men and women who have "no feelings at all of honor, justice, and humanity." Given his unsentimental view, Kames predictably showed little feeling when he delivered his sentences. When he issued a death sentence against someone with whom he had once played chess, Kames blurted out to the condemned man, "And that's checkmate to you, Matthew!"[26]

Was Kames aware of this savage side to his character? His long stream of strictures to Boswell, warning that he must put aside his brute pleasures and devote himself to serious work, suggests that, if only dimly, he was alive to his own inner desires. For Kames, industry was the lone road to a secular form of salvation; by industry, he meant the practice of a profession that benefited the commonweal as well as the individual. For Kames, to be an "improver" was "the noblest plan for the conduct of life."[27] As a result, while he encouraged Boswell to write "lively" pieces, Kames thought this ultimately little more than a sideline, not the life goal of a modern Scot. He of course enjoyed Boswell's written accounts of his adventures, but he also warned his companion—nearly fifty years younger than him—that such pleasures are transient. What truly abides, for Kames, is devotion to the improvement of one's property and people: "If you always keep in view the old seat of Auchinleck," he told Boswell, "you will never deviate far from your course."[28] Boswell, it turns out, never deviated from his course. Moreover, he was wed to the notion of improvement. It just so happened that the course toward which he was groping dovetailed neatly with the goal of improvement: the writing of a journal. Like Paul on the road to Damascus, all that was left was the road to London in order for Boswell to have this revelation.

— 3 —

A JOURNAL IS BORN

*I have discovered that we may be in some
degree whatever character we choose.*

IN NOVEMBER 1762, as he prepared for a year's stay in London, Boswell launched with self-conscious fanfare his journal: "The ancient philosopher certain gave a wise counsel when he said, 'Know thyself.' For surely this knowledge is of all the most important . . . But grave and serious declamation is not what I intend at present. A man cannot know himself better than by attending to the feelings of his heart and to his external actions, from which he may with tolerable certainty judge 'what manner of person he is.' I have therefore determined to keep a daily journal in which I shall set down my various sentiments and my various conduct, which will be not only useful but very agreeable. It will give me a habit of application and improve me in expression; and knowing that I am to record my transactions will make more careful to do well. Or if I should go wrong, it will assist me in resolutions of doing better. I shall here put down my thoughts on different subjects at different times, the whims that may seize me and the sallies of my luxuriant imagination. I shall mark the anecdotes and the stories I hear, the instructive or amusing conversations that I am present at, and the various adventures that I may have."[1]

Boswell had managed, probably with the help of Lord Kames, to strike a deal with his father: in exchange for taking his civil law examination in Edinburgh, Boswell could then travel to London and try to win a commission in the King's Guards. Even before he left Edinburgh on November 15, Boswell was already anticipating his separation from both his father and Kames. The journal would remind him, Boswell made clear, of his duties and responsibilities.

But the journal was far more than a pile of quarto leaves meant to echo paternal advice. The above introduction reveals a far greater ambition—or, more accurately, ambitions. That improvement looms large in his justifications was only proper for a Scot born in the mid-eighteenth century. By then, the improvement of the individual and society had become a virtual obsession. Numerous civic societies, like the Improvers in the Knowledge of Agriculture in Scotland, had been founded. In 1726, the Board of Trustees for Arts, Fisheries and Manufactures was created, followed the next year by the Royal Bank of Scotland, and in 1728 the establishment of the city's Musical Society. It is not accidental that Boswell's early mentor, Lord Kames, wielded tremendous practical and intellectual influence over this movement.

Of course, Boswell was less interested in improving the production of flax and more interested in improving the production of the self. But what was the particular self that Boswell sought to burnish and improve upon? As his citation of the Socratic imperative reveals, Boswell will use the journal to plumb his self. Boswell's inward turn was not unusual—by the end of the seventeenth century, personal diaries were commonplace. As the social historian Lawrence Stone notes, "there bursts on to paper a torrent of words about intimate thoughts and feelings set down by large numbers of quite ordinary English men and women, most of them now increasingly secular in orientation"—an activity that "was greatly stimulated by

Calvinist theology and morality."[2] Yet, while Boswell continues this tradition of self-probing, he also transforms it. In a sense, he takes it out of the closet—that is, the praying closet where his father's generation retreated in order to wrestle with their souls.

While Alexander Boswell was a Calvinist *tout court,* his son was a Calvinist *malgré lui-même.* In Boswell's journal, the line between fashioning the self and saving the self is largely erased. Calvin would not have approved of this blurring, no more than he would have approved of Boswell's belief that just as "a lady adjusts her dress before a mirror, a man adjusts his character by looking at his journal."[3] Yet such sentiments, widespread by the mid-eighteenth century, reflected a broader concern with politeness. By this term, Boswell and his contemporaries did not understand, as we do today, the practiced gestures and words that skim the surface of social relations, but something far deeper and more important. Rather than the cosmetics of social intercourse that hid the warts and wrinkles of daily life, politeness then had a more radical aim: to reshape lives, even the world. As David Hume asserted, without politeness "no human society can subsist." Good manners, he observed, were invented "to render conversation and the intercourse of minds more easy and agreeable."[4]

Politeness was not a solitary occupation; it was, instead, a profoundly social activity. Moreover, it was an activity that, like painting and music, one practiced with great care and consistency. Joseph Addison and Richard Steele were explicit on this score: not only did they accept the notion that the world is a stage, but they mostly collapsed the distinction in their writings between actors and audience, scripted and sincere language. As with any actor, true gentlemen and gentlewomen lived—or, rather, performed—their lives with an audience in mind. The rule, Steele told his readers, was to keep "your Desires, your Words, your Actions, within the Regard your Friends have for you." While the longing for admiration might strike some observers as vanity, Addison added, don't pay them heed. Such a passion "is not wholly to be discouraged, since it often produces very good Effects." The "commerce of discourse," in Steele and Addison's eyes, was designed both to impress others and impress ourselves; by acting well, we pleased others and thus pleased ourselves. Once the world becomes a stage, even those spaces once thought of as private—the home, the boudoir, even, or especially, one's own thoughts—become public. As John Brewer writes, social knowledge—how others see us and how we wish to be seen—"had become a form of self-understanding."[5] In turn, this form of self-understanding was then recycled into one's public performances.

Private journals and diaries, which flourished during this era, were the means to review one's performance given earlier that day, as well as to rehearse the performance slated for the following day. By re-creating through words the events they had just lived, journal writers were able to judge and when necessary correct their performance. As Boswell reassured himself, "if I should go wrong, [the journal] will assist me in resolutions of doing better." Yet it is not entirely clear what Boswell meant by "doing better." For Brewer, journals like Boswell's "were meticulous in their daily detail because reflection on the social world was seen as a better way of understanding oneself." This differed from earlier Protestant accounts in which a "moral struggle between the forces of darkness and light, between the depraved body and the religious spirit, overshadowed all else."[6] Yet, as we will see, the distinction proposed by Brewer does not always hold. In Boswell's case, at least, God (and our relationship with him) was in the very details of everyday life.

———————

Boswell rarely worries about correcting himself in the pages of his Harvest Jaunt; he is instead content with a self-portrayal that alternates between the clownish and clever. But as Boswell already knew from his earlier visit, London was not the Lowlands. Indeed, London was not like any other place in Europe. It required a different kind of response, both personal and philosophical, that appears in the opening pages of the journal.

With nearly 750,000 inhabitants, London dwarfed every other European city, with the exception of Paris. It was nearly twenty times the size of Boswell's native Edinburgh and within its vast sprawl contained a variety of peoples, places, and experiences that left few visitors indifferent. For Boswell's fellow Scot, Tobias Smollett, London was more splendid than "Bagdad, Diarbekir, Damascus, Ispahan and Samarkand [of] the Arabian Nights," while for Jonathan Swift it was a pit that exhaled "Filth of all hues and odors."[7] Samuel Johnson's celebrated remark—when a man is tired of London, he is tired of life—is less fulsome and more factual than commonly thought: life in its nearly infinite number of registers, from grand to ghastly, was found in London. It was, for Daniel Defoe, quite simply a "great and monstrous Thing."[8]

While the characters in Smollett's novel *Humphrey Clinker* praise the closely knit and intimate nature of Edinburgh, they gape at the sublime spectacle offered by London. Arriving in the city, Lydia Melford is overwhelmed by the great press of pedestrians and assumes that a "great assembly was just dismissed, and wanted to stand aside till the multitude should pass." But she quickly discovers she was wrong: she was witnessing the everyday concourse of people on London's streets. Her uncle, Matt Bramble, so fond of Edinburgh, is less kind to London: this "overgrown monster" threatens all notion of public and private order. "All is tumult and hurry," he announces; Londoners seem "impelled by some disorder of the brain, that will not suffer them to be at rest." Once he manages to escape the vast hubbub of the streets, Bramble declares "the whole nation seems to be running out of their wits."[9]

What better welcoming committee for Boswell than this constant swell of humankind? Four days after leaving Edinburgh, his chaise slowly climbed the gentle slope of Highgate. While another traveler named Stewart watched him in wonder from inside the coach, Boswell, all "life and joy," quickly clambered out to view the great sprawl of London below. After reciting a soliloquy on the immortality of the soul from Addison's popular tragedy *Cato,* he sang several songs, including one that he improvised on the spot, containing the refrain: "She gave me this, I gave her that / And tell me, had she not tit for tat?" The chorus was a far cry from the earlier invocation of Rousseau and Voltaire from the summit of Arthur's Seat. Unable to restrain himself, Boswell then gave three great huzzas before returning to the chaise and his thoroughly bemused fellow voyager.[10]

As the chaise entered the city, Boswell grew even more animated. Staring out the window, he was "agreeably confused" by the "noise, the crowd, the glare of shops and signs." Rather than being repulsed by the hubbub, as was Matt Bramble, Boswell welcomed it. In this great stew of people and activities Boswell knew he had a freedom largely absent in Edinburgh: the liberty to re-create or refashion himself. Just days after arriving in London, Boswell himself registers this change: "Since I came up, I have begun to acquire a composed genteel character very different from a rattling uncultivated one which for some time past I have been fond of. I have discovered that we may be in some degree whatever character we choose. Besides, practice forms a man to anything. I was now happy to find myself cool, easy and serene."[11]

In the "genteel lodging" he quickly found on Downing Street in Westminster—very near the present-day residence of the country's prime minister—Boswell yoked himself to a daily regimen. He had decided to retrain, or recast his character, and thus become a very different James Boswell to the one who acted in the

Harvest Jaunt.[12] Most days, either before going to bed at night or before rising in the morning, Boswell jotted down a memorandum in which he reminded himself of upcoming errands and social calls, lunch or dinner engagements, bills, visits to his banker or tailor. But the memoranda were more than a daily schedule of things *to do*: they were reminders of things *to be*. Thus, "Be comfortable yet genteel, and please your friend Captain Erskine." But when he was not with a man he was trying to be genteel to, but with a woman to whom he was laying siege, Boswell proposed a different set of counsels. Now, he reminded himself, "be warm and press home . . . Acquire an easy dignity and black liveliness of behavior. Learn, as Sheridan said, to speak slow and softly."[13]

The precept "Be retenu" weaves through the memoranda and journal entries.[14] This repeated reminder reveals the tensions at the heart of Boswell's scheme: How does one negotiate the difference between the Socratic injunction to know oneself and the Addisonian exhortation to hide or refashion oneself? The spiritual exercises embodied by Socrates presuppose an ideal self or soul, while the lessons contained in the *Spectator* assume a self that seems infinitely malleable. Addison underscores this point: "There is scarce a State of Life, or Stage in it, which does not produce Changes and Revolutions, in the Mind of Man." In a manner of speaking, he concludes, change "destroys our Identity."[15] While Addison was seemingly unperturbed by this state of affairs, it was a source of anxiety for some individuals. As Lord Shaftesbury repeatedly asked himself in his private diaries: "Who am I?" His answer was less than reassuring: "I [may] indeed be said to be lost, or have lost My Self."[16]

Boswell, though, often reveled in this process of what he clearly thought was creative destruction. He was a bricoleur of the self, borrowing from various models present and past in order to better present himself. In a typical entry, he wrote: "I hoped by degrees to attain to some degree of propriety. Mr. Addison's character in sentiment, mixed with a little of the gaiety of Sir Richard Steele and the manners of Mr. Digges were the ideas I aimed to realize."[17] That his friend Digges was best known for his performances of Macheath suggests that Boswell's understanding of personal *retenu* was rather generous.

But "retaining" oneself is not the same as destroying the self. The notion of bricolage offers an alternative to, say, Shaftesbury's despair over the durability and consistency of the self. While he juggled various models and masks in London, Boswell believed there was a *there* within: a true Jamie Boswell, a self or soul uniquely and recognizably his own. Early in his stay in London, he lamented how easily he allowed himself to play the buffoon and rake back in Scotland. He was then, Boswell writes, "a character very different from what God intended me and I myself chose."[18] It is only with his "independent situation" in London that the "real" James Boswell begins to reemerge. The "immense crowd and hurry and bustle of business and diversion . . . agitate, amuse and elevate [my] mind. Besides, the satisfaction of pursuing whatever plan is most agreeable, without being known or looked at, is very great."[19]

But Boswell had no intention to remain a passive observer of the London scene. Instead, he quickly became the most engaged of spectators—in an important sense, a stage director of the city. He learned how to choreograph an encounter between unlikely individuals, just as he became practiced at the cultivation of conversation. With pride, Boswell noted the observations made by friends on his ability to provoke his interlocutors. Though he taunted friends, he did "with so smiling a countenance" that they could not show their anger. "I must remark," he confided to his journal, "that I have a most particular art of nettling people without seeming to intend it. I seldom make use of it, but have found it very useful."[20]

His friend Andrew Erskine went straight to the heart of the matter. One day, after the two friends had dined and were strolling across the Haymarket, Boswell suddenly asked: "Erskine, don't I make your existence pass more cleverly than anybody?" Erskine quickly agreed, but Boswell insisted on more: "Don't I make you say more good things?" To this, Erskine replied: "Yes. You extract more out of me, you are more chemical to me, than anybody."[21] Oliver Goldsmith, with whom he later became acquainted, told Boswell that he "had a method of making people speak." Never burdened by undue humility, Boswell agreed: "I must say indeed that if I excel in anything, it is in address and making myself easily agreeable."[22]

Of course, not everyone always agreed with Boswell's self-assessment. While Hume was pleasantly impressed when Boswell unexpectedly called on him in Edinburgh a few years earlier, he was not always so even-tempered. There occurred a contretemps involving a mutual Scottish acquaintance, David Mallet, whose tragedy *Elvira* had been lambasted in a published pamphlet by Boswell, Erskine, and their fellow student George Dempster. The young men quoted Hume in support, which outraged the older Scot. In a scalding letter to Boswell, he demanded to know how "came it into your heads, or your noddles, for if there had been a head among you, the thing had not happened . . . to publish in a book to all the world what you pretend I told you in private conversation."[23]

This hardly boded well for Hume's reaction toward Boswell's journal, of course. Oddly, though, Hume exercised a great deal of influence over Boswell's writing. Commentators have observed that contemporary novelists make their way into Boswell's journal and, indeed, his life.[24] Boswell had read Henry Fielding with relish, as he had Samuel Richardson. But in 1762, it was Hume who Boswell declared to be "the greatest writer in Britain."[25]

By then, Hume was indeed a lion of the British literary establishment. Of course, Hume was also the era's greatest skeptic. This, in part, was the great appeal Hume held for the young Boswell when, still a student at the University of Edinburgh, he visited the philosopher's lodgings on High Street. By then Hume had weathered several confrontations with the High-Flyers, a group of obstreperous Protestants joining in a desperate last stand against the inroads of secularism and materialism. Though Boswell's father was not particularly fervent and had little to do with the extreme elements in the Kirk, he remained a right-thinking Protestant. While Lord Auchinleck did not care for the dim worldview of the High-Flyers, he also disapproved of the worldview of a reputed atheist like Hume. What better reason, then, for Boswell to call on Hume? And what better reason to be surprised, as was Boswell, to discover that Hume was in fact a most "discrete and affable" host?

Boswell was surely aware, even if he had not read Hume's philosophical works, that the philosopher looked askance at the Socratic injunction with which Boswell had introduced his journal. For Hume, the difficulty resided less in the task of wrestling with the self than in simply locating it. Know thyself? For Hume, the oracle at Delphi begged the question. The command assumes the existence of a self—an "I" standing somewhere in there, minding the operations of my mind. Yet Hume questioned this very assumption: "For my part, when I enter most intimately into what I call myself, I always stumble on some particular perception or other, of heat or cold, light or shade, love or hatred, pain or pleasure. I never can catch myself at any time without a perception, and never can observe any thing but the perception." To insist that we can glimpse our selves in the buff, stripped of particular perceptions or emotions, is as nonsensical as asking our shadows to stand still while we step back better to observe them. In an image that would surely have pleased Boswell, Hume compares the mind to a kind of theater "where several perceptions successively make their appearance; pass, re-pass, glide away, and mingle in an infinite variety of postures and situations."[26]

Why, then, do we assume an "I" surveys these activities? Hume answered that our minds assure the continuity of our selves. Thanks to the resemblance of various experiences in our lives, we come to believe in the existence of a single mind and a unified self. To Shaftesbury's plaintive "Who am I?," Hume calmly replies that "I" is little more than a "quality" that we attach to sundry perceptions "because of the union of their ideas in the imagination, when we reflect upon them."[27] Yet this union no more exists in the external and objective world than does causation, yet another concept he revealed to be a fiction.

But it was less Hume's treatment of the mind's fictions than his treatment of past facts that interested Boswell. After publishing his major philosophical treatises, Hume turned to history writing. The first volume of his *History of England* appeared in 1754 (shortly after Boswell had entered the University of Edinburgh); eight years later, the last of the six volumes was published while Boswell was gadding about the Lowlands.

As a historian, Hume reached out with stunning success to the growing audience of general readers. His essay "Of the Study of History," while largely concerned with female readers, reflects Hume's broader ambitions: "There is nothing which I would recommend more earnestly to my female readers than the study of history, as an occupation, of all others, the best suited both to their sex and education, much more instructive than their ordinary books of amusement." The paternalistic tone of this essay obscures a critical point: historical perspective readjusts not only a woman's understanding of public affairs but a man's as well. As with the ancient Roman historians Tacitus and Sallust, history cultivated virtue by strengthening the reader's desire to excel among his peers. For this reason, Hume believed that works of history, and not fiction, cultivated virtue. With both feet in the world of experience, historians taught their readers how to distinguish between the credible and incredible, the probable and improbable. In the process, they offered their readers the proper models to emulate (or avoid).

Little wonder Hume became indispensable to Boswell in the days and weeks following his arrival in London. Boswell devoted a few hours every day to reading him; in a note to the earl of Eglinton, he announced that Hume has become his companion; in letters to his father, he included observations on each of the volumes; in his journal, he exulted that the *History* "enlarged my views, filled me with great ideas, and rendered me happy."[28]

The *History* reminded the young Scot about the great acts in the public realm he wished to match. Hume emphasized the "masculine eloquence" and "undaunted love of liberty" of Viscount Falkland, who had rallied to Charles I during the Civil War, but also the aristocrat's "enjoyment of every pleasure." Yet what Hume underscored, and Boswell responded to, was Falkland's moderation: "When civil convulsions proceeded to extremities, and it became requisite for him to choose his side, he tempered the ardor of his zeal."[29] This was also the case with Elizabeth I, a woman who displayed consummate skill in restraining her passions in order better to rule the kingdom. She received "with affability even those who had acted with the greatest malevolence against her" and deliberately extended this kind of performance to the rest of the realm.

Elizabeth oversaw the development of "innocent artifices" designed to reinforce the court's popularity: "Open in her address, gracious and affable in all public appearances, she rejoiced in the concourse of her subjects, entered into all their pleasures and amusements, and without departing from her dignity, which she knew well how to preserve, she acquired a popularity beyond what any of her predecessors or successors ever could attain."[30] And while Boswell thrilled to Hume's portrayal of Charles I on the eve of his execution—determined, tragic, and, well, majestic—he must have been equally taken by Hume's subtle insistence on Charles's "frailties" that made him fail where Elizabeth succeeded: "his beneficent disposition was clouded by a nature not very gracious; his virtue was tinctured with superstition . . . his moderate temper exempted him not from hasty and precipitate resolutions."[31]

Boswell was all too aware of his own frailties: he had picked up the *History of England* more or less at the same time he picked up a severe case of the clap. He had begun Hume's work in the midst of his determined pursuit of "Mrs. Lewis," an actress he calls Louisa in his journal. Boswell had plotted out the seduction with the same application that he had brought to the other aspects of his social and private life. But he soon came to regret the success of his amorous siege. Several days after his epic night at the Black Lion Inn with Louisa—"A more voluptuous night I never enjoyed. Five times was I fairly lost in supreme rapture"—Boswell was a surprised and unhappy host to "Signor Gonorrhea."[32]

Recalling a favorite remark of his old professor at Glasgow, Adam Smith, that "a time of indisposition is not altogether a time of misery," Boswell resigned himself to a long and painful mercury treatment that would force him to keep to his lodging. Though friends frequently called, Boswell left his rooms just a few times over the next six weeks. Not only was the prospect of such prolonged detention a source of despair for someone so sociable, but it was also a source of concern for someone so eager for material to add to his journal. "What will now become of my journal for some time?" he wrote soon after having sequestered himself. "It must be a barren desert, a mere blank. To relate gravely that I rose, made water, took drugs, sat quiet, read a book, saw a friend or two day after day, must be exceedingly poor and tedious. My journal must therefore, like the newspapers, yield to the times."[33]

But it was during this period of forced convalescence that Boswell realized that the journal's importance lay not just in collecting material, but also in the improvement of his writing. His friend Erskine, paying call one evening, reminded him of this unlikely stroke of fortune. When Boswell read aloud a few passages from the journal, Erskine found the writing to be lazy and careless. "Take more pains upon it, Jamie," he told his friend: "turn periods and render yourself ready at different kinds of expression." "He is very right," Boswell wrote later that day. "I shall be more attentive for the future, and rather give a little neatly done than a good deal slovenly."[34]

His friend's advice worked more quickly on Boswell's writing than the mercury did on his illness. Just days after Erskine's visit, sitting gingerly at his writing table with a cup of green tea to ward off the chill, Boswell exulted: "Upon my word my journal goes charmingly on at present. I was very apprehensive that there would be a dreary vacancy in it for some weeks, but by various happy circumstances I have been agreeably disappointed." Tellingly, many of the entries from this period are not reconstructions of meetings and conversations, but reflections on his friends and himself. With a flash of insight, Boswell laments his weakness to sacrifice "almost anything to a laugh, even myself." This weakness is so great, he confesses, that were Dempster and Erskine—the subjects of earlier and brutally candid entries—to suddenly call on him, "I might show them as a matter of jocularity the preceding three or four pages, which contain the most sincere sentiments of my heart; and at these we would laugh immoderately."[35]

At times, the more immoderate the sound of Boswell's laughter, the more immoderate was his sense of despair. Long plagued by passages of melancholy, Boswell grew especially vulnerable to the "foul fiend" during the spring of 1763. His convalescence from gonorrhea ended at the end of February, but by late April Boswell was experiencing recurrent bouts of "dullness." He plunged into frequent episodes of heavy drinking; and despite repeated vows against "low street debauchery," he could not restrain himself. Even Hume's *History* no longer had a tonic effect: after Boswell had it read to him in bed, he lay awake "in sad concern."

Moreover, by spring he seemed to be the last individual in London to know that his plans to join the King's Guards had been from the very start a fool's errand: his father had made it perfectly clear to anyone who could help his son that they must not. But there was a corresponding obtuseness on Auchinleck's part. He alone in Edinburgh and London seemed unaware that his son was keeping a journal. One, moreover, that he was eagerly sharing with friends. When a family friend informed him of the journal's existence, Auchinleck was stunned. In a searing letter, Auchinleck told his son that the jottings might pass as an "entertaining rant" between two intimate friends, but as nothing less than a source of family shame when they were shared with the public. Pushed to extremes by his son's thoughtlessness, Auchinleck exploded: "Finding that I could be of no use to you, I had determined to abandon you, to free myself as much as possible from sharing your ignominy. I had come to the resolution of selling all off, from the principle that it is better to snuff a candle out than leave it to stink in a socket."[36]

No doubt through the intervention of Euphemia, and perhaps Kames, Auchinleck then stepped back and offered a truce of sorts: he would forget his son's past indiscretions and imbecilities if Boswell desisted from any further "mimicry, journals and publications" and settled down to his law studies and life in Edinburgh.[37] All that a browbeaten Boswell salvaged was his father's permission to tour Europe before completing his studies and practicing law in Edinburgh. Ever the practical man, Auchinleck insisted that his son begin the tour with a winter's term spent at the University of Utrecht in order to study civil law. As Boswell gamely told John Johnston, by falling in with his father's schemes "I make him easy and happy, and I have a better prospect of doing well in the world."[38] Yet as Johnston well knew, the decision did not make Boswell himself happier and easier.

— 4 —

ENTER JOHNSON

*You will smile to think of the association of
so enormous a genius with one so slender.*

ON MAY 16, 1763, BOSWELL called on his friend Tom Davies, an
actor who also kept a bookstore at Covent Garden. While the two
men chatted over tea in the back room, Davies caught sight of a
huge figure lumbering through the shop's front door. Davies's face
lit up and, donning the role of Horatio at the moment he calls Hamlet's attention to his father's ghost, he declared: "Look, my Lord, it
comes." Much to Boswell's distress and excitement, "it" was none
other than the individual whom he had been trying to meet ever
since his arrival in London: Samuel Johnson. His appearance, Boswell discovered, was "dreadful": a huge man on whom hung ill-
fitted clothing, Johnson's eyes were swollen, his body subject to
palsy-like quivers, and his skin pocked by childhood scrofula.
Knowing Johnson's hostility toward the Scots, a mischievous Davies
immediately revealed Boswell's nationality. Undone by his friend's
treachery, Boswell blurted: "Mr. Johnson, I do indeed come from
Scotland, but I cannot help it." Johnson was merciless: "That, Sir, I
find, is what a very great many of your countrymen cannot help."[1]

It turned out, of course, that Johnson could not help but take to Boswell, in spite of his Scottish handicap. As Davies assured his friend at the end of the visit: "Don't be uneasy. I can see he likes you very well." To be well liked by Johnson, as Boswell understood, was no mean achievement. By 1763, Johnson was the most celebrated literary figure in London. He had established his reputation with a variety of works, ranging from his poems "London" and "The Vanity of Human Wishes" through the philosophical tale *Rasselas,* to the collections of moral essays known as *The Rambler* and *The Idler.* And, to be sure, the *Dictionary,* which brought Johnson not just fame, but a degree of financial security he had never before known. Yet all of these works—even the *Dictionary,* or at least its "Preface"—are shot through with stark insights into the human condition. As social beings, Johnson observes, we are driven to compete for honors and glories and renown that, once achieved, quickly lose their luster. We are driven by pride and envy to outdo others, forever reaching for something more, something greater than what we have just achieved. With a degree of vigor matched only by that of ignorance, we devote our lives to the feeding of this bonfire of vanities. As Johnson made clear in "The Vanity of Human Wishes," this predicament is true not just for politicians and generals, athletes and actors, but even the obscure academic: "When first the college rolls receive his name / The young enthusiast quits his ease for fame / Through all his veins the fever of renown / Burns from the strong contagion of the gown." Yet desire for fame, even within the walls of the academy, collapses when set against the weight of life: "Yet hope not life from grief or danger free / Nor think the doom of man reversed for thee / Deign on the passing world to turn thine eyes / And pause awhile from letters, to be wise."

Such wisdom is rare, though. With a surer grasp than any contemporary, Johnson captures the delusive character of lives: our tireless pursuit of the trivial and inconsequential. He does not slight the objective horrors of injustice, disease, and poverty. How could he, having survived a childhood blighted by scrofula and much of his adult life burdened by material want? But Johnson in particular dwells on the subjective ills that mine our lives—the traps we lay for ourselves as a result of our desires and passions. The inevitable failures and failings, the loss of love and loved ones, the dreams revealed to have been illusions, and hopes turned to nightmares—these are inevitably our lot. Perhaps the only thing worse than our fecklessness is our ignorance—an ignorance of which we are blissfully ignorant. "Where then shall Hope and Fear their objects find?" he asks in "The Vanity of Human Wishes": "Must dull Suspense corrupt the stagnant mind? / Must helpless man, in ignorance sedate? / Roll darkling down the torrent of his fate?"

But Johnson never accepted that we are either wholly helpless or irredeemably ignorant. He insists on a moral equilibrium in human nature. On the one hand, we will always be vulnerable to the passions of society. As he notes in lapidary fashion, "we desire, we pursue, we obtain, we are satiated; we desire something else, and begin a new pursuit."[2] On the other hand, we will always have the capacity to recognize and moderate this weakness through the honest examination of what he called the "stratagems of self-defence." This is why, he famously declared, "men more frequently require to be reminded than informed."[3] Reason must be always on guard against not just the passions, but itself. Johnson insists on the "importance of keeping reason a constant guard over imagination, that we have otherwise no security for our own virtue."[4] Reason is a frail thing, but it is not inconsequential: "Though the boast of absolute independence is ridiculous and vain, yet a mean flexibility to every impulse, and a patient submission to the tyranny of casual troubles, is below the dignity of the mind."[5]

Vital to Johnson's conception of man's character was the centrality of the soul. "That the soul always exerts her peculiar powers with greater or less force," he wrote in one of his *Rambler* essays, "is very probable."[6] Indeed, for Johnson, the human being was an "incorporated mind," the human body serving as a vehicle, of unpredictable dependability, for the soul. The distinction between these two entities, spirit and matter, was absolute, as well as an absolute mystery that reason could not pierce. As Roy Porter notes, it was a distinction setting Johnson at odds with the age's belief in a natural science of man, as well as highlighting his muted expectations of human happiness.[7]

But what import happiness, when lucidity is most valuable? Johnson was fond of saying that the first step to greatness is honesty. This claim certainly applies to his moral writings. "Whether to see life as it is will give us much consolation," he wrote, "I know not. But the consolation which is drawn from truth, if any there be, is solid and durable; that which may be derived from error must be, like its original, fallacious and fugitive."[8]

By the way his mind worked on these questions, Johnson himself set a profound example of this insight. As Walter Jackson Bate has observed, he "energizes hope not only by what he thinks, but also by the way he goes about thinking it, and the hope his example activates is a hope for human nature, for ourselves."[9] Johnson's moral aims are not epic or exalted, but instead focus on our everyday experiences. He warns his *Rambler* readership that while our standard for moral progress must be absolute, our expectations must be modest. Once we "set positive and absolute excellence before us, we may be pardoned though we sink down to humbler virtue, trying, however, to keep our point always in view, and struggling not to lose ground, though we cannot gain it." He echoed this position in his essay on epitaphs: "The best subject for such writing is private Virtue; Virtue exerted in the same Circumstances in which the Bulk of Mankind are placed, and which, therefore, may admit of many Imitators. He that has delivered his Country from Oppression, or freed the World from Ignorance and Error, can excite the Emulation of a very small Number; but he that has repelled the Temptations of Poverty, and disdained to free himself from Distress at the Expense of his Virtue, may animate Multitudes, by his Example, to the same Firmness of Heart and Steadiness of Resolution."[10]

While the world may not have been freed from ignorance and error by Johnson, at least Jamie Boswell would be. This, at least, was the young Scot's conviction. The older man—Johnson was fifty-three when he lumbered into Davies's bookshop—had an incalculable effect on the twenty-two-year-old Boswell. So great, indeed, that Boswell hesitated to act upon his feelings. He waited a week before calling on Johnson at his unkempt lodgings in the Temple, a densely built neighborhood in central London thick with law offices. Welcomed with undisguised delight by Johnson, Boswell joined a small group of other visitors and mostly observed and listened. When the others prepared to leave, Boswell followed suit, but Johnson insisted that he stay longer. What could Boswell do but assent? "I was proud to sit in such company."

Proud, but also perplexed. Johnson marked his contemporaries not just by the range and power of his thoughts, but also by the variety and peculiarity of his behavior. While he talked, Johnson's face and body rippled and shuddered with countless tics and reflexes. Spasms would rake across his vast bulk, rocking his great head as he moved across a room. Johnson's twitches and fits were so dramatic that, upon meeting him for the first time, the artist

William Hogarth thought him an "ideot." No less impressed was the novelist Fanny Burney, who marveled over Johnson's habit of "almost constantly opening and shutting his mouth as if he was chewing," as his body was in "constant agitation, see-sawing up and down."[11]

When he wrote his *Life of Samuel Johnson*, Boswell emphasized the physicality of his subject's speech: "I cannot too frequently request of my readers, while they peruse my account of Johnson's conversation, to endeavor to keep in mind his deliberate and strong utterance. His mode of speaking was indeed very impressive."[12] And impressed Boswell was as he listened to Johnson hold forth on a variety of topics. But Boswell took particular note of his host's defense of Christianity. As was most often the case with Johnson, his defense was in fact an attack—in this case, though he was not named, on David Hume. In 1748, Hume had published his *Enquiry Concerning Human Understanding*, which was largely a reworking of his *Treatise of Human Nature*. In the *Enquiry*, Hume included material he had omitted from the earlier work on the worried advice of friends. In particular, there was Hume's skeptical treatment of miracles. When it was eventually published, the fears of Hume's friends turned out to be prescient: the chapter sparked an ultimately failed effort by the High-Flyers in Edinburgh to condemn the book and censor the man.

One need not read between the lines to discover what the Calvinist faithful found so scandalous. In his discussion of miracles, Hume claimed that, when confronted by two improbable events, we must always give greater weight to the one that seems less improbable. History shows that claims on behalf of miracles—spurred as they were by superstition, desire, peer pressure, ignorance, or hypocrisy—have always been less probable than the basis for rejecting those claims. "Where a supposition is so contrary to common sense, any positive evidence of it ought never be regarded," Hume told his fellow doubter Edward Gibbon: "Men run with great avidity to give their evidence in favor of what flatters their passions, and their national prejudices."[13]

Clearly, Johnson would have none of this. His massive body athwart his chair, he declared to Boswell that Christianity "has very strong evidences." Johnson allowed that some of this evidence "appears in some degree strange to reason," but what of it? Rather than adopt the position of, say, the ancient Christian apologist Tertullian, who believed *because* it is absurd, Johnson instead insisted on a rational and empirical basis for miracles. No doubt with Hume's critique in mind, Johnson told Boswell: "In history we have many undoubted facts against which a priori in the way of ratiocination we have more arguments than we have for them; but then testimony has great weight, and casts the balance."[14]

The moral weight of Johnson's words and physical weight of his presence overwhelmed Boswell. In his journal, he called his newly made friend the "Stupendous Johnson." It quickly became apparent that the older Englishman was no less taken. Scarcely a month after first meeting, the two men were dining at one of Johnson's favorite taverns, the Mitre, on Fleet Street. In the midst of their conversation, Johnson stretched his huge arm across the table, grabbed Boswell's hand, and declared: "Give me your hand. I have taken a liking to you!"[15] There was more than one level to the attraction they felt for one another. Most simply, they needed one another. Though Johnson had become, in the words of one observer, a "publick oracle whom everybody thought they had the right to visit and consult," he was not close to most of these pilgrims.[16] Moreover, he vastly preferred the company of younger men: "I love the young dogs of this age," he exclaimed, "they have more wit and humor and knowledge of life than we had." As for that young dog

Boswell, few friendships better caressed his vanity than Johnson's. It was no mean achievement by an obscure twenty-two-year-old Scot newly arrived in London to be befriended by England's most celebrated man of letters. As a giddy Boswell wrote to a family friend in Edinburgh, Sir David Dalrymple, "You will smile to think of the association of so enormous a genius with one so slender."[17]

But deeper reasons also girded their friendship. At the time he met Boswell, Johnson was suffering from writer's block. His edition of Shakespeare's plays, started in 1756 and expected to take less than two years to complete, was still undone. The expectations of his publishers, his subscribers, and his king—who had earlier given Johnson an annual pension of three hundred pounds—only served to burden him further, as did the notorious gibe from an envious contemporary: "He for subscribers baits his hook, And takes their cash—but where's the Book?"[18]

But writer's block was just one symptom of a more general paralysis of will. Like Boswell, but to a deeper and darker degree, Johnson suffered from what had come to be known, by the eighteenth century, as the "English malady": melancholy. This was, in fact, the title of George Cheyne's popular book, published in 1733, and which Johnson urged Boswell to read.[19] While melancholy was a condition as old as civilization, by the late seventeenth century, the English seemed to have claimed a monopoly. Mr. Spectator spoke of "that gloominess and melancholy of temper which is so frequent in our nation."[20] At the same time, a burgeoning class of experts like Cheyne emphasized that nervous disorders, rather than instances of coquetry or self-indulgence, are "without doubt real and unfeigned."[21]

Johnson certainly had no need to be convinced of melancholy's reach. He feared he was on the verge of a nervous breakdown similar to the catastrophic one he underwent when he was in his early twenties. As he wrote in his journal shortly before he met Boswell, "I have led a life so dissipated and useless, and my terrors and perplexities have so much increased, that I am under great depression . . . Almighty and merciful Father look down upon my misery with pity."[22] In the tattered remnants of the journal he kept during these years—Johnson destroyed nearly everything from this period shortly before his death—certain phrases, like "vain terrors," recur with grim regularity, as do the sentiments of dislocation and despair: "A kind of strange oblivion has overspread me, so that I know not what has become of last year, and perceive that incidents and intelligence pass over me without leaving any impression."[23]

"To have management of the mind," Johnson informed Boswell, "is a great art, and it may be attained in a considerable degree by experience and habitual exercise."[24] Yet once such management was attained, it remained, for Johnson, a struggle to maintain. Night held particular terror for him; the moment he would quit his friends at the Mitre to return to his lodgings was heavy with dread. As he wrote in an *Idler* essay, a man in his state trembles come the moment to leave his friends so that they "may sleep."[25]

Boswell's nights were often sleepless, too, though, as we saw in Chapter 3, for different reasons. After his five-week cure for the clap ended at the end of February, he dashed back into polite society. When not visiting old friends and calling on powerful individuals whom he hoped would become new friends, Boswell trekked across the city streets and parks. As he approached Regent's Park, he felt as if he were "launched into the wide ocean." While he "exulted in moving again freely about," he also worried that he was "rather too keen, and had too great a hurry of spirits."[26]

This state of mind was only natural for a young man suddenly released from a kind of captivity. But it also was the work of a spirit overwhelmed by professional ambitions mostly beyond Boswell's ability to realize. He still clung to the dream of winning a commission in the King's Guards, despite the several obstacles placed in his way by his father. Lord Auchinleck had warned away those individuals who might exercise influence on his son's behalf. Thus, Boswell's repeated and increasingly desperate calls on aristocrats like the Duke of Queensbury and Lady Northumberland elicited responses that were goodwilled, but maddeningly vague.

All the while, Boswell privately expressed doubts about his fitness for such an appointment. His "noble reveries" of cutting a fine figure in the Guards were frequently checked by "dispiriting reflections on my melancholy temper and imbecility of mind."[27] Several times over the course of the late winter and early spring, Boswell was stricken by bouts of depression and would often seek the company of friends in the hopes of ridding himself of it. One of his closest companions, George Dempster, a Scottish lawyer whose unflappable character often calmed Boswell, advised his friend to run around his lodgings a few times. To his happy surprise, Boswell found that the exercise worked: "It expelled the phlegm from my heart, gave my blood a free circulation, and my spirits a brisk flow." But Boswell worried that the burden of "unhappy dissipation" can at times become so great that one would lack the strength to undertake such exercises in the first place.[28]

He was right to worry. In early May the miasma of melancholy engulfed Boswell. So thick was the murk that even Hume's *History* was unable to lift Boswell's spirit, leaving his friend William Temple to shake his head: "Poor man! He can't help it!"[29] As if decided to find a setting suitable for his state of mind, Boswell returned to a

pastime he first acquired in Scotland: attending the public hangings of convicted criminals. For much of the eighteenth century,
the gallows was the site of public entertainment and edification in
England. Eight times a year, great crowds gathered at Tyburn to
witness the final moments of those sentenced to hang for crimes
ranging from theft to murder. Johnson himself decried the decision, in 1783, to transfer the gallows from Tyburn to Newgate, thus
veiling the once-public event. Even Tyburn, he expostulated, was
not safe from the "rage for innovation." Executions, he argued, "are
intended to draw spectators. If they do not draw spectators, they
don't answer their purpose. The old method was most satisfactory
to all parties; the public was gratified by the procession; the criminal was supported by it."[30]

Contemporary observers noted the irony that these spectacles,
whose official justification was to educate the public on the consequences of crime, were also occasions for further criminal activity.
Pickpockets roamed the crowd, prostitutes plied their trade, and
the crowds often ransacked taverns as they followed the carts
carrying the condemned from Newgate Prison to Tyburn. Once at
the gallows, spectators often fell into brawls for the best places to
witness the event, then frequently fought over the bodies after they
were hanged: the diseased and handicapped believed that the
corpses of hanged criminals were endowed with healing powers,
while the clerks of surgeons tussled with one another to claim the
bodies for their masters' dissection classes.[31]

Yet Boswell's attraction to public executions was exceptional even
among his contemporaries. He first learned about Tyburn when,
still a child, he read *Lives of the Convicts,* a book no doubt designed
to shock and awe its youthful readership. Moreover, the twice-yearly
procession in Edinburgh of condemned prisoners, tracing their via
dolorosa from the Tolbooth Prison to the gallows at Haymarket,

would pass by the windows of Boswell's grammar school in the West Bow. It is inconceivable that such an event would pass unnoticed by the students: sitting at their benches and learning Latin by rote was poor competition for so dramatic an event.[32]

On May 3, Boswell, unable to shake off his "low spirits," decided to visit the prisoners held at Newgate. Entering the prison's court, which was open to the public, Boswell surveyed a three-storey block of cells, each furnished with barred windows. This "most dismal place" upset Boswell and he refrained from entering the cellblock. Yet he dawdled in the court, observing the interactions between the prisoners and visitors. In particular, he was taken by Paul Lewis, a young man who had served gallantly in the navy, but thereafter became a highwayman. In an exchange between Lewis and a visitor, Boswell overheard the prisoner reassure his friend that he was "very well." Lewis's quiet courage deeply impressed Boswell, as no doubt did the flair of his person: he was dressed "in a white coat and blue silk vest and silver, with this hair neatly queued and a silver-laced hat, smartly cocked." As he watched the "poor fellow" rattle his chains, Boswell "took a great concern for him, and wished to relieve him."

After a restless night during which impressions of his visit had hovered over him like a "black cloud," Boswell returned the next day to Tyburn to witness Lewis's execution. Not content to hang back, Boswell pressed forward, through a "prodigious crowd of spectators," to the gallows in order to see better the hanging of this "perfect Macheath." But unlike the hero of John Gay's play, there was no last minute reprieve for Lewis, who died only after several minutes of dangling from the cord's noose. Another condemned prisoner, a woman named Hannah Diego, actually freed her hands from the rope knotted around them and, to the cheers of the crowd, briefly wrestled with the hangman. All of this, predictably, further depressed Boswell: "I was most terribly shocked, and thrown into a very deep melancholy."[33] Afraid to spend the night alone, he went to his friend Andrew Erskine's lodgings and shared his bed.

While not as dispiriting as his experience at Tyburn—one that he would repeat several times, both as an onlooker and lawyer for condemned clients—other prospects weighed Boswell down as well. The idea of returning to Scotland and shouldering the "drudge" of a law practice never stopped rankling him. At moments, he nearly convinced himself that such a future was not all that grim. Not only was the practice of law in some sense a family obligation, but it also would be a profitable duty. If he were successful at the bar, Boswell would have the means to travel to London and Europe. But he was unable to maintain such practical resolutions very long, inevitably lapsing into his dream of military glory—or, more accurately, the sartorial and social glory such a military appointment would bring. Caught between his father and his ambitions, Boswell writhed and wept. "Alas, alas, poor Boswell!" he moaned, "to what an abject situation art thou now reduced!"[34]

Boswell's melancholy was compounded in May by his earlier collision with his father. As he confided to his friend John Johnston, "I have indeed a tolerable cause of low spirits . . . My father's displeasure hangs over me; the airy forms of gaiety and pleasure that glittered before my fancy are vanished or hid in clouds of discontent; and wherever I turn my thoughts I can find no certain joy."[35] It was in the midst of his negotiations with both his father and his "daemon of Melancholy" that Boswell met Johnson, who was wrestling of course with his own demons. The timing could not have been better for either man. In the weeks that followed their initial meeting at Davies's bookshop, Johnson impressed upon Boswell the justice of his father's expectations. The older man was not just a great advocate of filial piety and ancestral claims, but his notions of the rights and duties of Scottish lairds were quite romantic. When Boswell opened his heart, describing his travails with Lord Auchinleck, Johnson weighed in immediately: "Sir, let me tell you, that to be a Scotch landlord, where you have a number of families dependent upon you, and attached to you, is perhaps as high a situation as humanity can arrive at."[36] That Lord Auchinleck's title was due to his position on the Scottish bench, not to a claim of nobility, and that he had no dependents outside of his own family, was immaterial for Johnson—and, for that matter, Boswell. For Johnson, who maintained a sentimental attachment to the House of Stuart, society requires hierarchy and subordination for its well-being and happiness; if such order had to be built on the will-o'-the-wisp of nostalgia, so be it.

Johnson, whose world was one of duties and burdens—a world, he observed, in which there is more to be endured than enjoyed—confronted Boswell's melancholy with his fierce common sense. He confided that he, too, had been "distrest by melancholy." Even more startling for Boswell, uttered as it was by the author of the *Dictionary*, was Johnson's confession that he "always felt an inclination to do nothing."[37] Idleness, Johnson believed, was the cause, not the consequence, of depression and was a "disease which must be combated." The cure, he felt, was "constant occupation of mind, a great deal of exercise, moderation in eating and drinking, and especially to shun drinking at night."[38] Boswell would devote a good portion of his life to ignoring this wise counsel. But Johnson did insist on one practice that deeply reassured Boswell—the keeping of a journal. But even here, Boswell failed to take all of his mentor's advice. While the younger man agreed with Johnson's observation that it "would be a very good exercise, and would yield me great satisfaction when the particulars were faded from remembrance," he was far more ambivalent over the admonition that he also "keep it private."[39]

When he learned of Boswell's plans to study and travel on the Continent, Johnson bellowed his approval. Not only did the decision display obedience to Lord Auchinleck's wishes, but it would also do wonders for Boswell's melancholy. Going abroad, he declared, would allow Boswell to "break off idle habits."[40] As for a plan of study, Johnson urged Boswell to wander rather than wed himself to a single subject. It was important, of course, to master a particular field. But that was not all: while Boswell listened intently, Johnson "ran over the grand scale of human knowledge" and urged him "to acquire a little of every kind [of] knowledge."[41] For Johnson, who had scarcely traveled beyond the limits of London, Boswell's trip should be a tour not of cities and cathedrals, but of learned writers and professors. He quoted Lord Essex's remark that he would "rather to go an hundred miles to speak with one wise man, than five miles to see a fair town."[42] Perhaps more than any other single piece of advice from Johnson, Boswell would follow this one with a passion.

———

In subsequent conversations with Boswell, Johnson frequently returned to the subject of journal writing, deepening his earlier remarks. For Johnson, a journal was much more than an archive for the storing of memories. This suggests that a journal is little more than a container—a passive object. Johnson recognized what Boswell had himself been groping toward: the journal was a tool that encouraged change no less than reminiscence. Journal writing,

Johnson told Boswell, encourages a man "to review his own mind."[43] The great thing, he asserted, is to record "the state of your own mind; and you should write down everything that you remember, for you cannot judge at first what is good or bad."[44]

Or, indeed, what is most consoling or most terrifying. In the cases of both Johnson and Boswell, the journal was the inner space where reason and faith wrestled over the meaning of death. During the winter of 1762–1763, childhood memories managed to breach the wall of distraction and dissipation Boswell had made for himself in London. Just a few days before Christmas, Boswell found himself weighed down by "dreary Tolbooth Kirk ideas, than which nothing has given me more gloomy feelings. I shall never forget the dismal hours of apprehension that I have endured in my youth from narrow notions of religion while my tender mind was lacerated with infernal horror." He immediately adds how surprised he is to have "got rid of these notions so entirely"—a claim more wishful than true.[45] The repeated descents into depression, the morbid fascination with public executions, the frantic efforts to avoid the responsibilities associated with adulthood, the "frightful imaginations" that periodically struck him with such ferocity that he would ask friends if he could share their bed: all of these traits suggest Boswell was whistling in the dark with such optimistic claims.[46]

For this very reason, it seems odd that Boswell found great relief in the company of Johnson. After all, as the tatters of his journal from this period reveal, the great defender of traditional religion was often flailing at demons as well. The cryptic remark he wrote in his journal several years later—"Faith in some proportion to Fear"—surrenders its mystery when placed in the context of this unremitting struggle.[47] For Johnson, like Boswell, it was less fear of hell than fear of nothingness—what both men called "annihilation."

To a friend who claimed that annihilation was a "pleasing dream," Johnson burst out: "It is neither pleasing, nor sleep; it is nothing. Now mere existence is so much better than nothing, that one would rather exist even in pain than not exist." When Boswell half-heartedly intervened, insisting that God would never allow for such a possibility, Johnson cut him short: it is in the "apprehension of it that the horror of annihilation consists."[48] Boswell does not record his response—most likely because he did not have one.

It was this capacity to make such telling distinctions, and confront the consequences unflinchingly, that set Johnson apart from other men. Boswell captured this quality: "His superiority over other men consisted chiefly in what may be called the art of thinking, the art of using his mind; a certain continual power of seizing the useful substance of all that he knew, and exhibiting it in a clear and forceful manner; so that knowledge, which we often see to be no better than lumber in men of dull understanding, was, in him, true, evident, and actual wisdom."[49]

Many long meals of beef and port in the clear and forceful presence of Johnson's mind, either at the Mitre or Turk's Head, had filled Boswell's weeks leading up to his departure for Holland. He often wondered at his remarkable luck. "Had it been foretold to me some years ago," he once blurted out to Johnson, "that I should pass an evening with the author of *The Rambler*, how I should have exulted."[50] Indeed, even Boswell needed time to accustom himself to the suddenness of this friendship with so "strange and somewhat uncouth," yet so celebrated a figure.[51] "Wrapt in admiration of [J] ohnson's extraordinary colloquial talents," Boswell at first struggled to record their exchanges with accuracy. It was only when Bos-

well's mind came to be "strongly impregnated with the Johnsonian ether" that he succeeded in re-creating their remarkable
conversations.[52]

Dining with Johnson was, in its way, no less remarkable. Few
words were spoken once the meal was served; instead, the huge man
gave his full attention to the plate set before him. Regardless of the
dish—though he could, once satiated, speak eloquently about the
art of gastronomy—Johnson would attack the plate so violently that,
Boswell relates, "the veins of his forehead swelled, and generally a
strong perspiration was visible."[53] Owning that others might find
this display repellent, Boswell did not seem to mind. In a sense,
Johnson was no less fierce in his attention to words as he was to
food. His conversations with Boswell ranged over dozens of topics,
but they frequently returned to Boswell's efforts to reconcile his own
ambitions with his father's expectations, centering as they did on
the upcoming stay in Utrecht. In mid-July, he confessed his wish
that he could be as comfortable with Lord Auchinleck as he now
was with Johnson. When Boswell wondered what explained this
difference, Johnson replied that, in part, it was due to the different
experiences of the older men. Whereas he, Johnson, was a "man
of the world"—by which he meant London—Lord Auchinleck
hailed "from a remote part of the island." How could he not, then
be blinkered to the horizons that inspired his son? But there was a
deeper reason: "There must always be," he pronounced in his typ-
ically loud and deliberate speech, "a struggle between a father and
son, while one aims at power and the other at independence."[54]

Rather than pretend that such relationships should be easy and
harmonious, and thus offer Boswell false hope, Johnson instead insisted on the natural, nearly adversarial bond between fathers and
sons. He spoke at times of his own difficult ties with his father,

Michael Johnson, a struggling bookseller nearly fifty-five years old when Johnson was born, and who bequeathed his "vile melancholy" to his son.[55] Johnson long resented how both his parents displayed—"bustled over," in his words—their son's precocious intelligence in front of strangers, an anger that led to youthful acts of rebellion. (Toward the end of his life, Johnson told Boswell that he sought to do penance for this behavior by standing bareheaded in the rain at the place where his father's bookstall once stood.[56]) Johnson did not advise Boswell to perform a similar act, but to instead accept that such conflict is inevitable. While Boswell would not be on easier terms with this father, he would at least understand why this was so. The palpable force that accompanied this commonsensical claim, uttered by a man who had long wrestled with the very same doubts that hounded Boswell and emerged battered but intact, must have deeply reassured the young man.

A great source of combustion between Lord Auchinleck and his son was, of course, the journal. For the crusty laird, Boswell's attachment to journalizing was little more than an apprenticeship of a wastrel. For this reason alone, Johnson's appearance in Boswell's life at this point was crucial. Here was an older man, one who ceded nothing to Lord Auchinleck in authority and gravity, urging Boswell to pursue precisely the path that angered Auchinleck. In one of his *Rambler* essays, Johnson had already sketched his justification for such a literary ambition. Readers, Johnson believed, would find value in any "judicious and faithful narrative" of a life, no matter how obscure. "Not only every man has, in the mighty mass of the world, great numbers in the same condition with himself, to whom his mistakes and miscarriages, escapes and expedients, would be of immediate and apparent use; but there is such uniformity in the state of man . . . that there is scarce any possibility of good or ill, but is common to humankind." The task of the biographer, he concludes, is to lead the reader's thoughts "into domestic privacies, and minute details of daily life."[57]

From biographer to autobiographer, from observer of other lives to observer of one's own life, there is but a small step. When Boswell worried that he had been filling his own journal pages with "too many little incidents," Johnson reassured him: "There is nothing, Sir, too little for so little a creature as man. It is by studying little things that we attain the great art of having as little misery and as much happiness as possible."[58] This was of a piece with Johnson's belief that the teaching of morality—a principal aim, after all, of biography—depends upon an honest appraisal of our everyday lives. As Boswell wrote about his "Philosopher, Guide and Friend" after his death, his "maxims carry conviction; for they are founded on the basis of common sense, and a very attentive and minute survey of real life."[59]

That this philosophical guide and newly made friend announced to Boswell, less than a week before he was to leave for Utrecht, his decision to accompany him to the port of Harwich, was thus an immensely reassuring, if unexpected offer. Yet the trip did not augur well at first. In the coach to Harwich, Johnson devoted much of his time to reading a Latin work on ancient geography. At one point, though, he struck up a conversation with a fellow passenger, a fat and fatuous woman, who prided herself on never having allowed her children to idle a single moment. Johnson clearly found irresistible the combination of subject and speaker. As the carriage swayed, Johnson bellowed above the rattling of the harness and creaking of the chassis, that he wished the woman had educated him, too: "I have been an idle fellow all my life." Relishing the moment, Johnson then pointed to a horrified Boswell, declaring that not only had this young man already been idle in Edinburgh, Glasgow, and London, but he was now "going to Utrecht, where he will be as idle as ever."[60]

Happily, Boswell found harbor in Harwich from Johnson's mischief. Nearly half a century before, Daniel Defoe had passed through the town, describing it as a place of "hurry and business, not much of gaiety and pleasure." This was perfectly fine for Boswell, who was in a hurry to tend to the business of drawing what wisdom and succor he could from his traveling companion before boarding his packet boat to the Dutch port of Helvoetsluys.[61] During a visit to the town's main church, Johnson urged Boswell, who was kneeling on the floor, to recommend himself to the "protection of your CREATOR and REDEEMER." As the friends then strolled toward the beach, Johnson gave another powerful, though indirect display of his roiling faith. Perhaps to pay back Johnson's earlier barbs, Boswell praised the ingenious metaphysics of George Berkeley, which "proved" by a series of a priori arguments that the world, and everything it contains, exists only when it is perceived by an observer. Insisting the claim was logically irrefutable, though practically nonsensical, Boswell succeeded in provoking Johnson. Lurching toward a large rock, the older man began to kick it until he rebounded from the effort. To a gaping Boswell, Johnson then victoriously declared: "I refute it thus."[62]

Of course, Johnson's refutation slides off Berkeley's glass-smooth idealism. In the realm of a priori reasoning, Berkeley's claim—to be is to be perceived—is incontestable; in the realm of a posteriori, however, all we need to perceive is Johnson being Johnson. Though Berkeley's reasoning was irreproachable, it was also irrelevant, perhaps even irresponsible. As Johnson insisted, "truth such as is necessary to the regulation of life, is always to be found where it is honestly sought."[63] If not dishonest, such metaphysical undertakings were disingenuous. Not only do we not live our lives by such axioms, but we cannot do so. Rather than seeking the principles of common life, philosophers like Berkeley juggled the subtleties of rarefied thought. Several years later, when Johnson told Boswell that Berkeley had a "fine imagination," it was less a compliment, perhaps, than a description.[64]

Johnson was reluctant to attack Berkeley who was not only a fellow Tory but also an Anglican bishop who inveighed against religious freethinkers. Yet Johnson's frustration with "skeptical innovators" like Hume also spilled into his attitude toward Berkeley's system. Was not the Anglo-Irish bishop as vain as the Scottish philosopher? Surely, Berkeley was no less liable than Hume to Johnson's dismissive back of the hand: "Truth will not afford sufficient food to their vanity; so they have betaken themselves to error."[65] Johnson's faith was as material, as rock-like, as his critique of Berkeley's immaterialism. Whether it was philosophical or religious skepticism, Johnson invoked the truth claims of everyday life and common experience. In one of their earlier conversations on faith, Boswell wondered about those who denied the truth of Christianity. His body quaking with impatience, Johnson replied: "It is always easy to be on the negative side. If a man were now to deny there is salt on the table, you could not reduce him to an absurdity." We cannot ignore, he impressed upon Boswell, "the weight of common testimony."[66] Salt or salvation: both are necessary to life just as both belong to the world of experience.

After their encounter with the large stone, Johnson and Boswell continued to the harbor and the packet boat preparing to sail to Holland. The friends embraced, and after Boswell wrung a promise from Johnson to write letters, as well as the vow he would not be forgotten, he boarded the boat. From the unsteady deck, Boswell later recalled that he kept his eyes on Johnson "for a considerable time, while he remained rolling his majestic frame in his usual manner: and at last I perceived him walk back into the town, and he disappeared."[67] *Essi est percipi,* indeed. Johnson would never disappear from Boswell's thoughts—a presence that proved critical come the young Scot's arrival in Holland.

— 5 —

DERELICT IN UTRECHT

Be retenu

AS HIS PACKET BOAT *Prince of Wales* sailed to Holland, Boswell clutched his copy of Johnson's *Rambler* essays as if they were a life buoy. In the memorandum he wrote a few days before his departure for Harwich, he wrote the first of many exhortations to himself: be more like his father, be more like Johnson, be more like any worthy model—in a word, exhortations *not* to be James Boswell. "Set out for Harwich like Father, grave and comfortable . . . Go abroad with a manly resolution to improve, and correspond with Johnson . . . See to attain a fixed and consistent character, to have dignity. Never despair. Remember Johnson's precepts on experience of mankind. Consider there *is* truth."[1]

To no avail: Boswell's manly resolutions wilted and his congenital despair flourished almost immediately upon his arrival in Holland. As he later wrote to John Johnston, "a kind of gloom" gripped his mind even before he embarked from Harwich.[2] It did not help matters that, upon disembarking in Holland, Boswell realized it was Sunday: the gloomiest of days in a country, devoted to business and faith, renowned for its gloomy character. After a week spent indifferently in Leyden and Rotterdam, Boswell slouched toward Utrecht, once again arriving on the weekend. Taking a room on Saturday night near the medieval cathedral, his despair deepened every hour on the hour when the great tower bells were rung. "A deep melancholy seized upon me," he confessed to Johnston. "I groaned with the idea of living all winter in so shocking a place." Sunday morning brought no relief—on the contrary. "All the horrid ideas you can imagine recurred upon me"; wherever he turned, "all seemed full of darkness and woe." Alone in a city where he knew neither a living soul nor the language, Boswell fell apart. Afraid of going mad, he convinced himself that he had done so. "I went out to the streets, and even in public could not refrain from groaning and weeping bitterly." As he stumbled along the narrow streets and canals, he cried aloud "Miserable wretch that I am! What shall I do?"—a question the startled burghers of Utrecht, on their way to church with their families, could no more understand than they could answer.[3]

When Boswell penned this letter to Johnston, more than a month had passed since the events he recounted. During this spell, he had time not only to reflect on these events, but, no less important, to rehearse them. Boswell's plunge into despair was real enough, of course. In a letter to William Temple, written immediately after he emerged, still shell-shocked, from his Sunday experience, Boswell's sincerity and anguish are unmistakable: "My mind was filled with the blackest ideas, and all my powers of reason forsook me. Would you believe it? I ran frantic up and down the streets, crying out, bursting into tears, and groaning from my innermost heart."[4] In his frenzy, Boswell also wrote to his friend George Dempster, who was then in Paris, begging him to come to Brussels. After posting the letter, however, Boswell accepted the invitation of an American medical student he had just met to join him for a "jaunt through Holland." As a result, by the time Dempster arrived in a great flurry several days later to rescue his friend, the friend was

nowhere to be found. Rather than flying into a fury, however, Dempster sent a long and sympathetic letter to Boswell, whom he rightly
addressed as "thou mass of sensibility."[5]

While Dempster was quite right in his estimation of his friend,
his letter suggests that Utrecht's character, and not Boswell's, was
the reason for the passing frenzy: "I foretold that your fund of patience and affectation was too small to bear living among a set of
Dutch professors in tartan nightgowns and long pipes . . . who consider mirth as a shame and rampaging as a sin."[6] Temple was closer
to Boswell and had known him much longer, and his letter captures both the authentic fears his friend felt and the aspect of performance to his behavior. Sympathizing with the "unhappy disposition of your mind," Temple does not make light of Boswell's
condition, but reminds him that he must take on the role expected
of him, urging his friend "to act a part more becoming yourself."
Allow reason to reestablish its mastery, he tells his friend, and "you
may still be whatever you please."[7]

At this point, however, it was not at all clear to Boswell what "becoming yourself" meant. As Temple implied in his letter, it entailed,
at least in part, becoming a son worthy of Lord Auchinleck's expectations. "There are many relations and dependencies to which
a proper regard must be paid. A father is a character to which much
is due." More immediately, it meant becoming like the friend who
had seen him off just a few weeks earlier at Harwich: "Think of
Johnson, and be again a man." Temple's exhortation was probably
unnecessary. In his memoranda, Boswell relentlessly reminds himself of the man whose presence, like a massive anchor, kept him
steady and away from the reefs of depression.

Turning to his copy of the *Rambler* essays, Boswell discovered
that "several papers seem to have been just written for me." In particular, Boswell was riveted by the thirty-second essay, in which

Johnson reflects on the proper response to human calamity. The Stoics, Johnson observes, are not the best of teachers: How can they be when they deny the reality of loss and suffering? Misery and pain are no less real than the boulder Johnson assaulted. Let us not, as a result, expend our "strength in establishing opinions opposite to nature." Instead, our task is to assess the human condition with lucidity and honesty. We will then recognize that the "cure for the greatest part of human miseries is not radical, but palliative." The man Boswell described to Temple as the "ablest mental physician I have ever applied to" prescribes patience and labor as the greatest balms for such moments. In fact, Johnson comes down hard on the necessity of action, the need to resist these evils, all the while recognizing the struggle's asymmetrical character. "The calamities of life, like the necessities of nature, are calls to labor, and exercises of diligence." We should no more submit to these calamities than a man dying of thirst "is to imagine that water is prohibited."[8]

In his *Life of Samuel Johnson,* Boswell compared Johnson's essays to "bark and steel for the mind."[9] In a letter to Johnston, Boswell begged his friend to buy a copy of the *Rambler* essays: "It costs twelve shillings. But it is worth much more." There was no book better suited for people with their similar temperaments. "It proceeds upon the supposition that we are here in a state where there is much gloom, and fortifies the mind to enable it to support the evils which attack it."[10] No doubt the essays helped, as bark does for leather, preserve and strengthen Boswell's mind against these assaults. But they also became the script for rehearsals to this part of his life. Committed to a yearlong course of study in Utrecht, Boswell turned to Johnson's essays as an actor seeking cues and guidance turns to a director. Returning to Utrecht from Rotterdam, where he had holed up at the end of his Dutch jaunt, Boswell hired a servant, rented rooms, and arranged courses at the university.

Utrecht was no longer a living hell, but quite simply was a "foreign city where I have the opportunity of acquiring knowledge" as well as a good distance "from all my dissipated companions."[11]

Boswell had set out an ambitious schedule for himself: French lessons (he wrote every day in French on themes ranging from his love of footbaths to his tendency to indolence), readings in Greek and Latin (Tacitus was a favorite, who "improves both the head and heart"), keeping up his correspondence and journal, reading widely in philosophy (Voltaire was a near constant companion) and theology (various English divines whose work Voltaire scorned), and engaging in polite conversation with the local notables. Not only do his law courses at the nearby university seem like an afterthought, but the content of his busy daily agenda is itself less important than the form itself. The schedule's great virtue was its mere existence, it was a series of, in Boswell's phrase, restraints. They provided, in effect, the seawalls to guard him against the inevitable and inexhaustible undertow of melancholy.

In Utrecht, Boswell continued the practice he had begun in London of writing a memorandum every morning. The memoranda were, more or less, directions for each day's performance: how to appear, what to do, when to speak. But unlike those written in London, each of the Utrecht memoranda included a review of the performance he had given the day before, paying heed to his language and appearance. "Mark what was right and what was wrong, then give directions for the following day."[12] Boswell was a merciless self-critic, frequently lambasting himself for speaking too little (or too much), being too gay (or too somber), or devoting too much time to various women (or, more rarely, too little). At times, he takes himself to task for having "talked too much in a vivacious style," and at other times for having been "absurdly bashful before Miss de Zuylen" (who will enter our story in due course).[13] He laments having fallen in with a group of Dutch students, with whom he drank toasts until the wee hours, and the next day compliments himself for having "recovered very well after your riot."[14] One morning, after having spoken too much and too loudly, he tells himself, in an observation that would have made his friends smile and his father sigh: "silence is your great refuge." In one memorandum, he vows to adopt John Locke's "prescription of going to stool every day regularly after breakfast."[15] (The following day's memorandum does not carry a review of this particular performance.)

The matrix for these memoranda was the "Inviolable Plan," which Boswell wrote in mid-October. Over several pages, he keeps circling back to the need for, well, an inviolable plan. Only that will save him from the bog of vacuity. "You have been long without a fixed plan and have felt the misery of being unsettled . . . You are to attain habits of study, so that you may have constant entertainment by yourself . . . Remember that idleness renders you quite unhappy . . . Without a real plan, life is insipid and uneasy . . . Keep firm to your plan. Life has much uneasiness; that is certain . . . Be assured that restraint is always safe and always give strength to virtue."[16] It is as if Boswell flips the traditional justification for education—habit and restraint are less the means than the ends while the ancient languages and civil law are less the ends than the means. For Boswell, his course of study is, ultimately, an exercise in self-discipline.

Not surprisingly, along with Johnson's name, the word that crops up most often in the memoranda is *retenu,* by which he understood calm, restraint, or poise. Boswell commends himself for being *"retenu* and on guard" against the wiles of a young widow, and lectures himself to "swear *retenue* and manners" after having failed to do so. He then counsels himself to "try silence one week"—a trial that lasted scarcely twenty-four hours.[17] In the dead of the Dutch winter, when Boswell's determination to cleave to the Inviolable Plan wavered, he grabbed himself by his own collar: "Fight out the winter here . . . Pray, pray be *retenu*. O man, thou has a sad inclination to talk; now is thy time to cure it!"[18]

"Pray, pray," a common eighteenth-century phrase used for emphasis, here underlines Boswell's desire to be *retenu*. But this particular use of the phrase is a happy coincidence, for Boswell's memoranda pick up where prayers leave off. Protestantism had transformed the largely ritualistic function of prayer. It continued to serve as the avowal of one's total submission to God, but it also demanded that Christians undertake a personal inventory. The review of one's past actions and thoughts was unforgiving—necessarily so, as it was done in front of God. Johnson was an old hand at this practice. According to his early biographer John Hawkins, Johnson kept a journal in order to "review his progress in life and to estimate his improvement in religion."[19] Johnson was especially brutal with himself; when he swore "to examine the tenor of my life & particularly the last week & to mark my advances in religion or recession from it," he would do so with little self-pity and even less self rationalization.[20]

While Boswell was no stranger to prayer, he was not at all on the same terms with it as his guide and friend. There are remarkably few allusions in his journal to praying (though he did take a nearly indecent interest in confession while he flirted with Catholicism). Prayers nevertheless filled his life and journals, but he calls them memoranda. These daily reviews played the same role for Boswell that prayers did for Johnson. They contained, of course, directions and goals for the coming day, but they also reviewed with a critical eye the day gone past. The great difference is that Boswell eyed his own self not from God's perspective, but that of the public. Or, perhaps more accurately, he did so from the perspective of a lesser god, the impartial spectator. In the notes and reviews he writes to himself, Boswell measured his actions with one eye on himself, the other on the public, ever striving to tune up or tune down his public self.

But Boswell's soul, stubbornly splenetic, required constant tuning. In the memoranda, we always find Boswell half-satisfied, half-chagrined by his performances. But they are almost always marked by a bracing lucidity, as well as a sense of the absurd. During a visit to Amsterdam, he spent an evening trawling a red-light district (whenever he left Utrecht, he also left the sexual *retenu* he practiced there). Boswell found himself in a room with a prostitute and a bottle of claret, but without "armor"—his word for the leather prophylactic he fitfully wore after contracting several bouts of gonorrhea. But never without words, the garrulous Scot then spent his allotted time chatting with the woman. In his memorandum, Boswell shook his head over the tableau: "It was truly ludicrous to talk in Dutch to a whore. This scene was to me a rarity as great as peas in February." But he was also critical of his action, disgusted to have spent time in "the sinks of gross debauchery." With severity, he concluded: "This was a proper way to consider the thing."[21]

Yet, no matter how proper or prolonged his reflections, Boswell was often unable to act the role he had assigned to himself. Even the invocation of Johnson's name at times proved inadequate. Everyone, including himself in his memoranda, urged him to be more like Johnson—everyone, tellingly, except Johnson. The Scot did not hear from his guide and friend until December, more than five months since they had taken leave of one another at Harwich. One of the reasons for the silence, Boswell discovered, was a frantic letter he had sent Johnson in August, penned when he wasn't busily ricocheting along Utrecht's streets, groaning and weeping aloud.

When Johnson finally wrote, he told his young friend that the first letter, which "gave me an account so hopeless of the state of your mind," did not merit a reply.[22] Boswell hardly flinched at the matter-of-fact remark; instead, he exulted to himself that he had heard from "the first author in England"—reason enough to make him "return still to the charge."[23]

In his elation, Boswell overlooked that Johnson had also ignored his second letter, written a few weeks later when he was again in control of himself and committed to remaining in Utrecht. Perhaps this was because Johnson had never been absent, at least in Boswell's churning mind. In late September, when he had finally wrestled down his frenzy and adopted his daily routine, he credited Johnson: "O Johnson! How much do I owe to thee! I now see that I can conquer my spleen by preserving just ideas of the dignity of human nature and never allowing sloth and idleness to get the better of me."[24]

Perhaps. Telling, though, is that Johnson's stubborn silence had less to do with Boswell's state of mind than his own. As we earlier saw, Johnson had fallen during this same period into one of the darkest nights of his soul. This has much relevance for Boswell, because the cures Johnson prescribed for the young man had failed Johnson himself. Though Johnson destroyed the pages from his journal that cover the period 1761–1763, both his subsequent entries, as well as testimony of others, underscore his dismal state of mind. A prayer from late 1764, in which he called upon God's mercy, makes visible the darkness of those years: "Let me not be created to misery . . . Deliver me from the distresses of vain terror."[25] Yet visitors to his rooms reported that deliverance was not yet nigh. One day, William Adams called on his old friend only to find Johnson dragging his massive frame from one room to another, sitting down and standing again, his lips moving without uttering a sound. Though a doctor, Adams was shocked. The sight, he reported, was "dreadful to see."[26]

Boswell did not himself see this awful sight, nor did he learn about it from Johnson. Instead, while gathering material for his *Life*, Boswell heard the tale from Adams. The experience still weighing heavily on the good doctor, Adams refused to say anything more about it, apart from offering a terrifying glimpse into his friend's misery. During a moment of lucidity, Johnson said he'd have a limb cut off if it would relieve his despair.[27] Johnson slowly recovered from this near-collapse into insanity, but the experience—not unlike Boswell's own repeated encounters with the "black fiend"— illuminates Johnson's understanding of the human condition, one that Boswell seems to have grasped.

In his *Life*, Boswell painted a celebrated portrait of his subject's defiance of doubt and despair: "His mind resembled the vast amphitheater, the Coliseum at Rome. In the center stood his judgment, which, like a mighty gladiator, combated those apprehensions that, like the wild beasts of the Arena, were all around in the cells, ready to be let out upon him. After a conflict, he drove them back into their dens; but not killing them, they were still assailing him."[28] By their very nature, these mental apprehensions, these beasts of the mind, could not be killed. By the mid-eighteenth century, faith could no longer be simple and unquestioned, while reason could only be complex and questioning. Charles Pierce has neatly summarized Johnson's predicament: "His deep respect for reason as the ultimate standard by which to determine thought and action impelled him to establish his religious life on a solid rational basis."[29]

Yet, in Johnson's mind, it proved as impossible for reason to justify religious faith as it was, in his heart, for him to consider Hume as anything other than an infidel. The intellectual and moral consequences of this failure were momentous. With Johnson, there was a constant tension between hope and fear, aspiration and desperation, unrelenting labor and unrelieved worry that he had fallen short of God's demands. During the conversation that had led Boswell to cast Johnson as a moral gladiator, Johnson had become increasingly agitated as Boswell pressed the question of what our proper response should be to the prospect of death. The Scot later realized that he "was in the wrong" because Johnson's "thoughts on this awful change were in general full of dismal apprehensions." Pushed once too often on a subject that terrified him, Johnson lashed out at Boswell: "No, Sir, let it alone. It matters not how a man dies, but how he lives." In a state of feverish agitation, his body shaking, Johnson then warned Boswell not to call the following day.

Boswell's reasons for pursuing the subject in 1769, when the conversation took place, were the same as they had been in 1763, when he struggled against melancholy and despair in Utrecht. His reasons were personal and persistent: like his guide and friend Johnson, Boswell could not accept the fact of annihilation. As he watched Johnson struggle in the Sisyphean task of battling down this particular fear, Boswell was not simply in the stands of the arena, a curious spectator and nothing more. Instead, he was in the same arena, uncertain whether even Johnson, with his great mind and great faith, could protect him from the prospect of annihilation. When Boswell, many years after the Grand Tour, implored Johnson for arguments for God's existence so that his "religious faith might be as firm and clear as any proposition . . . when it should be attacked," Johnson could not satisfy him: "Sir, you cannot have all the objections. You have demonstration for a First Cause: you see he must be good as well as powerful, because there is nothing to make him otherwise, and goodness of itself is preferable. Yet you have against this, what is very certain, the unhappiness of human

life." Only "positive revelation," he concluded, can offer such certainty: a qualification that hardly eased Boswell's fears—or, for that
matter, Johnson's.[30]

Through the fall of 1763, Boswell clung tenaciously to his Inviolable Plan. He followed his courses, wrote his French themes, made
the rounds of the local aristocracy, and exhorted himself to show
retenu. He read copiously, and not just the ancient historians and
moralists; his memoranda are larded with references to religious
works and, incongruously, the works of Voltaire and Hume. Acting
on Johnson's suggestion, Boswell read Samuel Clarke's *Discourse
Concerning the Being and Attributes of God*. A disciple of Isaac
Newton, Clarke declared solemnly that no "article of the Christian
faith is opposed to reason."[31] Not only did he offer an array of traditional a priori and a posteriori arguments for God's existence,
but also claimed that moral laws based upon God's existence were
no less irrefutable than mathematical laws. Yet, there was an odd
kind of uselessness to his work—one that he seemed himself to acknowledge. With some asperity, Clarke allowed that even his bat-
tery of arguments would prove useless for those modern men and
women burdened with a "presumptuous Ignorance which despises
Knowledge." As for those who instead approach the subject with
an "unprejudiced Apprehension and an uncorrupt Will," they already know in their hearts that God exists.[32]

It was perhaps for this reason that his contemporary Anthony
Collins made the famous dig that no one had doubted God's existence until Samuel Clarke tried to prove it.[33] Another English theologian, Joseph Butler, aware that rational Christianity was riven by
this inner contradiction, worried about the impact of deism on
young and inquiring minds. The problem with yoking God's existence to rational proofs is that they always seemed to lead to skeptical doubt. How could it be otherwise when critical inquiry is the

raison d'être of reason? Hence Butler bundled together the truths of reason and revelation, determined to do battle against the age's tendency to conclude that Christianity is fictitious.[34]

Yet Boswell, judged at least from the references in his journal, seemed more taken by Voltaire and Hume, in particular their work as historians, than by English theologians. While Boswell does not always identify the works he is reading, one that does crop up a few times is Voltaire's *Essay on Universal History*. Just as Copernicus and Newton had yanked the earth away from the center of the universe, so too did Voltaire seek to assign Europe its proper place in his history. He not only devotes the opening chapters of his history to the civilizations of China, Persia, and India, but also mocks earlier historians who portray Christianity as the epicenter of world history. In a word, Voltaire's own account presented itself as universal because it was based on reason, and it would thus serve the aims of religious tolerance, unlike the bogus universalism of Christianity, serving only the aims of rapacious and brutal religious leaders. Any historian worth his salt was a philosophical historian. As he told his friend Damilaville, he wanted his histories to "make people see how we have been deceived in everything; to show how much of what is thought ancient is modern; how much of what has been given out as respectable is ridiculous."[35]

This was a goal shared by Hume, whose *History of England* returns time and again to the catastrophic consequences of religious enthusiasm and superstition. It was hardly a secret that Johnson thought poorly of both men. The history written by the Scottish "infidel" was merely "an echo" of the history written by that "petty wit" across the Channel. (That Johnson, as he later told Boswell, had not read Hume's history did not prevent him from judging it.) Yet Boswell had been deeply impressed by Hume's work as a historian. As we saw in Chapter 3, he had begun reading the *History* while laid up in London with the clap, taking notes that he would then send to his father. But the young man's favorable impression of Hume began to fade, no doubt under the influence of Johnson. In a letter sent to Temple in early December 1763, Boswell declared rather prissily: "People may talk of David Hume as they please. I maintain his style is far from being good. He fritters it away like a French marquis."[36]

We can overlook the fact that Boswell did not also mention to his friend that, just a few months earlier, Johnson had condemned Hume on the very same grounds: "Why, Sir, his style is not English; the structure of his sentences is French." More important, however, was the substance of Hume's writings. Under the influence of Johnson, Boswell was now uneasy with his fellow Scot's skepticism. This is made clear in his response to Temple's suggestion that Boswell spend the winter in Paris. Hume had just arrived there, Temple reported, as the private secretary to the British ambassador, Lord Hertford. To find himself not only in the company of Hume but also the great philosophes, certainly fired Temple's imagination: "Indeed, I think it the luckiest incident in the world for you; and you certainly would be much to blame to slight it."[37]

But Boswell would have none of it: "Think you that I would learn prudence for my conduct in this world at Paris, or would d'Alembert and the other infidel Academicians help me on in my journey to happiness in the next?" Hume, of course, was at home among these infidels—a prospect that alarmed Boswell, who had been clinging tenaciously to his Inviolable Plan and had recently achieved emotional stability. Reminding himself on a daily basis to be more like Johnson, poring over the *Rambler* essays for spiritual reassurance and respite, welcoming with euphoria the arrival of Johnson's first letter, Boswell simply could not afford, emotionally or intellectually, to entertain Temple's suggestion. Write what you wish about Hume, Boswell replied dismissively to his friend, but "read the work of Mr. Johnson."[38]

Despite his embrace of Johnson's strictures, Boswell was unable to shake the "black fiend" of melancholy. After the initial shock he suffered in Utrecht, Boswell had managed to impose upon himself a thick and regular routine of sustained study and sober socializing. In his correspondence and journal, he exhorted himself to maintain this pace. In late September, he portrayed himself to Temple as prepared to join "the warfare of life." In an exultant state, he continued: "Let us never yield a moment to Mental cowardice . . . Let us persist with unremitting fortitude . . . We ought to consider that God has placed us here in a state of probation, where we have got abilities, which if we exercise properly, we may have immediate happiness."[39]

Boswell had received a steady barrage of variations of this same message, though usually without the promise of immediate results. A few days earlier, Temple had urged him "to break in pieces the fetters of dissipation and sloth," reminding his friend that "he who is most active for the good of his country and of mankind, that merits the glorious character of a man of virtue."[40] Less high-minded, but no less concerned, Dempster told Boswell that he had better roll up his sleeves: "Spleen is like a bullying boy at school: insupportable till he is once heartily thrashed, and for ever your humble servant."[41] His older friend, David Dalrymple, who helped mediate his earlier negotiations with his father, agreed that applying to God was "right and wise," but not enough: Boswell must also find "the proper means for [his] own relief." Along with the study of French and law, Dalrymple suggested frequent carriage jaunts and ice-skating, though it ought to be done in company so that Boswell would "run no danger of drowning, nor much of ducking."[42] Lord Auchinleck was no less practical. Replying to his son's earlier letter, in which Boswell had described his recovery from his dire state of mind, Auchinleck once again prescribed activity. "I would recommend to you as the best preservative against melancholy and vice never to be idle but still to be employed in something." And while taking notes on Tacitus was a fine activity, Auchinleck also encouraged his son to take notes on how the Dutch managed their cattle: "I would wish to be informed of the method by which they keep their cows so clean, for my remembrance of it is dark."[43]

Boswell never reported back to his father on Dutch dairy hygiene, perhaps in part because his own particular brand of darkness was again soon upon him. In early March, John Johnston wrote with tragic news: a son that Boswell had fathered two years before in Edinburgh with a "curious young little pretty" named Peggy Doig had died. Boswell had never seen the boy—he had already left for London when Charles Boswell, the name he gave his illegitimate son, was born. But he had provided both a nurse and ample money for the child's upbringing, and asked his friend Johnston to keep an eye on matters.[44]

The child's death terrified as well as saddened Boswell. In a series of poems, he tried to describe his loss—as well as a premonition he had of Charles's death—recalling that religion and activity alone could provide relief. Yet for naught: the following day, during a stroll, he "melted with tender distress," and a debate that same evening about Calvin's notion of predestination left him "faint and gloomy." In his memorandum, he castigated himself for having engaged such a conversation: "Did you not determine to keep mind fixed to real objects, and to expel *speculations*, which you *know* to be uncertain?"[45] Yet the grim speculations, particularly when he was alone, proved persistent. Though he continued to act on his Inviolable Plan, dining with acquaintances, writing his French themes, and studying his books, Boswell's taut nerves were straining. On March 14, 1764, he stunned his dinner companions when he blurted out that he "had so bad a view of life that [he] could almost do anything." On the following page of his journal was another, even bleaker poem addressed to Temple:

Oft I the warmest resolutions make
That the great road I never will forsake
But oft I find that I have gone astray
Nor can I tell how I have lost my way.[46]

Like Johnson, Boswell dreaded annihilation, by which they understood the state of nothingness that follows death. As Johnson told Boswell during their Scottish tour: "No wise man will be contented to die, if he thinks he is to fall into annihilation: for however unhappy any man's existence may be, he yet would rather have it, than not exist at all."[47] Boswell thus did his best not to think of this prospect, reprimanding himself when he allowed the possibility that God either did not exist, or that, if He did, was indifferent to his own existence. In a heated conversation with a fellow Scot named Rose, also in mid-March, he clung tenaciously to Clarke's proofs for God's existence and benevolence: "You receive a revelation from a Being whom you have the strongest proofs that he is, and he promises to make the good happy. Just keep to this. Be quiet and never own waverings, for then you're moulded by every hand . . . Say not another word to Rose on speculation."[48]

Yet Boswell wavered even as he wrote this passage. In the first sentence, he seems to lose his train of thought between the first and second clauses. He might have simply been affirming God's existence, or instead attributing certain characteristics to God, but instead quickly skipped to his own situation. Understandably so, as his situation continued to worsen. Within days, Boswell could not leave his bed—"You was direfully melancholy and had the last and most dreadful thoughts"—and was goading himself to spring up.[49] His inertia had grown so heavy that, as a French theme, he conceived a bed that, upon pulling a cord, would raise up at one end and deposit him on the floor: "Thus I should be gently forced into what is good for me."[50]

Though he soon returned to society, accepting invitations to dinner and stroll, he was incapable of wrestling down his "splenetic" thoughts when alone. He again turned to verse, asking himself "must I not have speculations sad / Who still am shuddering lest I grow mad?" Memoranda and poems were not enough, however. In a rare instance in the journal, Boswell noted that he also prayed.[51] Finally, on March 23, Boswell turned to Temple, the one friend with whom he felt he could be fully candid. In a remarkable passage, he observes that his "affliction [is] of an uncommon nature." As though anticipating Temple's reaction, Boswell then acknowledges that he had never seen his son: "I mourn for an idea." An idea of what might have been for Charles, of course; an idea, perhaps, of what was to come of Charles, and Boswell, once they passed these lives. How could he not speculate over this ultimate question? Indeed, with his "mind sadly clouded," he had "been tormenting [himself] with abstract questions concerning Liberty and Necessity, the attributes of the Deity, and the origin of evil." No answers were forthcoming, though, as he confessed, "I have truly a dark disposition."[52]

For the next several weeks Boswell's disposition remained dark. He once awoke in the middle of night in a sweaty tumult, shouting "There's no more of it!'Tis all over," and several days later "awaked shocked, having dreamt [he] was condemned to be hanged."[53] Public hangings had long compelled Boswell's attention no less than did the pomp and circumstance of religious rituals—he had taken communion in the Anglican Church at the Hague that same Christmas—but the scaffold now towered over the altar. Faith seemed powerless to prevent Boswell's spasms of anxiety over his annihilation. As Boswell wrote to Johnston, who had reported the news about Charles's death, the "black foe" had overpowered his religious beliefs. "When I am attacked by melancholy, I seldom enjoy the comforts of religion. A future state seems so clouded, and my attempts towards devotion are so unsuitable, that I often withdraw my mind from divine subjects."[54]

By "comforts of religion," Boswell could not have meant the Calvinism of his childhood. That particular brand of Christianity, of course, had been anything but a comfort; in fact, it seems to have been one of the culprits. As Boswell told Temple a few months later, "What variety of woe have I not endured? Above all, what have I not endured from dismal notions of religion?" In case Temple didn't understand the allusion, Boswell spells out these dismal notions: "The meanest and most frightful Presbyterian notions at times recur upon me."[55] A few weeks later, he returns to the charge: "Spleen brought back to my mind the Christianity of my nurse, and of that could I *not* doubt? You know how miserably I was educated with respect to religion . . . My dear Temple, how great is the force of early impressions!"[56] Though many years and many miles distant from his upbringing, from the pious and fearful mother who begged her young son to undergo conversion, from a father whose beliefs girded his relentless activity and severe expectations of himself and his spawn, from a world steeped in the horror of hellfire and hope of eternal happiness, Boswell was still in Calvinism's thrall.

———————

And yet, it is important to recall that frightful Presbyterianism was not the only Presbyterianism to be had in eighteenth-century Edinburgh. The city teemed with Protestant clergy who sought to stake a middle position between the dim and dour worldview of the so-called High-flyers and the freethinkers championed by Hume. Many of these moderate clergymen were, in fact, close friends of Hume—more a testament to their civility, perhaps, than to any common ground. The best-known figure, and lifelong friend of Hume, was Hugh Blair, who was not only the celebrated minister of St Giles Church in Edinburgh, but also professor of rhetoric at the city's university. Though the post was created in 1760, a few years after Boswell's fitful stay at the university, Boswell came to know Blair—an occasional source of regret for the self-regarding minister. In 1761, the young Scot had been invited to join the Select Society, of which Blair was a founding member. The Select was a group of eminently clubbable men who represented the best and brightest of the Scottish Enlightenment. Founded in 1754, the Society brought together Adam Smith, David Hume, Lord Kames, the painter Allan Ramsay, political theorist Adam Ferguson, and jurist and philosopher (and notorious eccentric) Lord Monboddo, as well as dozens of other, lesser literary figures to discuss the great ideas of the age. The one forbidden subject, however, was religion, for fear that it would turn toxic the atmosphere of great and claret-lubricated conviviality.

Yet Boswell was blissfully unaware that even conviviality had certain limits. In early 1763, he and Andrew Erskine published a collection of their correspondence. The cheekiness of two obscure young men who had neither written nor done anything notable enough to justify such a publication was compounded by the outrageousness of the contents: the correspondents poked fun at nearly all the luminaries orbiting in the Select's solar system. Lord Eglinton, one of the book's many targets, summed up the general reaction to the book: "By the Lord, it's a thing Dean Swift could not do—to publish a collection of letters upon nothing." There was one enthusiastic review, published in the *London Chronicle*, which announced "this collection as a book of true genius." Detracting from the review's value, however, is that its anonymous author was James Boswell.[57]

A vexed Blair had also scolded Boswell with "What are you to the world?" He then proceeded to answer the question: "It appears to those who do not know you as if you were two vain, forward young men that would be pert and disagreeable and whom one would wish to keep out of the way of."[58] Blair was right on three of the four counts against Boswell: he was vain, forward, and pert, but rarely disagreeable. On the contrary: as with most everyone else who met Boswell, Blair was deeply attached to, if frequently exasperated by, the volatile young man. In return, Boswell considered Blair, along with Kames and Johnson, as one of his "Mentors." The minister, Boswell remarked, "would stop hounds by his eloquence."[59] (Johnson shared this opinion, telling Boswell that, upon reading one of Blair's sermons, "To say that it is good, is to say too little."[60])

There was more than mere eloquence in Blair's sermons and lectures; a manual of sorts for the forming of character also lay there. Though some of his contemporaries dismissed Blair as a philosophical lightweight, the minister strove to mediate between Calvinist doctrine and Enlightenment thought. In particular, Blair made an intriguing case for the collaboration between moral philosophy and

Christian faith, affirming that we are "inhabitants of the earth" as well as "candidates of heaven." These roles, he insisted, were "only different views of one consistent character."[61] Unlike Smith, who claimed that while we could not truly know another's feelings or thoughts, this did not matter thanks to the work of imagination, Blair could not accept the self's fundamental opacity to others. While the other sees us in one way, and we see our own self in another way, neither succeeds in seeing our self as it truly is. God alone, Blair argued, could fill the essential moral function of knowing who we are. Without this divine, merciful, and engaged spectator, we would otherwise be condemned to a world of mirrors and masks. In a passage that echoes the language of Jean-Jacques Rousseau's *Second Discourse,* Blair described society as a place "where everyone appears under an assumed form; possesses esteem which he does not feel; and bestows praise in order to receive it."[62]

But whereas for Rousseau our predicament was the result of stepping out of nature and into society, for Blair it was the consequence of our stepping away from God. He measured this distance by the age's increasing attachment to reason and skepticism in regard to revelation. But to dismiss the truth of revelation, he claimed, was to undermine the only certain source we have for self-knowledge and self-correction. Revelation provides, in the end, the existential foundation for what we were, what we are, and, most important, what we need to be in order to secure our salvation. "Without the belief and hope afforded by divine Revelation, the circumstances of man are extremely forlorn."[63] But with too clear an understanding of that same revelation, our earthly actions would become merely instrumental. Fortunately, Blair observed, our understanding of the afterlife was dim. Why fortunate? Because if we knew the exact return in the next world of our moral investment in this world, the investment would be, in a deep sense, fraudulent. For Blair, our earthly course was the crucible of moral character, and it was right and proper "that difficulty and temptation should arise in the course of duty."[64]

Strikingly, in one of the French themes he wrote during his gray winter in Utrecht, Boswell echoed Blair's sermonizing on moral character and salvation. We are unable, he declared in his quickly improving French, "to form an idea of that felicity [of salvation] . . . and if it were not for the hope of another [life], we should be in a most deplorable case."[65] In a second French text, he affirmed "It is a certain truth that the harder I work, the happier I am" and ends with a hoorah worthy of Blair: "Rouse yourselves, wretched mortals! Remember that you have the honor to be men."[66]

By mid-April, Boswell had mostly recovered from his paralyzing bout of depression. It is not clear, of course, how greatly the appeals made in letters by his father and friends, or in essays and sermons by Johnson or Blair, to devote himself to industry and activity helped pull Boswell from his deep slough. Did Boswell's reengagement with common life precede or follow his reemergence from his long state of despair? Perhaps a little bit of both. Was this reengagement a guarantee against future personal crises? While certainty was impossible, hope was not. In a letter to Temple, Boswell marveled at his recovery: "Good heaven! What is Boswell?" Yes, he was a being subject to "melancholy," suggesting that his condition was chronic. And yet, at the same time, Boswell believed that he had emerged from his harrowing experience as a new person, hammering into being the beginnings of a new self. "I look back with astonishment on my history since I came abroad," he tells Temple—a history that has shown him that he could not just withstand "the most grievous shocks," but also learn from them. Utrecht had taught him not just civil law, but also the ways of reserve, calm, and "uniformity of mind." I am forming, he assured his friend, "into a character which may do honor to the ancient family which I am born to represent."[67]

It was this same character, however, who was readying himself, as he announced to Temple, to ignore his father's command that he make short shrift of his European tour: "I could wish to see you'gainst winter at home."[68] Instead, Boswell conceived "an excellent plan": a foray into Germany, followed by a lightning strike on France and Switzerland, all with an eye on visiting Voltaire and Rousseau.

— 6 —

BELLE DE ZUYLEN

She is much my superior. One does not like that.

ON JUNE 14, 1764, AS HE PREPARED to leave Utrecht for Germany, Boswell donned his best coat in order to pay a *visite de congé*. He was taking leave of Belle de Zuylen, his name for Isabella Agneta Elisabeth van Tuyll van Serooskerken, a young woman with whom he had flirted for months. (Belle had Gallicized her name following her French studies in Geneva: her French, to her parents' pride and chagrin, was more fluent than her Dutch.) This remarkable woman, who would later in life become one of the literary lights of the Republic of Letters, the author of several epistolary novels under her married named Isabelle de Charrière, had mesmerized the young Scot. Though he was determined to break free of her spell, he never fully succeeded. To his friend Temple, Boswell wrote that Belle's "lightning" mind "flashes with so much brilliance [that it] may scorch."[1] On this score, he was lucid: Upon leaving Holland, though Boswell would never again see Belle, yet this gifted and independent woman left lasting clear scars on him.

Boswell was as ignorant of Belle's literary past as he was of her future work. In 1763, she had anonymously published a slyly provocative novel, *La Noble*. The work's heroine, clambering out of her bedroom window to meet a forbidden lover, uses as her ladder a

pile of ancestral portraits she had taken from the wall for this purpose. "She had never believed that one could get so much support
from one's grandfathers." Predictably, her father, Diederik Jacob,
baron van Tuyll van Serooskerken, scion of Utrecht's oldest aristocratic family and inspector of the country's dikes—a mark of the
man's unimpeachable character and reputation—clawed the book
back from the publisher upon learning his daughter was the author.[2] But Boswell's volatile mix of emotions and thoughts over this
remarkable young woman, over whether to propose to whom he
long dithered, suggests that he sensed Belle de Zuylen would never
be content as wife to the Laird of Auchinleck.

The first meeting between Boswell and Belle was hardly momentous. In late October, he met her at a soirée, but seems not to have
left much of an impression on the young woman: "At night you was
absurdly bashful before Miss de Zuylen." Matters hardly improved
after he took leave and joined a fellow Scot with whom he "put on
foolish airs of a passion" for Belle.[3] The next encounter was scarcely
more promising, if only because Boswell had taken a sharp turn
to the other extreme. He spent three hours in Belle's company at a
dinner, but could not help but be Boswell. "You was too much off
guard, and gave way too much to instantaneous fancy and a little
lightheaded," he berated himself. "Be busy this day to atone."[4] At
times, Boswell believed that Belle, not he himself, needed to atone.
He was nonplussed by the witty and willful woman. Sitting down
to a game of cards with Belle and a local aristocrat, Boswell records his amazement at her behavior: "You was shocked, or rather
offended, with her unlimited vivacity. You was on your guard; at
supper you was retenu."[5] In fact, Boswell would repeatedly accuse
Belle of undue vivacity. Thus he would lecture her that she was "too
vivacious" and really needed to show "a little decorum."[6] During
the depths of his depression over the death of his illegitimate son

Charles, Boswell was perhaps even more sensitive to Belle's "un-hinged" behavior, distressed by her "eternal laughing" and shocked by her joy in shocking the *bien-pensants* of Utrecht.[7]

Vivacity came naturally to a woman who, many years later, re-marked "Life is made of moments."[8] Belle's governess, a remark-able individual named Jeanne-Louise Prévost, would gently remon-strate with her charge: "What's become of that little girl who laughed in her sleep?"[9] As she grew, Belle not only laughed easily in the com-pany of men, but also made them laugh with her sharp and sar-donic sense of humor. In fact, a man had to be terribly self-confident not to be shocked by the young woman's sallies. Before she met Bos-well, she had already launched a clandestine correspondence with David-Louis Constant d'Hermenches, a dashing Swiss-born mili-tary officer several years her senior. A staunch collaborator of Vol-taire's in the effort to *écrasez l'infâme*, d'Hermenches had himself become infamous as a womanizer. (He was also the uncle of a far more famous Constant, the political theorist and novelist Benjamin Constant, who twenty-five years later would pick up where his uncle left off, beginning with Belle one of the century's great epistolary friendships.)

D'Hermenches, seduced by Belle's original and bright mind, found himself trying to field her questions about his mistresses. More outrageously, she would guess at the odds that her own fu-ture husband would contract a sexually transmitted disease from one of *his* mistresses. But as Belle had warned d'Hermenches: "My friendship knows no etiquette; it has its highs and low like my moods, and I have not composed my feelings into a code of con-duct." In a word, "I am not sociable—I am bizarre, difficult, un-obliging, and any kind of constraint seems to me a torture."[10] Indeed, Belle's scorn of traditional expectations shocked even this veteran of battlefields and boudoirs. "Your imagination is everything," he declared in a half-admiring, half-admonishing fashion.[11] But he was not so shocked as to end their correspondence, which stretched over sixteen years.

In a self-portrait she had earlier written for her friends—Boswell took the pains to transcribe it into his journal—Belle, who gave herself the name "Zélide," dwelt on this very trait: "Blest Sensibility! Zélide will never disown thee, thou sole offset for the misfortune of nice discernment and exacting taste . . . Thou art highly dangerous, perhaps, but thou art always a positive good."[12] Like so many others in mid-century Europe, Belle had fallen under the spell of Rousseau's thought, albeit less his savage critique of society or espousal of republicanism than his idealization of sentiment and authenticity. She may even have tried to visit Rousseau, without success, at nearby Neuchâtel at the start of his wanderings as an exile.[13]

The Rousseauian cult of nature justified Belle's contradictory attitude toward the world and others. "When she is mild and affable," she wrote about Zélide, "be grateful to her; she is making an effort. When she remains for any length of time civil and polite to those whom she does not care for, redouble your esteem: she is a martyr."[14] As for her physical beauty, Belle was sublimely elusive: "I do not know. It all depends on your loving her or her wishing to make herself beloved."[15] Decades before Stendhal wrote *De l'amour*—which describes the act of falling in love as the work of the lover's imagination, not the beloved's reality—Belle de Zuylen had already sketched the essay's perspective.

Boswell's biographers point to his idealized conception of his Scottish ancestry to explain his chronic unease with Belle. There was, to be sure, scarcely room in his feudalistic fantasies for free spirits like her. No doubt this explains in part Boswell's horrified fascination, but only in part. Something else, deeper and closer to the bone was at play. Boswell dimly understood that he and Belle were all too alike. Rebellious and ribald, dreaming of careers in literature, scheming to make advantageous marriages, endowed with seductive and engaging personalities that transformed their fairly plain physical features: Boswell and Belle were mirror images of one another.

Between late winter and early spring, Boswell gyrated like a weathervane when his thoughts traveled to Belle. One day those thoughts are devoted to the possibility of marriage with her, the next day to the catastrophic consequences of such a marriage. One day he makes a "pact of frankness" with her, only to berate himself that night for having then talked too much. Yet the next day, he accused her of the very same fault, annoyed by her "imprudent rattling and constant grin." Chagrined by the trust he had placed in her just the day before, Boswell dismissed her as "foolish and raised."[16] It did not strike him as comic or inconsistent that he was penning these thoughts in a journal to be read by his friends. That Belle had herself raised this issue at a dinner party—"You write everything down," Belle remarked, either as an observation or accusation—did not prod Boswell to any reflections deeper than to avoid the subject in the future.[17] Of course, Boswell also forgot, if only for the moment, that he was himself something of a grinning rattler.

But Boswell nevertheless knew with whom he was dealing—no less with Belle as with him himself. In a missive to his friend William Temple, he revealed an awareness of his own strengths and flaws in his analysis of Belle. "She is a charming creature. But she is a *savante* & a *bel esprit* & has published some things. She is much my superior. One does not like that."[18] Yes, Boswell did not like that. But here, precisely, was the rub: Boswell *did* like Belle. A great deal. He liked her though she was his intellectual superior. Indeed, he defended her against a mutual friend's barb that Belle was more alarming than a poorly trained battalion of soldiers: "Mademoi-selle de Zuylen deserves a great deal more fame and love than she gets."[19] He liked her despite the fact that, after Boswell asked for her support following the news of "the death of a friend"—namely, his son Charles—she could not help but revert to her "eternal laughing."[20] He did like her despite her mocking his plans, never realized, to write a dictionary of Scottish terms. When Belle dis-missed, no doubt with a laugh, Boswell's ambition as "trifling," his response, recorded in one of his memoranda, was immediate and movingly sincere: "You said the words were your children, and you'd protect the family."[21] Finally, Boswell continued to like her, indeed love her, even in the wake of Belle's slap-down to a senten-tious lecture in which he baldly insisted that she loved *him*, but also advised her to better govern her "libertine" ways. "I was shocked and saddened to find," she announced, "in a friend whom I had conceived of as a young and sensible man, the puerile vanity of a fatuous fool, coupled with the arrogant rigidity of an old Cato."[22]

Of course, all of these foibles belonged to Boswell. But as Belle herself recognized, they hardly defined him. Soon after Boswell had left for Germany, Belle reported to d'Hermenches that the Scot, be-fore taking his leave, had lectured her in front of her family on mo-rality and religion—all of which left a deep impression not just on her parents, who had nearly leapt to their feet to applaud Boswell, but also on her. "He is so good a man that he looks odd in this per-verse age."[23] Their last meeting was not the first time the friends had discussed these topics—on the contrary. On several occasions, Belle and Boswell debated religious faith—a subject on which Bos-well was especially sensitive, and one on which Belle could not help but be skeptical.

It is tempting to suggest that because Holland's Protestantism was marked not by the harsh vision of Knox but instead by the humane spirit of Grotius, the seventeenth-century legal philosopher and statesman, Belle was less burdened than Boswell by the question of faith. But Belle found the Protestantism of her youth as dour and dim as Boswell found his. Revelation, a matter so crucial to Boswell, left Belle dubious; the gospel's claim that those who believe will be saved, while those who don't will be damned, shocked her. While Boswell found reassurance in a friend's insistence that "damnation" meant only that unbelievers never would have "the happiness to hear of Christ," he also insisted on believing Belle believed as he did.[24]

In an exchange of letters just days after Boswell left Utrecht, Belle raised the subject of religion so that her friend "would carry away a right idea of me." In a passage marked by her recent reading of Rousseau's *Emile,* in particular the long section devoted to the Savoyard vicar's profession of faith, Belle pointed to nature and her heart as evidence for God's existence and his goodness: "Everything tells me that there is a God, an eternal, perfect and all powerful being." At the same time, however, she remained dubious about revelation, and, it appears, all institutionalized forms of Christianity. While revelation has "qualities of grandeur, goodness and mercy," Belle also insisted on the contradictions that this belief entails. "I am incapable of forcing my mind to believe what it does not understand." For good measure, she then returned to the doctrine of predestination, warning Boswell that she could never force her heart "to subscribe to a religion which I can never love so long as I find it denies promised happiness to a part of God's creatures." While these questions made her doubt, she also reassured Boswell that she kept her doubts to herself: "I should think it a crime to destroy the belief of others when I can replace it only by an anxious doubt." As for her own state of indecision, Belle concluded, she would wait patiently for truth to arrive and enlighten her eyes.[25]

It is difficult to read these lines, at least today, and fail to catch a scent of playful skepticism, the scarcely subdued vivacity that so frustrated Boswell. No less striking is the omission, in her self-portrait, of any reference to faith or religion. For someone who placed so great a weight on living in the present moment, reflections about the possibility and nature of an afterlife were, for Belle, simply weightless. Yet Boswell seemed unaware of his friend's emotional and intellectual detachment from the questions that caused him so much torment. In his reply, Boswell agrees with Belle's generous understanding of religion. He reassures her, and no doubt himself, that he had foresworn the grim Calvinism of his childhood: "I do not believe that a few only shall be made happy in another world. My notions of God's benevolence are grand and extensive." Moreover, as someone who had nearly converted to Roman Catholicism and now frequented the Church of England, Boswell was sincere when he claimed "As to systems of faith, I am no bigot."[26]

But, ultimately, this subject was of far greater moment for Boswell than Belle. Moreover, whatever opportunity there was to pursue it was spoiled by Boswell's inability to carry his open-mindedness into his attitude toward women. How could it be otherwise when Boswell urged Belle to avoid the realm of metaphysics? His reasons were two. First, it was a pointless enterprise since David Hume, who "thought as much as any man who has been tortured on the metaphysical rack," had already pronounced that the business of man (and, it seems, woman) is the business of everyday life. Second, metaphysical exercises are simply unsightly in a woman. Such speculations "are absurd in a man, but in a woman are more absurd than I choose to express."[27] To be sure, Boswell was hardly exceptional in this conviction. Dr. Joseph Gregory, the influential authority on feminine conduct, was elected to the chair of Medicine at the University of Edinburgh at the very moment that Boswell was lecturing Belle. In his works, Gregory expressed the general wisdom of his era: nature endowed men with a stronger intellect, while women were given a greater sensibility and moral sentiment. The fair sex, he declared, will gain "from our conversation, knowledge, wisdom and sedateness; and they would give us in exchange, humanity, politeness, cheerfulness, taste and sentiment."[28]

Ultimately, Belle declined to pursue this exchange with Boswell. Even had she acknowledged its intellectual legitimacy—which was far from the case—Belle found that Boswell had failed to fulfill his half of the agreement. He was neither wise nor knowledgeable, but instead narrow-minded and foolish. When Boswell wrote to Belle's father, inquiring as to whether she had received the letters he had sent her, to which she had never replied, the baron's reply captured the great intellectual chasm that lay between the two of them: "My daughter says she will not forget your counsels, but to follow them is another matter."[29]

Yet Boswell would not surrender his confusion over Belle. Despite her frustration with Boswell, and her clear unwillingness to suppress what she was in order to become what he believed she should be, Boswell would not relent. Nearly two years later, after he had quit Holland and was preparing to return to Scotland, he still entertained the wild hope that Belle would become his wife. No less wildly—indeed bizarrely—he continued to insist that Belle would need to conform to his exacting expectations. Rather than sharing his hopes directly with Belle, however, Boswell instead relayed them to her father. Would the baron be so generous as to consider Boswell a candidate for his daughter's hand? Rather like a nation soundly defeated and then ignored by its conqueror, Boswell then insisted on writing the terms of the treaty. They were as onerous as they were outlandish. Not only would Belle need to swear before her family that she would always remain faithful to Boswell, as well she must swear never to see or write to another man, or publish any literary works, without his approval. Perhaps most remarkable, Belle would have to promise "never to speak against the established religion or customs of the country she might find herself in." If she signed on the dotted line, Boswell assured Monsieur de Zuylen, "I would marry her tomorrow."[30]

Of course, it was Boswell's good fortune that de Zuylen never relayed Boswell's proposal to his daughter. Nevertheless, more than a year later, when Boswell brought the matter up in an evasive manner to Belle herself, she put paid to it once and for all: "I do not know your Scotland. On the map it appears to me a little out of the world . . . I have seen it produce decidedly despotic husbands and humble, simple wives who blushed and looked at their lords before opening their mouths." Having settled accounts, Belle then exercised the sympathy her age attributed to her sex: "A strictly sensible person who read our letters would perhaps not find you too rational, but I do not wish to put my friend under constraint." Instead, she read Boswell's singular proposal "with pleasure, with a smile."[31]

At the end of the day, we are left with Belle de Zuylen's smile rather than the grin Boswell insisted upon. It is a smile that resembles Hume's smile in the famous Allan Ramsay portrait. Belle's smile is that of a woman who grasped the futility of grasping for truths beyond the world of everyday life. Like the Scottish infidel, the Dutch aristocrat was undisturbed by this particular and particularly harsh truth. In her novel *Honorine d'Userches,* Belle has the eponymous heroine express a longing for God—or, more precisely, a longing to believe in God. Toward the end of the novel, she tells her lover: "I miss God: with him I was not as alone as I am now."[32] Raised by a father who practiced the most severe skepticism, Honorine is condemned to disbelief. While the fictional father has little in common with Belle's real father, Honorine does resemble her creator to a certain extent. There is her remark to Boswell about refusing to teach doubt to believers, as well the sense that she also felt this loss of transcendental solace. Unlike her erstwhile Scottish suitor, though, she refused to be tormented by it.

To another of her correspondents in the mid-1760s, Adolf van Pallandt, Belle described her relationship to religion as one of *incredulité formelle,* or formal disbelief.[33] She would not and, indeed, could not, be a freethinker: her world would not tolerate a woman to harbor such a belief, or disbelief. But Belle also held a deep and abiding intellectual distaste for atheism, as she did for any school of thought that was dogmatic and blinkered. To d'Hermenches, she confided that while theologians merely bored her, freethinkers horrified her.[34] She understood, as did Voltaire, the social and moral necessity of religion; but she also understood that true skepticism entailed, as Hume believed, a kind of humility and intellectual modesty. Belle would never be free of doubt, but unlike her friend Boswell, she would also always be free of the temptation to seek certainty.

— 7 —

WAITING FOR FREDERICK

*'I was not at ease with myself. My Faith was con-
fused. Objections rose thick against Revelation.*

HAVING ENTERED UTRECHT agitated and alone, Boswell quit it
for Germany one year later animated and accompanied. Indeed,
as his coach rattled out of the city on June 18, 1764, he could hardly
believe his company. Sitting across from him was George Keith,
better known as Earl Marischal of Scotland, whom Boswell's father, learning that Keith was to pass through Utrecht on his way
to Berlin, prevailed upon to take along his son. The news dazzled
Boswell: "I was now to travel with a venerable Scots nobleman who
had passed all his life abroad, had known intimately kings and great
men of all kinds, and could introduce me with the greatest advantage at courts."[1]

Boswell got most of that right. Lord Keith was the tenth, and last,
Earl Marischal, one of the most honored titles in Scotland. Seventy-
five years old when Boswell met him, he had joined the Jacobite
rebellion of 1715 that aimed to return James Francis Edward
Stuart—the Old Pretender—to the English throne. When that rebellion failed, Keith then threw himself into the 1719 uprising, which
was an even greater flop. But Keith's courage was unquestioned,
as was his fidelity to the Old Pretender's cause. At least, that is, until

the uprising of 1745, under the Old Pretender's son, Prince Charles Edward Stuart, or Bonnie Prince Charlie, which also failed. Giving up on the dashing, but hapless Stuarts, Keith joined the Prussian court and soon became one of Frederick the Great's most influential advisors. Once banned from Great Britain for his Jacobite activities, but pardoned in 1759, Keith was in fact returning to Germany from a visit to his properties in Scotland.

Adding glow to the Lord Marischal's romantic aura was his adopted daughter and companion, Madame de Froment. The good woman was in fact a Turk whom, Boswell breathlessly jotted in his journal, Keith had taken prisoner during a battle. This, at least, was what Boswell believed, but the truth was even more fantastic: it was Keith's brother, a general in the Prussian army, who had found her. While he was slowly riding through a massacre of Turks by Russians, a child grasped the stirrup of the general's horse. He saved the child, but he died soon after in a subsequent battle, leaving the girl's upbringing to his brother Lord Keith. By the time she too was sitting across from Boswell, Madame de Froment was middle-aged, morose and mostly taciturn.[2]

But neither Keith's long silences—he most certainly knew he would never again see his native Scotland—nor Froment's long sighs dampened Boswell's excitement. The ride was often rude: due to the absence of ancient Roman engineering and a modern centralized bureaucracy, German roads were mostly abysmal. Most of the vehicles banging along these gutted and gouged scars across the landscape were no less dismal, whether they were *journalières,* open carts made of wood slats that left passengers prey to low-lying branches and birds, or wagons that, though covered, were little more than torture chambers. Traveling to Frankfurt, Boswell found himself imprisoned in one of these "monstrous machines." With cracks pretending to be windows, it had iron bars bolted across the cabin against which the dozing Boswell periodically rapped his skull. "I was really in danger of having my head broke."[3] Even the sturdier coaches often fell victim to the boggy and bruised conditions of the roads. On a cold and wet night outside of Cassel, a deep rut bit into the wheel of Boswell's carriage and nearly overturned it. Despite the arrival of the nearby stationmaster with an extra horse, the carriage refused to be pried loose—much to the chagrin of Boswell and his fellow passengers, who were watching these efforts in a driving rain. Yet Boswell's spirits were not dampened: he walked to the nearest village, found an inn, and slept soundly.[4]

Though he did not comment on this particular inn, Boswell found that, in general, the rusticity of lodgings rivaled those in the Highlands. In 1722, one British newspaper reported that in Germany "a man may travel many days and not find a bed to lie upon."[5] Forty years later, Boswell found this still to be the case. When he was not given, as he was on one occasion, a table for a bed with a giant mastiff as a companion, Boswell flopped for the night on stacks of moldy hay. When the stars aligned, he did have a bed, though it often came with one of his traveling companions. These trials of travel were certainly less onerous than his bouts of depression, yet Boswell also versified these experiences, if only to make light of them: "Here am I sitting in a German inn / Where I may do penance for many a sin / For I am pestered with a thousand flies / Who flap and buzz about my nose and eyes."[6] The litany of woes trails on for another six lines.

Bumping across Germany—a geopolitical fiction behind which lay the reality of some 300 kingdoms, duchies and cities, some large, some small, all jealously guarding their independence—Boswell ricocheted among various religious communities. This was not always to the taste of British travelers, who were primed to despise Roman Catholic countries. Thus one tourist, having watched a convert take the veil at the convent in Duderstadt, sighed, "Thank god it is my happy lot to be of a nation a long time since by the protection of heaven delivered from such pernicious bigoted and mistaken zeal."[7]

Boswell did not share this very English prejudice. Catholicism responded to Boswell's hunger for meaning that, in the case of this Church, was made manifest in costume and theatrics. No less important, these theatrics were not the work of everyday drama, but instead the drama of salvation—one in which the protagonist could play a critical, if not decisive role. Thus a mass Boswell attended in Minden buoyed him so much so that he had "not one Scots Sunday idea." The experience revealed, if not the certainty of salvation, at least the "probability for the truth of Christianity."[8] Whenever Boswell's spirits waned, a visit to a Catholic church helped to reignite them. In Mainz, he went to a cathedral, most probably the dramatically gothic Saint Stefan, where his "Soul was elevated to Devotion by the solemn Vespers."[9] A few months later, Boswell met a French Jesuit inside a medieval church in Mannheim. After a few minutes of conversation, Boswell told the Jesuit that he was "of no sect" and took his devotion where he could. Besides, he added, "I found my devotion excited by grand worship & that I was happy to worship in a Romish church." Won over by Boswell, the priest blurted how he wished his interlocutor were Catholic. Touched by the priest's candor, Boswell also regretted he wasn't.[10]

The Catholics did not, of course, have a monopoly on pomp and pizzazz. The profane theater of the courts also transfixed Boswell's romantic imagination. Even when they did not offer a lasting answer to the questions of sin and salvation, they did provide temporary succor. One night at the court of Brunswick, the dinner table was laden with sparkling glasses and plates, while the guests equally sparkled in their uniforms, their conversation rising above the strings of a small orchestra playing in the same room: "I confess that I was supremely elevated," Boswell recorded. But he could not help but think then about home: "I had the utmost pleasure of contrast by considering at this hour is assembled the Auchinleck Kirk, and many a whine and many a sad look is found therein."[11]

The Duchy of Brunswick, a small and enlightened kingdom in northeast Germany, especially entranced Boswell. In fact, shortly after Boswell's stay, Prince Ferdinand—who so impressed Boswell that no amount of "speculation could annihilate the satisfaction of this interview"—invited the philosopher, theologian, and dramatist Gotthold Ephraim Lessing to take the position of librarian at the Wolfenbuttel Library in Brunswick.[12] Mostly remembered today as the friend of Moses Mendelssohn and author of the philo-Semitic play *Nathan the Wise,* Lessing used the library's holdings to publish later in life his *Beitrage,* or *Fragments,* in which he argued that revelation was an early, but valuable stage in humankind's relationship with God. The evolution of belief among Christians, Jews, or Muslims, Lessing declared, ultimately leads them to what, in effect, is humankind's starting point: the reasonableness of faith. Religion is not true "because the evangelists and apostles taught it, but they taught it because it is true."[13]

The young Scot would have welcomed the German thinker's spirit of toleration. During his visit to the library—a "noble" room that contained nearly 11,000 books and 5,000 manuscripts—Boswell marveled at the dented inkhorn with which Luther beaned the devil while he was translating the Bible into German. It was, he declared, a "very just emblem of the outrageous temper of this Reformer."[14] As he moved from Catholic to Protestant courts and cities, Boswell was a perfect illustration of the confusion that occurs when religions and revelations collide. The stew of different sects and religions— not just the various Christian sects, but Islam as related by Madame de Froment—gnawed at Boswell's belief, hammered home by Johnson, in the importance of revelation. In a letter to William Temple, then preparing to become an Anglican minister, Boswell fretted about the truth of revelation: "The Subject is really a matter of knowledge where all Nations put in different claims and are equally firm in their faith." This had made Boswell not only "very doubtful," but also of course made him very anxious as well, given his "early prejudice of thinking unbelief a dreadful crime." The basso continuo of questions that thrummed inside Boswell pulled him even farther from his Presbyterian background, indeed from most every established Church and denomination. "I make it a rule to keep my sentiments to myself," he told Temple, "for I have been conscious of such diversity that I really cannot have much certainty beyond what I have given you as my Creed."[15]

Parts of Boswell's creed in fact resemble Lessing's own stance. By the end of his life, Lessing felt bound to no single creed or sect—a position echoed by Boswell, when he told Belle de Zuylen that he was no bigot when it came to systems of faith.[16] As for the rest of Boswell's creed, it was, he acknowledged, "very general." To Temple, Boswell declared: "I believe firmly the existence of a Supreme Being. I adore him with all the powers of my mind and I study to recommend myself to his favor by a manly and amiable Behavior. I have also the most lively hopes of Immortality. Thus far I am constant, for, thus far I have strong reasoning or strong sentiment to support me." He then pushed away the glowering God of his Calvinist upbringing, embraced the "mild System" of Jesus Christ, and volunteered that "religion is the duty of every individual."[17]

In the jumble of religions he found in Germany, the young Scot tried to piece together a creed that could fit the demands of both his reason and his fears. This effort explains the immediate liking he took for Brunswick's court chaplain, Johann Friedrich Wilhelm

Jerusalem. The aptly named minister was a leading figure of neology, a theological movement that, by applying critical historical method to scripture, sought to find a common ground between deism and pietism. Jerusalem was supremely confident about his method. Give me two hours with Frederick, he told Boswell, and the notoriously skeptical king would confess of the truth of Christian faith. (When Boswell in turn told this story to a British diplomat, Andrew Mitchell, the reply was neat and true: the king has heard all of Jerusalem's arguments, Jerusalem has heard all the king's, and "after they have said a great deal, each will retain his own opinion."[18])

Reputed for his tolerance and faith, Jerusalem was rather like a Prussian Frances Hutcheson, insisting in his sermons upon man's innate benevolence.[19] In the neological scheme of things, there was no place for original sin: the very idea flew in the face not just of ethics, but also of the God these theologians had reconceived. In the heart of the heart of Lutheran Germany, the neologists moved away from the fiery fomenter of the Reformation and moved closer to his nemesis, the great humanist Erasmus.

Boswell's conversations with the abbé—in his journal, he used this title rather than the German "abt"—were marked by warmth and humor. Jerusalem, he found, was an "agreeable Man with a pleasing simplicity of manners" who nevertheless spoke forcefully on a wide range of subjects. In particular, Boswell was struck by Jerusalem's confession that, twice when he thought he was dying, he had turned to Plato's *Phaedo* for solace. Yet both times he found the dialogue, which nevertheless was the "bible" of Stoics, unsatisfying and "weak." As a result, in both instances of extreme compunction Jerusalem had turned "to the Religion of Jesus, and had full contentment of mind." Boswell deeply enjoyed the story and regretted that he was scheduled to leave the next day for Potsdam. Nevertheless, he also found something wanting in Jerusalem's words—an intellectual guarantee of sorts that would set his mind at rest was missing: "I was not at ease with myself. My Faith was confused. Objections rose thick against Revelation."[20]

This was no small matter: Johnson had himself urged Boswell to turn to revelation whenever he was besieged by doubts. The short sermon the older man had delivered in the church at Harwich no doubt still echoed in Boswell's mind. The Bible, for Johnson, was quite simply the revealed word of God in which we are "taught to know the will of our Maker . . . by messengers inspired by himself."[21] The pages of scripture formed the stairway to salvation—a stairway that, if the individual willed, she or he had the power to climb. No less than Boswell, Johnson found repellent the determinism at the core of Calvinism. Instead, his understanding of man's relation to God owed much to Arminianism, an early modern theological movement that insisted upon man's capacity to assist in his own salvation and, as a result, dwelt on the importance of the self-examined life. Yet as Boswell knew, the one element Johnson refused to examine was revelation: without it, he feared, his faith would founder on the reefs of reason.

Neither Johnson's exhortations nor Jerusalem's explanations eased Boswell's qualms. As for the "neat summary of the proofs of Christianity which might always keep his mind settled" that Jerusalem had promised to give Boswell, but never got around to doing so, they would not have erased Boswell's unease either.[22] The Scot's doubts bled into even the most sparkling of occasions. During a meal at the court of Brunswick, Boswell found himself sitting across from Prince Ferdinand, duke of Brunswick, celebrated for his actions on the battlefield. Boswell was "electrified," declaring: "Every time that I looked at him, I felt a noble shock." Yet the repeated shocks were not enough to fend off Boswell's habit of "abominable speculation" that once again melted "all into insipidity at last."[23]

Yet Boswell mostly succeeded in disguising these thoughts, even when they were horrid, as they were one afternoon while he took tea with Keith. The Lord Marischal related with great verve a story about the Marquis d'Argens, a philosophe who belonged to Frederick the Great's court and who lived in dread of death. Fearful that he would catch cold, the first step to pneumonia, the marquis had not removed his waistcoat in several years. Yet when d'Argens, persuaded by Frederick, began to remove the item of clothing, he couldn't: with years of sweat and dirt pasting it to his skin, the waistcoat had to be scraped off. Having told the sorry tale, Keith "as usual laughed at religious gloom." Boswell, who was then wrestling with his own religious demons, was stunned: "I told him he had the felicity of a sound mind, which everybody has not. Good heaven! How fortunate is one man above another!"[24]

Boswell was also overtaken by these restless thoughts on more mundane occasions. One night while Boswell was riding in one of those cursed post wagons, he was slapped in the eye by a tree branch. The collision, which nearly blinded him, paradoxically gave him insight into the mysterious ways of Providence. "I had time in the dark silence of the night to ruminate on the great question concerning Providence. Should I now have said that Providence preserved my eye? But I pray you why did Providence permit the branch to strike me?" After several more lines in which he tries to trace the fallen dominoes to a divine source, Boswell brings the futile effort to something of an arbitrary end: "Yes—the Universal eye perceives every thing in the Universe. But surely, the grand and extensive System employs the attention of God, & the Minutiae are not to be considered as part of his care."[25]

———————

If theologians could not deliver the lasting answers, perhaps philosophers could. In Potsdam, Boswell happened to find such a thinker: his fellow Scot, Thomas Reid. While wandering through Lord Marischal's library, Boswell stumbled across a "treasure": a copy of Reid's *Inquiry Into the Human Mind, On the Principles of Common Sense,* which had been published that same year. With Reid's book, Boswell believed he had found a cure to skepticism. Reid, he discovered, "insisted much on the original Principles of the Mind, which we cannot doubt of, and which cannot be proved; because they are really Axioms: He drove to pieces the skeptical Cobweb. I found myself much refreshed and very happy."[26]

By "Cobweb," Boswell meant the tissue of skepticism that David Hume had woven and from which his critics tried to extricate themselves. As Boswell told Temple, Reid's book "has relieved me from the uneasy universal Scepticism into which David Hume led me, and from which I absolutely could not escape."[27] Like so many contemporaries dismayed by Hume's seemingly irresistible assault on the supposed powers of reason, Boswell embraced Reid's energetic reply. Tellingly, when Reid's follower James Beattie was inspired to write *An Essay on the Immutability and Nature of Truth,* the portraitist Joshua Reynolds, an intimate friend of Johnson's, celebrated the occasion by depicting Beattie triumphantly holding a copy of the essay in the foreground, while behind him an angel is manhandling three dubious figures, one associated with Hume, a second with Voltaire. Appropriately, the portrait now hangs in the University of Aberdeen's Marsichal College, founded by one of Keith's ancestors.

Having followed his father's path as a minister, Reid was well loved by his parishioners for his sensibility and piety. Both of these traits were challenged, however, when Reid read Hume's *Treatise of Human Nature*. As he exclaimed, Hume's skeptical assault on reason "leaves no ground to believe any one thing rather than its contrary."[28] He devoted the rest of his life to refuting Hume's work, and his principal weapon was what he called "common sense." By this phrase, Reid understood something quite specific, namely an innate rational faculty found in all human beings. It was, he wrote, "that degree of judgment which is common to men with whom we can converse and transact business."[29] As Boswell telegraphed in his journal entry, Reid argued that this faculty of common sense requires no philosophical proof: it is "axiomatic" insofar as it is part and parcel of our human constitution. This faculty serves both as conduit and guarantor of the world's reality, as well as the self's. To reason against their existence is as absurd as to reason against our faculty of sight. Should a skeptic ask why I believe in the existence of an external object, Reid declared, I must reply that the belief is not of my making: "It came from the mint of Nature; it bears her image and superscription; and, if it is not right, the fault is not mine: I even took it upon trust, and without suspicion."[30]

Though Reid moved to Glasgow in 1764 to fill the chair of Moral Philosophy left vacant by Adam Smith, he never moved from his grounding in Christian faith. It seems, in fact, that he believed that religious beliefs could be founded on principles of common sense. This was certainly the use that many Christian apologists, both in Great Britain and America, made of his work.[31] In fact, not just traditional Christians, but also deists: Thomas Jefferson almost certainly borrowed the notion of "self-evident truth" from Reid's writings.[32]

While Boswell did not pull anything nearly so grand from Reid's work, his discovery of Reid occurred at a pivotal moment in his inner life. Throughout his stay in Holland, whenever he felt he was backsliding and at odds with himself, he would scold himself to be more *retenu* or more Johnsonian. Yet such exhortations grow scarce in the pages of his journal after he arrives in Germany. In their place appears a growing acceptance of who he is—which, he declares, is not at all bad. On July 20, just one day after he had found and devoured Reid's essay, Boswell reflected joyfully on the performance he had just given at a ball: "I was rather too singular. Why not? I am in reality an original character. Let me moderate & cultivate my Originality. God would not have formed such a diversity of men if he had intended that they should all come up to a certain standard . . . Let me then be Boswell and render him as fine a fellow as possible."[33]

In a letter to Temple written a few days later, Boswell returned to this realization. Explaining his determination to be introduced to Frederick, Boswell declares: "I will let him see that he has before him a man of no uncommon clay. You see me now Temple restored to Myself; quite the great man. Don't laugh."[34]

The subject seemed inexhaustible, for he again returned to it several days later: "I saw my error in suffering so much from the contemplation of others. I can never be them; therefore let me not vainly attempt it, in imagination; therefore let me not envy the gallant and the happy, nor be shocked by the nauseous and the wretched. I must be Mr. Boswell of Auchinleck and no other. Let me make him as perfect as possible . . . I am all to myself. I have but one existence. If it is a mad one, I cannot help it. I must do my best."[35]

We can never know, of course, if the meeting between Reid's common sense and Boswell's uncommon sense of himself resulted in the latter's declaration of independence. But it is significant that, for Reid, personal identity was not, as Hume affirmed, a fiction we slap on a bundle of passing impressions. Instead, our sense of self is also "minted in Nature," a first principle that cannot be doubted. As Reid declared with a conviction he hoped would brook no dissent: "Whatever this self may be, it is something which thinks, and deliberates, and resolves, and acts, and suffers." There is no place for doubt or hesitation when it comes to first principles: they are, we are. Coupled to this tonic affirmation was Reid's insistence that, more so than reason or reflection, it is activity that defines human nature: "In the right employment of our active power consists all the honor, dignity and worth of a man; and in the abuse and perversion of it, all vice, corruption and depravity."[36]

Boswell's heart must have skipped as he read these passages. In a library in central Europe, he discovered a Scottish thinker who seemed Hume's equal, yet refused to buy his skeptical bill of goods. Indeed, this same Scot, who was a Presbyterian minister as well as a philosopher, reached out from his book, collared Boswell, and reminded him that he not only had a self, but that he must exercise it. At that moment, Boswell must have looked up, startled. Had he not been doing precisely that in his journal? It cannot be a coincidence that, as he explains to himself and others his decision to be himself, Boswell also justified why he "gives himself so much labor" to keep the journal. "Does it not," he writes, "contain a faithful Register of my variations of mind?"[37] His mind, his register, his self: in Berlin, Boswell begins to cohere.

———————

Yet Germany also afforded several occasions for another kind of activity, one Boswell studiously avoided in Holland: sex. Despite several close encounters in The Hague and Amsterdam, the dike of celibacy Boswell had erected when he arrived in Holland held remarkably fast. Unremarkably, it collapsed almost immediately once he quit the Lowlands for Germany. Just days after settling in Berlin, Boswell seduced his laundry woman with the promise that he would take her to England. "Her beauty thrilled my frame. I thought I might be an old Patriarch upon occasions and could not see any harm in taking her with me." Yet Boswell had enough residual *retenu* from Holland and held back from "debauching her to give myself a few days pleasure." As it happened, the young woman politely declined Boswell's spontaneous and strange invitation.[38]

When a young woman called at his lodgings a few weeks later, however, such *retenu* melted like the chocolate candies she was selling. Flirting with her, Boswell discovered that she was both married and pregnant. His reaction was immediate: "Oho! A safe piece." He invited her into his closet, where their brief encounter left Boswell feeling "cool and astonished." Predictably, it also left him reflective, wondering about the consequences of his act: "Should I now torment myself with speculations on Sin and on losing in one morning the merit of a year's chastity?" Not at all, was Boswell's answer: "Let it go. I'll think no more of it. Divine being! Pardon the errors of a weak Mortal."[39]

A number of other encounters occurred during Boswell's travels across Germany, duly noted in the journal. But the most important encounter in Berlin for which Boswell planned and schemed in fact never took place: a meeting with Frederick the Great. The Prussian king, it turned out, was one of the few great historical actors who proved indifferent to the Scot's irrepressible efforts at presenting himself to them.

By the time the Scot's carriage lumbered into the Prussian capital, the city was only beginning to recover from the vast costs, financial and human, of the Seven Years War. The population had thinned dramatically; when Frederick returned to the city following the war's end, he lamented that he found nothing but "empty walls and the memory of those he had loved."[40] This sentiment, of course, sounds hollow when one recalls that Frederick helped launch the war when he recklessly invaded Silesia, then part of the Austrian empire, soon after coming to power. This act of aggression sparked the war that eventually enveloped not just Europe, but North America as well.

Just as the war was politics by other means for Frederick, driven to ratchet up Prussia's status, so too were culture and city planning. During his long reign (1740–1786), Frederick force-marched Berlin from its sleepy backwaters, best known for its barracks culture, to the center of European art and thought. This marked a dramatic change from his father's reign. The harsh and pious Frederick Wilhelm enjoyed nothing better than to watch his corps of giant grenadiers—who had to be at least six feet tall—high-step through his palace and have them listen to the sermons he delivered every Sunday morning from the pulpit of the military church. By the same token, Frederick Wilhelm enjoyed nothing less than just about anything associated with France, beginning with its language and culture. Indeed, the king despised culture *tout court*: he dismissed intellectuals as "dog food" and professors as unworthy of sentry duty.

But all of this changed under his son. At the very moment Boswell, living in Berlin, was determined to be more like Boswell, Berlin was determined to be more like Paris. Frederick the Great not only acknowledged Paris's cultural superiority, he eagerly imported it to Prussia. With the same energy and focus his father devoted to Prussia's military, Frederick turned to Berlin, transforming it into a vast site of urban renewal. The Unter der Linden was extended and improved, the Tiergarten utterly refashioned, and the new opera house, festooned with state-of-the-art stage machinery, water pumps for artificial lakes, and waterfalls, attracted scores of visitors when still under construction. Sans Souci, Frederick's rococo retreat from the rigors of statecraft in Berlin, was also built in nearby Potsdam.

At the start of his reign, Frederick bolted out of the blocks, determined to realize the great hopes held by his contemporaries for a truly enlightened ruler. Few imagined that the king would prove over his long reign to be far more despotic than enlightened. He energetically threw state support behind new industries and transformed the civil service into a model for modern states; he also sought to reform the justice system and took steps to curtail censorship. This achievement, however, also reflected the ambiguous nature of enlightened despotism: official censorship may well have been superfluous in a state that placed so great a premium on obedience and conformity. As the philosopher Johann Gottlieb Fichte remarked in different circumstances, "If you want to do anything with men you must mold them so that they are unable to want anything except what you will that they should want."[41]

Nevertheless, the young king was quite willing to tweak the noses of other monarchs equally committed to imposing obedience and conformity in their own realms. In early 1748, Frederick welcomed to Berlin the Continent's most controversial thinker, Julien Offroy de la Mettric. A physician who began to speculate about the human bodies on which he worked, la Mettrie published anonymously in 1747 *L'homme machine*, or *Man: A Machine*. The book was a radically materialist portrayal of the human body, in which everything, including the mind, was reduced to mere matter. In such a mechanistic scheme, there was little place for spirit or soul—or, indeed, for God. While la Mettrie was careful not to draw this conclusion, the Church did, condemning him as an atheist. When the good doctor was forced to flee France, Frederick quickly invited him to pitch his tent in Berlin. It was the least the king could do for this innocent victim of "theologians and fools."[42]

La Mettrie died suddenly in 1751 from food poisoning—a game and truffle pâté tart had been left standing too long—but his star had already been on the wane. Many of his fellow philosophes, not to mention theologians, were repelled by his radical materialism— one whose roots led, among other places, to the remarkably post-modernist claim that morality was little more than a convenient fiction or, in his words, "the arbitrary fruit of political neces-sity."[43] But his place was taken by other itinerant philosophes, drawn by the financial and institutional recognition Frederick was eager to offer them. In order to attract the age's great thinkers, Fred-erick, with one eye on the "New Rome" that Paris was thought to be, subjected the Academy of Sciences to the same overhaul he gave his capital. In effect, he gallicized the institution, making French its official language, drafting French philosophes to fill its seats, and holding up the Académie française as its ideal. The mathematician Pierre-Louis de Maupertuis was named as permanent secretary of the academy—although the position's permanence faltered during the Seven Year War, when even Maupertuis's mathematical skills were not great enough to square the circle of a Frenchman presiding over a Prussian institution while the two countries were at war with one another. Another important figure was the Marquis d'Argens, a feisty freethinker (and the man who refused to disrobe for fear of catching his death of cold) whom the historian Peter Gay perhaps too harshly describes as a "versatile literary errand boy," but who was an unabashed admirer of his employer, the Prussian king.[44]

As Voltaire quipped, Berlin was a place where only soldiers and horses spoke German.[45] But as we will see, even Voltaire was ex-pected to speak, even in French, only at the pleasure of the king.

For many observers, when it came to Prussia's variation on enlightened despotism, it was the noun, not the adjective that carried the day. By the time Boswell was scurrying ever more desperately to meet Frederick, many thinkers already had the king's number. For this reason, Lessing angrily wrote to a Berliner in 1769: "Don't talk to me of your freedom of thought and publication in Berlin. It consists only of the freedom to publish as many idiotic attacks on religion as one wants—a freedom of which any honest man would be ashamed to avail himself. But just let anyone try to write about other things in Berlin . . . let him attempt to speak the truth to the distinguished rabble at court, to stand up for the rights of the subject, to raise his voice against the despotism as now happens in France and Denmark, and you will realize which country, up to the present day, is the most slavish in Europe."[46] Perhaps. But it is clear that Frederick's definition of enlightened rule was that whenever the interests of the state and those of the individual collided, the latter had to give way.

Yet by the bloody light cast by the religious wars that had convulsed the Continent, Frederick was very much enlightened. His attitude toward religion—"Here everyone must be allowed to go to heaven in his own way"—had a tremendous impact on the age. While skeptical about the existence of this particular destination, Frederick was not at all skeptical about the political benefits of toleration. Hence the active role the king played in the design and construction of Saint Hedwig's, the domed Catholic cathedral in the Protestant city's center. Even the city's Jews, to whom Frederick granted full control over their schools and synagogues, benefited from his rule—though he did not annul many of their other disabilities and taxes.[47]

When he first arrived in the city, accompanying Madame de Froment in Lord Marischal's coach, Boswell gaped at the buildings and homes. "I was struck by the Beauty of Berlin. The Houses are handsome and the streets wide, long and straight." He was especially taken by the palace and opera house, marveling at Frederick's inscription (in Greek) to Apollo that was carved on it.[48] Even the canal—a feature of Utrecht's cityscape that generally depressed Boswell—was in Berlin a source of delight.

In Germany, Boswell spoke the court vernacular—French, not German—which undoubtedly added to the charm that Berlin exercised on him. (During his German travels, Boswell wrote many of his journal entries, either transcriptions of conversations or his own reflections, in French.) But an equally important element was the charismatic presence of the French-speaking king. Boswell first glimpsed Frederick in mid-July at a military parade in Potsdam. The king was standing at the front of his troops—"a glorious sight," exclaimed Boswell, all the more because Frederick was dressed in his trademark blue suit, to which a single star was pinned, and a plain hat festooned with a white feather. Striving for the epic, Boswell wrote: "The Sun shone bright. He stood before his Palace, with an air of iron confidence that could not be opposed. As a Loadstone moves Needles, or a Storm bows the lofty oaks, did Frederick the Great make the Prussian Officers Submissive bend, as he Walked majestic in the midst of them."[49]

Boswell's language is, predictably, freighted with the awe Frederick inspired in so many of his contemporaries. His fearlessness in battle, his identification with German peasants (and ability to speak their language, though he was most comfortable in French), his insistence on being "the first servant of the state" (by which he meant his willingness to sacrifice his own desires on behalf of the state's interests), his unrelenting energy all left their mark on his contemporaries. One Prussian nobleman, Ludwig von der Marwitz, who as a child was held up to see Frederick pass by in a carriage, spoke for many of his contemporaries: "I was only a foot or so away from the King and I felt as if I were looking at God."[50]

Yet six months later, as he prepared to leave Germany, Boswell had still not been introduced to God. As always with Boswell, it was not for want of trying. As he wrote to one of the king's counselors: "I am not satisfied with having seen the King. If it is possible, I should like to hear him speak . . . It is certain that I am not a great man, but I have an enthusiastic love of great men, and I derive a kind of glory from it."[51] His hopes that Keith would introduce him to Frederick were utterly unrealistic. The old Scot knew that his sovereign despised the usual social protocols and activities and preferred the company of his flute or his closest advisors. As a result, Keith deftly ignored Boswell's pleas, as did other officials Boswell approached. His doomed efforts in London to become an officer seemed, in comparison, infinitely more realistic. Yet his desperation was as great: when he saw the king at a garden in Charlottenburg, Boswell felt the great urge to throw himself at Frederick's feet, begging him to speak.[52]

For a man who made a career of throwing himself at others, Boswell might well have acted on this urge. But whether it was the sight of the cane in the king's hand or the staying hand of the courtier with whom he had been speaking, Boswell managed, if only for a moment, not to be Boswell. He held himself back, concluding that this "King is feared like a wild beast. I am quite out of conceit with the Monarchy."[53]

By then, however, Boswell had another wild beast in his crosshairs: philosopher of nature, political exile, and mountain recluse, Jean-Jacques Rousseau.

— 8 —

THE DISTANCE BETWEEN
MÔTIERS AND FERNEY

Monsieur Rousseau, will you assume direction of me?

DEEP IN THE VAL DE TRAVERS—a valley forming a right angle to the Jura Mountains—nested the village of Môtiers. A village of 400 souls, its setting was bucolic, but also misleading: many of the villagers no longer farmed, having turned their energies to more profitable enterprises like lace-making, clock-making, or the mining of asphalt. Môtiers nevertheless struck visitors as a place perfectly suited for the poet of nature, Jean-Jacques Rousseau.

Yet, it so happened that Rousseau was less than thrilled by the view. A resident of Môtiers since mid-June 1762, he informed his former protector, François-Henri de Montmorency, the duc de Luxembourg, on whose estate just north of Paris he had lived for five critical years: "Grand though the spectacle is, it seems rather bare. The mountains slope steeply and show gray crags in many places, and the darkness of firs breaks the gray with a cheerless tone."

Perhaps Rousseau's eye had grown jaundiced because Montmorency had, in fact, failed him as a protector. Just weeks before, the philosopher had had to flee the estate, and France, for his life. The Paris Parliament had just condemned his pedagogical treatise

Emile—which along with *Julie* and *The Social Contract* Rousseau had published over the course of sixteen months—and ordered it to be burned outside the Palais de Justice. The backlash, engineered by hardliners within the Church, was inevitable. The section of the novel known as the "Profession of Faith of the Savoyard Vicar" denied every dogma they held dear. Not only does the vicar dismiss the doctrines of revelation, miracles and, perhaps, original sin, and denigrate the role played by priests, he also questions Christ's very divinity.

For Rousseau's vicar, nature alone is divine. The mountains and meadows, like the prompting of our conscience, is all the revelation we need. The rest, when it comes to religious faith, is worse than superfluous—it is destructive. Religious doctrines lead not to God, but instead to oppression and war. The vicar thus urges the reader: "Behold the spectacle of nature. Listen to the inner voice. Has God not addressed everything to our eyes, to our conscience, to our judgment? What more can men tell us?"

It happened that a number of men, powerful and outraged, were telling Rousseau quite a bit. None of it was complimentary and not all of it came from Paris. Any thought Rousseau gave to returning to his native Geneva quickly dissolved with the news that the city's Calvinist elders, as irate as their Catholic foes in Paris, had also condemned *Emile* to the flames. (For good measure, they also torched *The Social Contract*.) Europe's most influential and celebrated writer had thus succeeded in the redoubtable task of uniting, if only on the subject of Jean-Jacques Rousseau, Catholics and Protestants, monarchic France and republican Geneva.

Tellingly, great figures of the Enlightenment felt as menaced as did the Church by Rousseau's work. His *Discourse on the Sciences and Arts,* published in 1751, had transformed Rousseau into a European celebrity. This was something of a paradox: Europe's

enlightened readers hailed an essay that mocked their very enlightenment. In a few dozen pages, the "Citizen of Geneva"—the
penname Rousseau adopted—questioned the advances made by
the sciences and arts. The more they advanced, he argued, the
deeper the damage they made in our lives. The values that made
for the greatness of ancient Greece and Rome—honor, duty, courage,
piety—have no place in a society devoted to personal gain and greed.
Blinded by science's useless wonders and society's empty spectacles, we scorn nature's wisdom and stifle our original selves. Rousseau urged his readers to reflect on the many vices born when we
no longer dare to appear as we truly are. "No more sincere friendships, no more real esteem, no more well-founded confidence. Sus-
picions, offenses, fears, coolness, reserve, hatred, betrayal contin-
ually conceal themselves behind . . . that much lauded urbanity we
owe to the enlightenment of our age."[1]

Yet for Rousseau there was no turning back. In 1755, he published
a second essay, the *Discourse on the Origin and Foundations of Inequality among Men*. As with the first discourse, Rousseau wrote
this in response to a competition announced by the Academy of
Dijon; as with the first discourse, Rousseau took up a question much
debated among his fellow philosophes; as with the first discourse,
Rousseau questions certain assumptions of his age. But here the
similarities end. While his contemporaries could, with effort, parse
the first discourse as a paean to ancient republican values, they
could not mistake the targets lined up in the second discourse. The
power of reason, the reality of progress, the benefits of civilization:
all of these claims, whose truths were axiomatic for the citizens of
the Republic of Letters, were slashed by Rousseau's lacerating prose
and left for dead. Rousseau dismisses the Enlightenment as a new
kind of obscurantism, its convictions misguided and its goals cat-

astrophic for humankind. Reason, he announced, is little more than the tool of desire, pursuing ends that can never be reached. Instead of representing progress, this mad effort to fulfill our desires drives us from nature (now despoiled) and our natural selves (long since repressed). As for civilization, rather than the source of our happiness, it is little more than a hall of mirrors where appearance reigns and misery abounds.

How did we wind up here?

Proposing a thought experiment, Rousseau leads us back to an age, one that resembles Eden, where man lived in nature and in isolation from other men. Natural man, or *l'homme sauvage*, knew only needs: food, shelter, and sex. But he did not know himself. How could he, Rousseau asks, if he does not know language, reason, or society? Instead, natural man knew nothing more than the brute sentiment of his existence, an existence, moreover, pinned entirely to the present moment. The past was as unthinkable as the future for this creature that did not think, but merely existed. With alarming eloquence, Rousseau described our dim and dumb ancestor: "Savage man, subject to few passions and self-sufficient, had only the feelings and the enlightenment suited to that state, that he felt only his true needs, looked at only what he believed it was in his interest to see, and that his intelligence made no more progress than his vanity. If by chance he made some discovery, he was all the less able to communicate it as he did not recognize even his children. Art perished with the inventor. There was neither education nor progress; the generations multiplied uselessly. And since everyone always started at the same point, the centuries passed by in all the crudeness of the first ages; the species was already old, and man remained ever a child."[2] Why alarming? Because Rousseau announces that everything we think to be true is false.

Alarming because we find natural man was happy precisely because he was dumb, unaware of himself and others; alarming because this state of ignorant bliss could not last; alarming for its consequences for the enlightened worldview of Rousseau's contemporaries.

Lodged in our small, nearly imperceptible stumble toward society is the fatal moment when we exiled ourselves from paradise. Men began to associate with other men, pursuing aims that benefited all of them. As they gather, Rousseau suggests, they dance and sing around a tree. At first the dancers and the dance are indistinguishable, but there comes a moment when the dancers glimpse themselves as individuals among other individuals. "Each began to look at the others and to want to be looked at himself, and public esteem had a value. The one who sang or danced the best, the most beautiful, the strongest, the most clever, or the most eloquent became the most highly considered—and this, then, was the first step toward inequality and vice."[3]

Humankind's descent from that distant fire to Facebook was a question of millennia, not maybes. The moment we caught sight of ourselves in the reflection of the other's gaze, we could never again go back. Back to an existence informed by nothing more than the sentiment of existence; back to a happiness shaped by the fulfillment of needs, not desires; back to a natural goodness not yet corrupted by society. Now, unable to think of others apart from our own desires, incapable to think of our own selves as distinct from the thoughts of others, we are forever yoked to our own selves—a work forever in progress, a work in constant need of revision. Our passion to perfect ourselves runs roughshod over our reason, bending it toward its own ends—ends which, by their very nature, are endless. This is how, Rousseau laments, the "human race, debased and dispirited, no longer able to retrace its steps, or renounce the unhappy acquisitions it had made, and working only towards its shame by the abuse of the faculties that do it honor, brought itself to the brink of its ruin."[4]

Where better to escape such ruins than Môtiers? Forgotten in these craggy expanses, Rousseau could return to the bliss of that earlier world. *Hélas,* the world would not leave Rousseau in peace. For that matter, neither could Rousseau leave the world alone. He could not stop writing that he should never have become a writer, could not stop pulling others to him to say he wished to be left alone, could not stop declaring his indifference to a public he had so skillfully created in his own image, nor stop telling these legions of admirers that he was the most misunderstood of men.

Indeed, ever since Rousseau's arrival in Môtiers, an unbroken stream of visitors wound its way to the ramshackle wood house where he and his companion Thérèse le Vasseur rented the upper floor. Many came simply to gaze upon the author of these works— readers, Rousseau muttered, who had not read his books and had too much free time on their hands. Or there were cases like the baron de Sauttern, a dashing Hungarian officer who struck up a quick friendship with the usually reticent philosopher. The two men shared many walks and conversations—that is, until the baron bolted town after having knocked up a local girl. Only then was it discovered, much to Rousseau's chagrin, that Sauttern was neither an officer nor a gentleman, but instead was simply Jean-Ignace Sauttermeister von Sauttersheim, a government clerk who had fled Prague just steps ahead of a pack of creditors.

But Sauttersheim's disguise hardly shocked the good folk of Mô-tiers, by then accustomed to the sight of Rousseau walking through town garbed in a lilac-colored, fur-edged robe and matching hat. The exotic costume had prosaic origins: suffering from a urinary tract problem, Rousseau found the robe, dubbed as an Armenian caftan, easier to negotiate than breeches during his forays to the chamber pot. At the same time, he began weaving silk ribbons, which he offered to local brides in exchange for the promise that they would breastfeed their infants. (Given the frightening mortality rate of infants farmed out to wet nurses, Rousseau's gesture was odd, but also deeply humane.) Exhilarated by his new self-image, Rousseau exclaimed to one of his many female correspondents: "I have thought as a man; I have written as a man and I have been called bad. Well, now I shall be a woman."

Gender and garb notwithstanding, Rousseau remained for his enamored readers "Jean-Jacques," the author of *Julie* and *Emile*. In the weeks leading to his assault on the reluctant recluse, Boswell had plunged into these epistolary novels. While crossing the German archipelago of independent states and kingdoms, the Scot spent his evenings reading *Julie* and its tragic tale of undying love unfolding against mountains as massive as the class differences that separated Julie and Saint Preux. The language galvanized the melancholic youth: "Rousseau gives me an enthusiasm of feeling which I thought was all over with poor melancholy Boswell. Thus agitated my heart expands itself & feels the want of an object to love."[5] But Boswell, inspired by Saint Preux's self-denial, was in no hurry to find such an object. When his thoughts began to wander along sensual and illicit paths one night, he recalled the goal of his travels: "I swore solemnly neither to talk to an Infidel nor to enjoy a woman before seeing Rousseau."[6] (His recollection of Rousseau alone did not suffice: still feeling "unhinged," he drank a glass of water and paced strenuously in the room of his inn until he fell back to bed, exhausted.)

Boswell's reading of *Emile,* in particular the profession of faith, helped as well. As with *Julie,* the effect was immediate: "I was struck with its clearness, its Simplicity and its Piety." Indeed, that clearness revealed that Christians had need of neither the Church's teachings nor Enlightenment's teachers; that they needed only their inner sentiment, which they could hear if they only learned to listen (preferably in nature); that one's conscience, unlike the words of our fellow men, never deceives; and that it speaks not in religious dogma or philosophical treatises, but through nature. As Rousseau's faithful but dry-eyed friend Alexandre Deleyre once remarked, the great man "deleted from the divinity anything that wasn't human, fatherly, and merciful."[7] Of course, none of this played well with Catholic or Protestant authorities: a magnet for those disenchanted with the institutions of religion and reason, Rousseau was persona non grata in Paris and Geneva.

Understandably, Boswell's anxiety was great. Finding his room too small, he threw on his overcoat—its green fabric setting off his scarlet and gold laced coat—and flung himself toward the forest, where he found himself "surrounded by immense mountains, some covered with frowning rocks, other with clustering Pines, and others with glittering snow." Inevitably, not only were Boswell's eyes colored by Rousseau's sensibility, but his mind was also filled with the man: "I recalled all of my former ideas of J. J. Rousseau, the admiration with which he is regarded over all Europe, his Heloise, his Emile, in short a crowd of great thoughts."

Buoyed by these thoughts, Boswell returned to the inn to find a reply from Rousseau: he would be glad to receive the visitor, but given his poor state of health, the visit had to be short. Shuddering at the word "short," Boswell again barreled out of the inn and straight to Rousseau's lodging. Out of breath, he was met at the door by Thérèse, who led him up a winding and dark staircase to the kitchen; moments later, Rousseau stepped into the room from the facing door, his caftan trailing along the wooden planks, as if he had just woken from an afternoon nap. (Indeed, Boswell thought the hat was a nightcap.) Rousseau invited his guest to promenade in the kitchen, and thus began the first of five improbable visits Boswell made over the next several days.

Boswell had once observed of himself: "I have the art to be easy and chatty." His art certainly worked wonders with Rousseau. Within minutes, the voluble Scot was punctuating his conversation by grasping the hand and grabbing the shoulder of his surprised, but curious host. Rousseau repeatedly insisted the visits be short, but for naught: resolute and relentless, Boswell pursued questions great and small, philosophical and personal. From the quackery of doctors ("I'm through with doctors") to the greatness of Samuel Johnson ("I would like to see him, but from afar, as I'm afraid he'd give me a good thrashing"), to the evils of society ("I cannot support the world as it is and live in my own world of daydreams") and the uselessness of history ("It's a mere amusement"), Rousseau replied to Boswell's increasingly frantic volleys of queries. Though fatigued by Boswell, Rousseau was also intrigued: he invited the Scot to stay for dinner during the last visit. Over a simple, well-prepared prepared meal of beef, turnips, and white wine, Rousseau practiced the egalitarianism he preached in his works. When Boswell asked if he could have a second serving of a dish, his host replied: "Is your arm long enough to reach it?"

But behind the scattershot of questions lay, for Boswell, a single target: how to reinforce the foundations to his faith. Convinced Rousseau alone could set his soul at ease, Boswell invariably bent the conversations in that direction. At a pivotal moment, as Rousseau recounted his youthful coming and going between Catholicism and Calvinism, Boswell interrupted him: "Tell me, though:

Are you a Christian?" Clearly, Boswell's doubts had been raised by the swirl of controversy over Rousseau's writings. Taken aback, his host stared at him, struck his fist against his chest and declared: "I am proud to say I am." The Gospels, he continued, were a source of great comfort. Yet, just as the Savoyard vicar affirmed nothing less—and nothing more—so too with Rousseau: faith has nothing to do with the mummeries of priests and philosophes. But, demanded Boswell anxiously, what about the expiation of my sins? His dark eyes fixed on his febrile guest, Rousseau was matter-of-fact: "Only by doing good can you undo evil."

Transfixed by Rousseau's words, Boswell blurted the question he no doubt meant to ask from the beginning: "Monsieur, will you assume direction of me?" Boswell of course meant spiritual direction, and a surprised Rousseau begged off: he was too ill for such a task. Besides, he added, "I can be responsible only for myself." In effect, this was the same answer Rousseau had given Boswell at the dinner table. When he asked if he could take a second serving, the canny host had replied you're on your own.

After dinner, as Boswell prepared to leave Môtiers, he sought reassurance from Rousseau that their meeting would endure. Pulling a hair from his head, he asked: "Can I tell myself that we're attached by even the thinnest of threads? By a hair?" Did Rousseau smile? Or stare hard? All we know, according to Boswell, is his reply: "Yes, remember there are always points where our souls are tied." Overwhelmed, Boswell bellowed "Bravo!" and declared "I shall *live* to the end of my life." To which, Rousseau responded, "That, most assuredly, is what we must do," as he watched Boswell lead his horse away.

The Scot had told his host, quite accurately, that he was headed to Yverdun. What he had failed to mention, however, was that this small town was a mere stop on the road to Geneva, then Ferney, where Boswell intended to lay siege to Rousseau's great nemesis, Voltaire.

When Boswell and William Temple bellowed to no one in particular "Voltaire, Rousseau, immortal names!" from the top of Arthur's Seat during their student days at Edinburgh, they did not know that few things would have appalled these two men more than the joining of their names. By the end of the 1750s, the Enlightenment's two most celebrated representatives were at war with one another. A war of words, of course, but nevertheless a war whose violence shocked their contemporaries. Voltaire, Rousseau announced, was a "mountebank" and "impious braggart"—a man "of so much talent put to such vile use."[8] Most famously, in 1760, he penned a venomous letter to Voltaire in which he stated "I do not like you, sir." A few lines later, whipping the letter to its conclusion, Rousseau thought better of his opening declaration—clearly, it did not fully capture his feelings. With a flourish of his quill, he lashed out: "In a word, I hate you—just as you intended I should."[9]

Voltaire did not bother to reply to Rousseau, but did bother to reply to most everyone else in the Republic of Letters. In a letter to Madame d'Epinay, Voltaire confided that "Jean-Jacques has gone off his head," concluding with a magnificent shrug: "What can I say?"[10] Being Voltaire, this was a tad ingenuous. The man whose rapier-like pen wounded countless victims always knew quite well what to say and, when it came to "le pauvre Jean-Jacques," said it quite often. "Ridiculous," "depraved," "pitiful," and "abominable" were just a few of the adjectives with which he described his nemesis, though they scarcely measure up to his description of Rousseau as a "bastard of Diogenes' dog" whom he would gladly see beaten senseless were it not for the fact that he was already insane.[11]

It had not always been this way. In the early 1740s, when Rousseau, then an aspiring composer and fervent citizen of the Republic of Letters, first arrived in Paris, Voltaire's name provoked from him only admiration. How could it be otherwise? The eighteenth century was already well on its way to becoming the Age of Voltaire.

But Voltaire had first to transform himself from the young, savvy, and sharp-witted courtier and versifier he was into something greater: an older, but no less savvy and sharp-witted philosopher. It all began with an insult. When an aristocrat, the duc de Rohan, scornfully asked the ambitious commoner named Voltaire just what his real name was, the man born François-Marie Arouet replied that regardless of his name, he at least knew how to bring it honor. When Rohan had his servants rough up the young upstart for his act of lèse majesté, the bruised but proud Voltaire prepared to challenge him to a duel. Fortunately, friends instead persuaded Voltaire that temporary exile was the better part to valor. In 1727, the poet crossed the Channel and settled in England.

Voltaire's choice of destination would have remarkable ramifications for the history of the Enlightenment. It was in England that he met Alexander Pope and Jonathan Swift, but even more important, it was there that he met Isaac Newton. Or, rather, where he met Newton's coffin. The author of the *Principia Mathematica*—which, in Pope's famous couplet, took God's laws that lay hid in night and suddenly all was light—had died shortly before the Frenchman's arrival. Submerged in a mass of mourners at Westminster Cathedral, his rapier-fine features straining to understand the great rumble of spoken English, Voltaire nevertheless grasped the event's true significance. All of this pomp and circumstance choreographed for a commoner, rather than a king or cardinal, though so unlike France, was so much like a world rightly ordered.

Suitably dazzled, Voltaire set himself the task of learning to write and speak English. This was no small matter: many years later, he spent roughly the same amount of time in Germany, yet did not bother to learn enough German to ask directions. But English allowed a freedom of expression that French simply did not, and his notebooks record his laborious efforts to tame the language, his lessons taken from the works of the men he called his "first masters": Shakespeare, Addison, and Pope.[12]

Tellingly, the subject of his first stab at expressing himself in English concerned religious toleration: "England is meeting of all religions."[13] The theme of religious toleration, coursing through so much of Voltaire's writings, first surfaces in his *Philosophical Letters*. In this work begun in London, drafted partly in English, and published upon his return to France, Voltaire translates the genius of English thought and science for his fellow countrymen. In nimble portraits of Francis Bacon, John Locke, and Newton, Voltaire implicitly compares their achievements, the fruit of grounded reason and empirical investigation, to those of René Descartes, the stuff of abstract reason and metaphysical speculation. For Voltaire, the latter, blinded by a priori rationalism, fails to make the grade. So, too, does French civil society, shackled by religious intolerance and arbitrary justice, fall short of the messy and liberating nature of English society. In London, Voltaire declared, one's religion was a matter of public indifference—though Catholics and Jews, subject to an array of civil disabilities, might have begged to disagree— whereas one's skills, talent, and intelligence were matters of public acceptance and concourse. With a bracing flourish, Voltaire affirmed: "Were there just one religion in England, despotism might arise; were there two, people would be cutting one another's throats; but as there are dozens, they are all happy and live in peace."[14]

Upon his return to France, Voltaire proceeded to conquer nearly every imaginable literary genre. From theater to history, opera to poetry, scientific treatises to fiction, he wrote clearly, constantly, and copiously: his works fill more than two hundred volumes.[15] And this does not include what some perhaps rightly consider his greatest achievement: his correspondence. His biographer Theodore Besterman collected and published 15,000 letters, but even this indefatigable scholar could not resurrect thousands of others, including the eight volumes between Voltaire and his great love, Emilie du Châtelet, which were either destroyed or lost.

But the magnitude of his epistolary feat must also be measured by its impact on his contemporaries. Voltaire rarely wrote for the sake of writing; instead, he wrote for the sake of informing and influencing. Rousseau was hardly exempt from the philosophe's reach. It was Voltaire's *Philosophical Letters* that introduced the young Genevan to the powers of English empiricism and French witticism.[16] It was Voltaire's play *Alzire*, about love, death, and a proper understanding of Christianity among the Incas, which gave Rousseau "palpitations."[17] And it was to Voltaire that Rousseau wrote in 1745: "For fifteen years I have been striving to make myself worthy of your attention and of that solicitude which you offer to young poets in whom you detect talent." With the magnanimity expected of the Enlightenment's recognized leader, Voltaire wrote back to express his esteem and respect for Rousseau's own work.[18]

By the early 1750s, however, as the nature of Rousseau's work changed, so too did Voltaire's attitude. While the Academy of Dijon awarded the *Discourse on the Sciences and Arts* first prize, a good many readers, most importantly Voltaire, were puzzled that Rousseau—an artist, musician, and contributor to the *Encyclopédie*, the great monument to the Enlightenment whose first volume was also published that year—should write so scathing a critique of the world in which he prospered. His anger with Rousseau's attack on the values of the Enlightenment was all the greater given the dangers the philosophes were then facing on various fronts. Just two years earlier, Denis Diderot, one of the co-editors of the *Encyclopedia,* and friend of both Voltaire and Rousseau, had been imprisoned for a spell after the clandestine publication of his pamphlet *Letter on the Blind,* whose materialist and determinist claims seemed to banish God from the cosmic order. As for the *Encyclopedia,* the first volume's success ratcheted up the determination of reactionary critics to bury the entire project. For a time, they were successful, but in 1752, after the publication of the second volume, the monarchy suspended further publication, temporarily throwing the entire enterprise into doubt.

All this while, Voltaire was himself, depending on one's perspective, either the guest or prisoner in Berlin of Frederick the Great. In 1750, the philosophe had accepted Frederick's invitation to come to Prussia, an offer Voltaire found difficult to refuse—all the more so as the king had cast it in verse and addressed it to "Old Apollo."[19] More prosaically, Old Apollo's preeminence had been on the wane in Paris, and Berlin offered him a new stage and audience, but also a trap. Dazzled by the king's attention and generosity, Voltaire discovered the promise of fame came at a catastrophic price: the loss of his intellectual and physical freedom. In a moment of thoughtlessness, the Frenchman enlisted in Frederick's service, thus becoming for all intents and purposes the imperious ruler's prisoner. Frederick gently, but forcefully kept Voltaire within reach, even after he began to tire of him. Hardly a year had passed when the king told one of his courtiers: "I shall have need of him for another year at most, no longer. One squeezes the orange and one throws away the peel."

Upon learning of the king's remark, Voltaire's thoughts suddenly flew to plans for escape. Writing to a correspondent, he confided "I am resolved to place the orange peel in safe keeping."[20] Yet the orange peel delayed his escape. If Berlin was a cage, the bars were gold-leafed, the food was excellent, and the visitors engaging. When Voltaire finally made his getaway in the early spring of 1753, Frederick's police found him in Frankfurt. Furious at Voltaire's escapade, Frederick kept him detained for several days, but perhaps persuaded that there was no more juice to be had, he finally ordered Voltaire's release.

Freed from Frederick, Voltaire now found himself homeless. Unable to return to Paris—Louis XV had made it clear he did not wish to see this freethinker on his doorstep—Voltaire had become a displaced person. Though this prefigured Rousseau's plight a few years later, Voltaire's response was quite different. Having made himself a rich man through canny investments, Voltaire refused to depend on the well-born and powerful for his freedom. Instead, he bought his liberty, first in the form of the chateau of Les Délices in Geneva, then Ferney, a forested estate just outside the Calvinist capital that Voltaire made a workshop of a truly enlightened rule. Though well into his sixties, besieged by real and imaginary maladies, and little more than a skeleton with pale white skin pulled tightly across his bones, Voltaire devoted himself tirelessly to the property and "his" peasants, imposing scientifically sound agricultural and artisanal practices. As he was fond of telling visitors, there was not a job, apart from that of lumberjack, he had not done at Ferney.[21]

———

While Rousseau's eloquence dazzled him, it also drove Voltaire to despair; his enlightened followers had enemies enough from without and the prospect of traitors from within was unbearable. In a letter to Rousseau, who had sent him a copy of his *First Discourse,* Voltaire made clear his ire and puzzlement (as well as his willful misreading of the work): "I have received, Sir, your new book against the human race. One acquires the desire to walk on all fours when one reads your work. Nevertheless, since I lost the habit more than sixty years ago, I unfortunately feel that it is impossible for me to take it up again."[22] In a letter a few years later to Jean d'Alembert, the mathematician and coeditor of the *Encyclopédie,* Voltaire confided his fears over Rousseau's influence: "The philosophes are in disarray. Our little troupe devours one another while the wolves are set on devouring us. It is with your Jean-Jacques that I am angriest. The sublime fool might have amounted to something had he allowed himself to be your disciple, but he has instead decided to stand apart. He condemns the theater after having written a bad play; he criticizes France, which nourishes him; finding four or five rotten planks of Diogenes' barrel, he has climbed inside and barks at the world."[23]

The chasm between these two remarkable minds deepened dramatically on November 1, 1755, when an earthquake leveled the city of Lisbon. The philosopher Susan Neiman has suggested that eighteenth-century Europeans used the word "Lisbon" in the way we use the word "Auschwitz" today.[24] The seismic convulsion, so great that tremors rippled the surface of Loch Lomond, collapsed the city's churches and cathedral, burying thousands of men, women, and children celebrating Sunday mass. As the ground continued to splinter and shift, a series of twenty-foot tidal waves heaved into the harbor, snapping ships and smashing warehouses, and surged through residential neighborhoods. Where the sea failed to reach, fires did not: flames engulfed parts of the city for several days, destroying both invaluable art and book collections, as well as commercial merchandise that mounted into the millions. All told, 30,000 residents of Lisbon lost their lives, and the significance of the disaster striking on All Saints' Day was not lost on Europe— it's just that few could agree on what, precisely, that significance happened to be.

Voltaire, though, had few doubts—or, more accurately, his doubts now deepened. At the very moment he received news about the disaster, he was in the midst of revising his *Discours en vers sur l'homme*—a sprightly variation on Alexander Pope's *Essay on Man* that had much impressed the Frenchman. Suddenly, though, Pope's faith that our world was the best of all possible worlds, designed and built by an omniscient and omnipotent god, seemed bankrupt. But was one, then, to abandon faith? Voltaire's enlightened position was nearly impossible to maintain. As the historian Jonathan Israel asks, "How does one express agonizing pessimism and skepticism and yet emphasize the role of divine creation, justice and providence?"[23]

With unsatisfactory, yet unsettling results, Voltaire attempted to do just that in his remarkable "Poem on the Lisbon Disaster, or an Examination of the Axiom 'All is Well.'" With classical restraint, Voltaire lambastes those who believed that an all-powerful and all-good being had wrought our world:

> Unhappy mortals! Dark and mourning earth!
> Affrighted gathering of human kind!
>   Eternal lingering of useless pain!
>   Come, ye philosophers, who cry, "All's well,"
>   And contemplate this ruin of a world.
>   Behold these shreds and cinders of your race,
>   This child and mother heaped in common wreck,
>   These scattered limbs beneath the marble shafts—

A hundred thousand whom the earth devours,
Who, torn and bloody, palpitating yet,
Entombed beneath their hospitable roofs,
In racking torment end their stricken lives.
To those expiring murmurs of distress,
To that appalling spectacle of woe,
Will ye reply: "You do but illustrate
The iron laws that chain the will of God"?

Was *this* the best God could do? Allow the walls and roofs of churches to crack and collapse upon his faithful as they were worshipping him? How could laws bind him, even those made of iron, especially if they result in a world where such disasters occur? Voltaire recoiled in horror at the rationalist's incapacity to acknowledge the fierce and seemingly arbitrary violence unleashed on humankind. Was the doctrine of optimism, decreed by Leibniz and popularized by Pope, which posited an infinitely wise and powerful God who did the best he could with the available materials, anything more than a bad philosophical joke? "Tranquil spectators of your brothers' wreck," Voltaire declaims, "Unmoved by this repellent dance of death / Who calmly seek the reason of such storms / Let them but lash your own security."[26]

Not only does Voltaire upbraid philosophical optimism, but he also comes terribly close to scorning the God enthroned by this doctrine. But coming so close, Voltaire is horrified by the view and steps back: he can no more banish God than God can banish evil—or, at least, what human beings perceive as evil. The distance between Voltaire and Leibniz is not as great as we often think. As Neiman observes, Leibniz has a compelling argument—one Voltaire famously parodied in his subsequent masterpiece *Candide*.

Leibniz never claims this is a good, much less a great world; instead, he simply asserts that any other world would be even worse. The roof is sagging, the plumbing is failing, the lighting is spotty, and the floor is uneven, but the dwelling we have is preferable to living in a cave. As for those who whine and resist, Leibniz showed little patience: these poor souls simply don't see far and deeply enough to judge God's work.

In the end, Voltaire might well have accepted this claim. But the heart of his argument with Leibniz and Pope had less to do with their interpretation of God's nature than with their lack of compassion for humankind's lot. With "optimists" such as these thinkers, he asks, who needs pessimists? For this reason, after detailing the litany of evils we face, and God's silence at the end of each and every one, Voltaire suddenly pivots at the poem's ending:

> A caliph once, when his last hour had come
> This prayer addressed to him he reverenced
> "To thee, sole and all-powerful king, I bear
>   What thou dost lack in thy immensity—
>   Evil and ignorance, distress and sin."
> He might have added one thing further—hope.

Upon reading the "Poem on the Lisbon Disaster," however, Rousseau returned this very same criticism at Voltaire. By then ensconced in the bucolic splendor of Montmorency, where he lived in a guesthouse on the estate of Madame d'Épinay, Rousseau penned a long letter to Voltaire, reminding him what his readers most needed in the wake of such a disaster: consolation, not criticism. "You reproach Pope and Leibniz for belittling our evils in their claim that all is for the best, all the while emphasizing the array of evils that deepen our affliction. In place of the solace I sought, you instead deepened my sorrow." For Rousseau, thinkers like Leibniz and Pope at least affirmed that God had, from all possible permutations, chosen that which combined the least evil and greatest good. As for the moral of Voltaire's poem, Rousseau says, it is simple and bleak: "Suffer forever, unhappy man. Since God made you, he is undoubtedly all-powerful and could have prevented all of these evils. Lose all hope, then, that these misfortunes will ever end: the only reason you exist is in order to experience them."[27]

In effect, Rousseau accuses Voltaire of taking the wrong side in the so-called Epicurean dilemma. For centuries, Christian thinkers had grappled with this theological impasse: If God is both omnipotent and benevolent, how is it that evil exists? The efforts at resolving the dilemma, without subtracting one of the two divine attributes, are legion. Most notably, the theological claim that humankind's willed sinfulness is the source of evil and the Neoplatonic argument that evil is nothing more than the absence of goodness—both of which Saint Augustine happened to make—did not prove decisive. No matter how convincing as formal arguments, they nevertheless fail to satisfy the fundamental conviction, at least in the West, that the world is simply not big enough for God and evil.

Voltaire's mistake, Rousseau argues, lays in plumbing for God's omnipotence, not his benevolence. The choice says more about Voltaire than God. If evil's existence forces us to alter one of the two traits we traditionally ascribe to God, benevolence and omnipotence, why choose the latter? He thinks there is no obvious reason, apart from one's particular prejudices, to do so. "If I had to choose between these two errors," he tells Voltaire, "I much prefer the former." After all, we owe our existence to the benevolence of this Creator—an existence whose very nature, despite the many afflictions we face, remains "precious." As he would later write in his *Reveries of the Solitary Walker,* "The sentiment of existence, stripped of any other emotion, is in itself a precious sentiment of contentment and of peace which alone would suffice to make this existence dear and sweet to anyone able to spurn all the sensual and earthly impressions which incessantly come to distract us from it and to trouble its sweetness here below."[28]

This is the sort of sweetness Rousseau had rediscovered at Montmorency—away from Paris and his fellow men. Indeed, when it comes to criticizing humankind, Rousseau proves as harsh as Voltaire. Rousseau's strictures, though, have a more practical bent. As one scholar has observed, Rousseau builds upon his *Second Discourse*'s claim that everything must be viewed not through our inevitably limited and prejudiced eyes, but instead from nature's perspective.[29] Had not men foolishly built a city in so vulnerable a place, he asserts, this natural disaster would not have killed thousands. Herein lies Rousseau's crucial distinction between those disasters that are the work of nature and those issuing from the hands of man. Cities are, he argued, inevitably corrupting and corrosive. As a result, it didn't much matter where they were built: regardless of their location, by their very nature they were unnatural. Cities were cauldrons of human pride—and what other than pride, Rousseau maintained, drove Voltaire's belief that man should be able to grasp God's reasons for Lisbon's experience? Or, for that matter, that man should believe that his desires should command nature's laws?

> You would have liked—and who would not have liked—the earthquake to have happened in the middle of some desert, rather than in Lisbon. Can we doubt that they also happen in deserts? But no one talks about those, because they have no ill effects for city gentlemen (the only men about whom

anyone cares anything). For that matter, desert earthquakes have little effect on the animals and scattered savages who inhabit such spots—and who have no reason to fear falling roofs or tumbling buildings. What would such a privilege mean to us? Will we say that the order of the world must change to suit our whims, that nature must be subject to our laws, that in order to prevent an earthquake in a certain spot, all we have to do is build a city there?[30]

Voltaire never replied to Rousseau's letter. But we might well wonder if it is coincidental that at the end of *Candide*—the work that Rousseau always believed was Voltaire's reply to his letter—its author settles his scarred and sobered troupe not in a city, but instead in the countryside where they attempt, in Candide's final words, to tend their garden.

On the eve of Boswell's siege of Ferney, however, its seigneur was still engaged in the greatest battle he would ever fight on behalf of the city: the Calas affair. This case, which burst onto the European stage in 1762, did more than establish Voltaire's enduring fame. In effect, the affair made Voltaire "Voltaire."

In March 1762, the Catholic authorities of Toulouse convicted a local Protestant merchant, Jean Calas, in the murder of his son. The motive, they concluded, was clear: Calas fils planned to convert to Catholicism—an act the father was resolved to block, even by murder if necessary. Lack of evidence for the charge was not a concern: torture would wring a confession from the accused man. Yet neither the rack, nor water boarding (Calas was twice forced to drink, in rapid succession, ten large jugs of water), nor the wheel (on which his arms and legs were broken) pulled an avowal from the man. Finally, the magistrates, embarrassed and uneasy, had Calas garroted and his body burned in public.

By month's end, news of the execution had reached Ferney. At first, Voltaire dismissed the event as little more than a footnote to the wars of religion: a pox on both Catholic and Protestant fanatics, he told visitors. But as additional visitors and missives carrying details of the case arrived in Ferney—the depressed young Calas, Voltaire learned, had most certainly hanged himself—the lord of Ferney changed his tune: "My tragedies are not as tragic as this death," he lamented.[31] On April 4, he wrote to his faithful disciple Damilaville that no event since the Saint Bartholomew's Day Massacre had "so dishonored human nature." Protest against this injustice, he urged Damilaville, "and may others protest as well."

Never in the business of penning idle hopes, Voltaire now donned the role of stage director. In orchestrating his campaign to proclaim Calas's innocence—and denounce what he called a "judicial assassination"—Voltaire mobilized his vast web of correspondents and acquaintances, reaching as far as the king's closest ministers and even his mistress, Madame de Pompadour, known simply as "la Pompadour." At the same time, Voltaire—accustomed to writing subversive works under various pseudonyms—churned out a series of pamphlets under the guise of firsthand accounts by Calas's wife and son. "If there is one thing that can stay the hand of fanatical rage," Voltaire observed, "it is publicity."[32]

As with any public relations campaign, a slogan was needed. Voltaire had already minted one several years earlier during his sojourn in Berlin: with a fierce flourish, he signed off his letters with the phrase "Ecrasez l'infâme!" By stamping out the "infamous thing," Voltaire did not mean religion but religious superstition and fanaticism. And, to be sure, the campaign seemed to succeed. Two years after he was broken and strangled by administrative fiat,

Calas's name was cleared by the royal court and the family was granted an indemnity. Poet and tragedian, historian and moralist, Voltaire thus added the title of publicist to his list of accomplishments. Indeed, this is the truest sense of the word "philosophe." While not an original or systematic thinker like Locke or Bacon, Voltaire was an immensely gifted translator of their work and method. Indeed, in the case of Calas, he did more than popularize their thought—he politicized it, revealing the tremendous stake a healthy society had in cultivating critical inquiry and religious tolerance.

This particular argument, no doubt, weighed less with Louis XV and his court than the need to mollify France's Huguenot community—another argument that Voltaire underscored in his letters. Within a matter of months Calas's daughters, who had been confined to a convent, were reunited with their mother; a few months later, Versailles showered them with royal grants as compensation for their unmerited suffering. Upon learning the news in Ferney, Voltaire broke down and cried. His tears flowed, no doubt, from the sense of triumph over the forces of *l'infâme,* but also joy that reason had carried the day.

But the day was short-lived. The same year that witnessed Calas's posthumous exoneration also saw the official execration of Voltaire's *Portable Philosophical Dictionary.* The book, which mocked the established religions yet at the same time offered a sincere defense of deism, was burned in Protestant Geneva and condemned in Catholic Paris. More troubling, it also appeared in the trial and execution in Abbeville, scarcely a year later, of Jean-François Lefebvre, chevalier de la Barre. This young man, accused and found guilty of blasphemous acts—which a conniving local magistrate, determined to settle a personal grudge, had cooked up—was beheaded on July 1, 1766. His body was then tossed into a bonfire; among the tinder was a copy of Voltaire's dictionary, which the court alleged had corrupted the young man.[33] This event, as Peter Gay observes, was "the source of Voltaire's greatest fright and greatest fury in his Ferney years."[34]

But in December 1764, these horrific events had not yet unfolded. Indeed, as he orchestrated the publication of his *Philosophical Dictionary,* Voltaire was supremely confident, delighting in the discomfort he was causing his Catholic and Protestant foes. This diabolical dictionary, he wrote, tongue in wrinkled cheek, to Jean d'Alembert, "appalled me, as it did you, but what pains me most grievously is the thought that there are Christians sufficiently unworthy of that fine name as to be able to suspect me of being the author of such anti-Christian work."[35]

Boswell, of course, was familiar with Christians worthy of the name, most notably Johnson, who firmly believed Voltaire was anti-Christian. The "big man," as Oliver Goldsmith called him, was as enraged by Voltaire's elegance as by his insouciance on matters of faith and God. The Frenchman's insistence he was a deist mattered little to Johnson: even if it were a fact, and not a fiction, such a creed must inevitably lead to atheism. This is why, in a conversation with Boswell, he lumped Voltaire and Rousseau together as "bad men." When Boswell pressed him on the point, Johnson exploded: "Why, Sir, it is difficult to settle the proportion of iniquity between them."[36]

As his carriage from Lausanne jogged into Geneva on December 22, Boswell must have been mulling over Johnson's remarks. Confiding to his journal that "Curious were my thoughts on entering this seat of Calvinism," the traveler unloaded his bags at an inn and immediately set about plans to call on Voltaire. At noon the following day, Boswell hired a coach, excitedly giving "Ferney" as his destination. Less excited was the coachman who, if he had been plying his trade for long, had carted to Ferney dozens of other young Scots and Brits making the same pilgrimage to the estate. Voltaire, who prided himself on being "the innkeeper of Europe," had by the end of life welcomed over 500 of Boswell's compatriots alone to his chateau.[37] "It would be scandalous," said one visitor, "to go home without having seen Voltaire."[38]

Boswell, however, was not like the others: to see "the illustrious M. de Voltaire" was not nearly enough. As his coach swayed along the snow-banked road, Boswell "called up all the grand ideas which I have ever entertained of Voltaire."[39] Some of these same grand ideas were those that, several years before, had prompted him and Temple to shout Voltaire's name from the top of Arthur's Seat. Ideas like Voltaire the tragedian, most notably of *Zaire* (translated and produced at the Drury Lane Theatre by David Garrick); or, more recently, the creator of *Candide,* published in English translation in 1759, just weeks after its French publication. Grand ideas of more recent mint, such as Voltaire the scourge of obscurantism, the hero of the Calas affair, must also have crowded Boswell's mind. Somewhere in that mix, though, was the idea, shaped by Johnson's animosity, of Voltaire the deist—"The Infidel, the Author of so many deistical pieces."[40] As in the case of David Hume, Boswell found both irksome and irresistible a thinker who thought of a world without revelation and redemption.

Once the coach entered the estate, Boswell gazed at the parish church that Voltaire had rebuilt; the pediment's inscription, "Deo erexit Voltaire," particularly struck him. What Boswell left unsaid was that the phrase—"Built for God by Voltaire"—allowed no one else, neither saint nor Holy Spirit, to come between the local and cosmic seigneurs. In fact, though it was engraved below the "Deo" and "erexit," Voltaire's name was much larger.[41] And Boswell did

not know that Voltaire, when he first bought the estate, hired a crew
to raze the dilapidated church: the crumbling pile spoiled the sight
lines from the chateau. Confronted by the resistance of local authorities, Voltaire was forced to drop his plans. But in a signature
move, he transformed this act of apparent submission into one of
implicit rebellion. Voltaire had the church renovated after his own
taste, which included commissioning a life-size sculpture of Christ
who, far from representing the torment of the Passion, "expressed
rather the Voltairean conception of Christ as a sage of antique
wisdom."[42]

When Boswell, garbed in his brilliant green overcoat and red
vest, called at the chateau, a squad of liveried footmen informed
him that their master was ill and unable to greet his guest. This
was the first of Boswell's many frissons at Ferney, but one that mer-
cifully did not last long. Shown to a reception room where, with
other guests he spent what seemed an eternity in polite conversation, Boswell wondered if he would ever set eyes on Voltaire. At
that moment, a second door to the room suddenly opened, framing
Voltaire in all his majesty. Transfixed, Boswell "found him just as
his Print had made me conceive him." In a word, the skeletal figure,
swathed in a slate blue night robe and wearing an elaborate wig—
both of which were less fashion statements than defenses against
the freezing rooms of the chateau—had the "air of the world which
a Frenchman acquires in such perfection."[43]

Yet even perfection à la française has its off days. In a letter he
wrote to Temple a few days later, Boswell noted the great man "was
not in spirits" that night.[44] No less telling, Boswell himself felt dull
and convinced he had little to offer other than rank banalities in
his Scot-burred French. (Voltaire refused to speak in English for
the very good reason that "one needs to put one's tongue against
the teeth, and I've lost mine.") The conversation, which lasted thirty

or so minutes, moved fitfully from Scottish painting—Voltaire dismissed the idea as oxymoronic, since artists must always have warm feet in order to paint—to Lord Kames, whose work, to Boswell's chagrin, Voltaire also dismissed. As for the wild Highlands that so inspired Rousseau, the urbane Voltaire was unimpressed. When Boswell described his plans to tour the region with Johnson, his host replied: "Please do so! I'll stay here." It was meager consolation for Boswell that the one thing Scottish that won Voltaire's approval was the infidel Hume: "un vrai philosophe," he declared.[45] Voltaire then drew the curtain on his performance, retiring to his quarters while his guests filed to the dining room for dinner. Disgruntled and disappointed—"I was by no means satisfied," he informed Temple, "to have been so little with the Monarch of French Literature"—Boswell ate and ran in order to reach Geneva before the city gates closed for the night.[46]

Just as those same gates were the bane of Rousseau's youth—he repeatedly was locked out of Geneva after losing track of time while wandering in the surrounding countryside—so, too, were they for Boswell. Yet he quickly hit upon an idea: he would plead with Voltaire's companion, Madame Denise, for an invitation to remain the night at Ferney. After he penned the letter, Boswell was much impressed by the result. Observing that the sun at Ferney, unlike nature's sun, rose not at day but night, might he not be granted, he asked Madame Denise, the favor of spending a night under the chateau's roof? Indeed, if need be, just below the roof: "I am a hardy and vigorous Scot. You may mount me to the highest and coldest garret. I shall not even refuse to sleep upon two chairs in the Bedchamber of your maid."[47]

For a man who, in his travels, had slept in stables and on tables, Boswell's declaration was genuine. But it proved unnecessary: taken by Boswell's genial effrontery, Madame Denise, with Voltaire's wink, invited the Scot to stay at Ferney. Two days later, Boswell again disembarked at what he called the "enchanted castle."[48] And yet, the enchantment threatened to remain as elusive as it had been during the first visit. To his dismay, Boswell was again shepherded into the same waiting room where several other guests were milling about, busily "soaping their own beards"—namely, making conversation or music, playing cards, or drawing portraits. Everything, in a word, one would expect in an Edinburgh drawing room and not in the dwelling of the "Magician." Rather than enchantment, Boswell felt the first tugs of depression: "All was full. The Canvas was covered. My Hypochondria began to muse . . . I had heavy ennui."[49]

But the clouds then gave way: from an adjoining room, Voltaire shouted: "Find Father Adam!" As Boswell had discovered, one of the evening rituals at Ferney was a game of chess between Voltaire and the Jesuit father who was part of the chateau's large and motley household. While they settled down to their game, Boswell stood near Voltaire and, as he put it to Temple, "touched the keys in unison with his Imagination." Some of the keys happened to be in English, as Voltaire, clearly unconcerned by the absence of teeth, swore with comic vigor, recited passages from the poetry of Dryden and Pope, and even sang a ballad he had learned during his stay in London. He praised Addison as a "great Genius," pummeled Johnson as a "superstitious dog," and proposed the English love Shakespeare because "they have no taste."[50]

The "brilliance" and "extravagance," the "bold flights" and "flashes of wit" that often made Boswell "start up & cry upon [his] soul this is astonishing" were merely a warm-up for the interview Boswell was the keenest to have. As the other guests filed out to the dining room, the Scot realized this was his one chance to have Voltaire to himself. Remaining behind in the drawing room,

Boswell effectively blocked Voltaire's escape route to his own rooms through his relentless questioning. For nearly two hours, the men took up the subjects—and frequently the cudgels—of religion and faith. With a Bible separating the two men, the conversation assumed epic proportions: "If ever two men disputed with vehemence we did."[51]

In his journal, Boswell noted his intention to write down the conversation in a separate document. Good as his word, he did so shortly after, but the eight pages he filled with his recollection of the tête-à-tête have since been lost. Based on the scattered remarks Boswell jotted in the journal as well as the account he gave Temple, vehemence there most certainly was—but also much vaudeville. Raging and trembling, Voltaire "stood like an Orator of ancient Rome"—that is, until he fell back into his chair, moaning: "O, I am very sick. My head turns round." What, precisely, made his head spin? Was it the subject of revelation? Providence? Theodicy? Might it have been sheer exasperation with Boswell's doggedness? Or, since Voltaire immediately recovered, nothing more than a theatrical turn by an old pro? Boswell doesn't say what, though he does refer to his eight-page account as "our important Scene."[52] No less tellingly, the young Scot, who knew a thing or two about self-dramatization, did not flinch. Rather than being alarmed by Voltaire's melodramatic swoon, Boswell most probably felt like applauding.

In any case, he certainly felt the need for clarity. Looking hard at his bewigged and bemused host, over whom loomed a large painting portraying Mars leaving the bed of Venus, Boswell took Voltaire to task: ""I did not believe him capable of thinking in the manner that he declared to me was 'from the bottom of his heart.'"[53] The Scot wanted to get to the bottom of Voltaire's soul: he was determined to know the philosophe's sincere belief on the matter of belief. Demanding from Voltaire "an honest confession of his real sentiments," Boswell got what he desired, but not what he had hoped. Voltaire confessed "his love of the Supreme Being, and his entire Resignation to the will of Him who is all-wise." Moreover, his host expressed his desire "to resemble the Author of Goodness, by being good himself." In a word, he got the world according to deism.

This was all well and good, but not enough for Boswell: he needed more from God than Voltaire thought God needed to give. His disappointment was great: "I was moved; I was sorry." Yet the old deist did not waver. With a smile that stretched tight the wrinkled parchment of his skin, Voltaire said he refused to "inflame his mind with grand hopes of the immortality of the Soul. He says it may be; but he knows nothing of it." Such imperturbability struck Boswell as yet another instance of playacting and he pressed Voltaire on the truthfulness of his claim. While the clatter and conversation from the dining room could faintly be heard, Boswell demanded to know if Voltaire was sincere. "Before God I am," Voltaire replied, then with the "fire of him whose Tragedies have so often shone on the Theatre of Paris, he said: 'I suffer much. But I suffer with Patience & Resignation; not as a Christian—But as a man.'"[54] Announcing he needed to retire to bed, Voltaire then drew the curtain on this remarkable scene.

For the next two days, Voltaire was hors de combat. Illness, Madame Denise reported, prevented the seigneur of Ferney from mingling with his guests. But it may well have been that Voltaire was too busy orchestrating from his bedchamber his two-front campaign against l'infâme and that reviled turncoat Rousseau. The Genevan, in fact, had just published his Letters Written from the

Mountain. In this pamphlet, Rousseau not only delivered a passionate defense of democratic politics, but also committed the unpardonable crime of identifying Voltaire as author of the *Oath of the Fifty,* a brutal and hilarious critique of Christian scripture. Enraged by this violation of his anonymity, Voltaire was at that very moment penning a vitriolic tract that revealed Rousseau as having fathered five children with Thérèse—which was true—but also of having murdered Thérèse's mother and "exposed his children at the gates of an asylum." Perhaps to Rousseau's chagrin, Thérèse's mother was alive and well, and while he did abandon his five children, Rousseau did not "expose" them, but admitted them to a foundling hospital—a truth awful enough without Voltaire adding his absurd accusations.[55]

Boswell was not, of course, privy to the cloak-and-dagger doings at Ferney. Had he been, they still would not have distracted him from what he called a "singular and solemn occasion." Sitting down with Voltaire for what would be the last time, Boswell told him that before coming to Ferney he had thought he would see "a very great, but a very bad man." Either amused or confused by this wonderfully tactless remark, Voltaire replied: "You are very sincere."[56] No less sincere—and no less tactless—was Boswell's last effort to persuade Voltaire that deism was not enough. Citing chapter and verse, not this time from the Bible, but instead from his host's *Philosophical Dictionary,* Boswell shared his "troubles" over the entry "Soul." This was not surprising: in the dictionary, Voltaire made clear that we can no more grasp the term than the blind can grasp the notion of light. Let us conclude, he wrote, that we are ignoramuses about such matters. "As regards ignoramuses who pride themselves on their knowledge, they are far inferior to monkeys. Now dispute, choleric arguers: present your petitions against each other; proffer your insults, pronounce your sentences, you who do not know one word about the matter."[57]

Boswell had neither insults to proffer nor sentences to pronounce, but he did propose a compromise. Was it not, he asked, more "pleasing and noble" to believe the soul was immortal? Of course, Voltaire replied, but what of it? "You have a noble desire to be King of Europe. I wish it for you and I ask your protection. But it is not probable." In essence, Boswell could do what Johnson did with the boulder, and kick this particular item of faith all he wanted, but doing so would not make it true. But he continued to kick none-theless. Citing a line from Addison's *Cato,* Boswell implored: "We can all say 'It must be so,' till death reveals the truth about immortality.'" The old magician refused this particular spell, however: "Before we say that this soul will exist, let us know what it is." For this, Boswell had no rejoinder. He instead wondered if he and Voltaire could, at the very least, find a common ground for worship—an invitation his host accepted, but with his own proviso: "Let us meet four times a year in a grand temple, with music, and thank God for all his gifts. There is one sun. There is one God. Let us have one religion."

For Boswell such an austere prospect, one that offered no place to revelation or personal salvation, was intolerable—even if accompanied by music. Perhaps this is why, in response, Boswell took his leave with one last question: "May I write in English, and you'll answer?" Voltaire said he would, no doubt relieved that his irrepressible, but increasingly irritating guest was finally on his way. Perhaps he thought Boswell would never act on his request. Yet this was not their final exchange. Less than two months later, Boswell wrote to Voltaire, again pressing Voltaire on the subject of the soul. Voltaire's reply was brief and blunt: "I know nothing of it, nor whether it is, nor what it is, nor what it shall be. Young scholars and priests know all that perfectly. For my part, I am but a very ignorant fellow."[58]

When Boswell returned to the charge a few weeks later, sending to Ferney yet another letter making the case for the soul's immortality, Voltaire did not bother to reply. Had he bothered, it might have made little difference. By then, Boswell was in Italy where his concern over the soul now competed with a fascination over the less immaterial forms of solace offered by women.

— 9 —

ON LIBERTINES
AND LIBERTY

The good in you amazes me as much as the bad.

THE COASTAL AREA SOUTH of the Swiss Alps was, for most continental tourists, the climax of the Grand Tour: Italy. "A man who
has not been in Italy," Johnson told Boswell several years after his
return, "is always conscious of an inferiority, from his not having
seen what it is expected a man should see. The grand object of trav-
elling is to see the shores of the Mediterranean." For Johnson, visiting these shores was a pilgrimage to our common past: it was this
part of the world that gave Europe "all our religion, almost all our
law, almost all our arts, almost all that sets us above the savages."[1]

To be sure, the common reason for visiting Italy was the classical artistic and political ideals held in common by the West. In
an age where Latin and the classics were part and parcel of young
men's education, Italy crystallized the lessons they had been taught
and values they had been given. To walk across Rome and its en-
virons was to walk back in time—like the golden bough in the *Aeneid,* the city's ruins served as the passport to a past still alive in
the imagination of its descendants. Tellingly, just a few months before Boswell reached Italy, Edward Gibbon had arrived in Rome,

where while he "sat musing amidst the ruins of the Capitol . . . the idea of writing the decline and fall of ancient Rome first started in [his] mind."[2]

While the glories of Rome's past were certainly on Boswell's mind as he left Geneva for Turin on New Year's Day 1765, they were soon crowded out by more immediate sensations. The most traveled road between France and Italy was by way of Savoy, where the town of Pont-de-Beauvoisin served as the base camp for passage through the Mont Cenis pass, which lay nearly 7,000 feet directly above. The path was too narrow and rough for wheeled vehicles, while heavy rains and snow often washed out bridges. (It was only in the latter half of the nineteenth century that engineers managed to construct a rail line along the path.) Deprived of carriages, travelers hired what Boswell called an "Alps machine": a web of leather cords hanging between two tree trunks and shouldered by teams of local guides. It was while ensconced in such a machine that Boswell confronted a landscape far more wild and sublime than anything he had seen before or even imagined possible. In an effort to capture the moment, he recalled a line from Virgil's Eclogues—"I have climbed the rudest heights and drunk the Alpine snow"—as he gazed on chamois clambering over boulders and snow drifts rising more than six feet. The prospect, he later wrote in his journal, "was horridly grand." The phrase may strike us as perfunctory, but we would be mistaken. Boswell's exceptional ability to re-create conversations did not carry over to his descriptions of the natural world, a fact he himself recognized. Moreover, his choice of words is telling: although he had not yet read Edmund Burke's influential *Philosophical Enquiry Into the Origin of our Ideas of the Sublime and Beautiful*, published in 1757, the book's ideas were "in the air" as much as the eagles that glided high above Boswell's Alps machine. By the sublime, Burke understood the astonishment, even terror that over-

whelms the mind upon seeing nature at its most disorderly and un-
tamed, from its great mountains to raging seas. Yet that frisson of
horror was welcomed, not shunned—as certainly was the case with
Boswell as his porters jogged him toward the pass of Mont Cenis,
then descended toward the Piedmontese plains.

Unlike most travelers who raced past Turin, the first stop once
they passed the Alps, for the wonders of Florence and Rome, Boswell lingered there for more than two weeks. His reasons differed,
at least in part, from those that drove him to Môtiers and Ferney.
As soon as he arrived in the city on January 7, he set about the conquest not of philosophers, but instead of lovers. Introduced to the
Contessa di San Gillio, an influential aristocrat who, according to
Casanova, orchestrated all of Turin's romantic intrigues, Boswell
began a series of frantic and unsuccessful sieges of the city's women.
The urgency of Boswell's efforts does not surprise, given his mostly
celibate passage through Germany and Switzerland. Besides, Italy's
reputation as a land of passionate women and louche mores
seemed confirmed the day after Boswell arrived, when he attended
a public ball. Every time an attractive woman caught Boswell's eye,
a French officer by the name of Captain Billon assured him: "Sir,
you can have her. It would not be difficult."[3] At first Boswell believed Billon was having him on, but the officer insisted he was quite
serious.

As it turned out, it was difficult, indeed impossible for Boswell
to seduce Turin's women—or, at least, its titled ones. Turin's high
society may well have been "openly debauched," as Boswell insisted,
but its members still expected a modicum of politesse and patience
that the hurried Scot would not observe. In rapid succession, he
attempted to seduce three aristocratic women—Mesdames di San
Gillio, di Borgaretto and di Scarnafigi whom he believed open to
intrigues; no less rapidly, the door was shut in his face all three

times. The Contessa di Scarnafigi, the wife of a diplomat, especially attracted Boswell—though this was not at all her intention. In their meetings, she showed herself indifferent to his efforts to win her attention, yet the poor Scot grossly misinterpreted her coldness as a ruse to inflame his passions. In a letter he had his servant deliver to Scarnafigi, Boswell assures her "We have the liveliest ideas, which we express only by our glances" and marvels over the "the exquisite delicacy" with which she avoided touching his hand. Deluded and desperate, he then assured her that the moment "we abandon ourselves to pleasures under the veil of darkness, what transports, what ecstasy will be ours!" As he learned the next day, the good woman's response was to throw Boswell's letter into the fireplace.[4] More or less simultaneously, Madame di Borgarato asked Boswell to stop sending her letters, while the Contessa di San Gillio sent a note that flattened the Scot: "You should not attempt the profession of gallantry, for if you do, you will be terribly taken in. Mind your health and your purse, for you don't know the world."[5]

It turned out that Captain Billon, who had encouraged him to pursue these noble women, moonlighted as a pimp. He procured a "pretty girl" for Boswell, but these "low pleasures" filled the young man with disgust.[6] These encounters, which did not match the romantic ideals he had about Italy, darkened Boswell's spirits. He had by then already suffered bouts of melancholy, moments when he felt "deeply hipped [a contraction of "hypochondriacal"] and knew not what to make of [him]self."[7] By January 21, Boswell was consumed by self-disgust, crying out in his journal: "O Rousseau, how am I fallen since I was with thee!"[8]

In a letter he wrote to Rousseau several months later, Boswell reflected on his time in Turin. With the hermit of Môtiers again cast as his confessor, Boswell dwells on the doubts that then gnawed at his soul. "I know my worth sometimes, and I think and act nobly. But then melancholy attacks me, I despise myself, and it seems to me a waste of time to try to improve so petty a thing." At such moments, he would recall Rousseau's remark to him at Môtiers—"Sir, all you lack is knowledge of your own worth"—but he would nevertheless often succumb to bleaker thoughts.[9] Unable to talk to Rousseau, Boswell succeeded in finding another interlocutor, John Needham, an Englishman and Roman Catholic priest serving as tutor to a local aristocratic family. A skillful casuist, Needham impressed Boswell with his defense of the Catholic faith; after listening to the priest's case for transubstantiation, Boswell was "convinced that it was not absurd." As for the orthodox view of heaven and hell, Needham was especially persuasive, taking his cue from Saint Augustine and defending eternal punishment as the "continual shade which must be in the universe." Clearly troubled by the priest's assurance that "to exist with a certain degree of pain was better than to be annihilated," Boswell struggled to recall Rousseau's more "liberal views of a benevolent Divinity."[10]

Though he finally quit Turin for Milan on January 22, Boswell found it impossible to leave behind the mortal questions he had entertained with Needham. As his carriage clattered past the docks lining the Po River, Boswell saw a throng of spectators converging on a gallows. A thief was about to be hanged—a spectacle that, as always, exercised a morbid fascination on Boswell. He jumped out of the carriage, pushed his way toward the front of the crowd and watched as the condemned man, noose tightened around his neck, was flung from a ladder by the executioner, who then jammed his foot against the man's head to complete the job begun by gravity. The hideous sight transfixed Boswell; though he had hoped "feelings of horror might destroy those of chagrin," he could not shake free of his "feverish agitation." He slipped into a neighboring church, kneeled in front of the altar, and "felt three successive scenes: raging love—gloomy horror—grand devotion."[11]

Boswell's effort to steady his mind inside the church had little effect: the next several days, as he made his way southward, were variously "grievous" and "deplorable." Following a rapid visit to Milan, Boswell hurried on to Parma to meet Alexandre Deleyre, a tutor in the duke of Parma's household who was a dedicated follower of Rousseau. Almost immediately, the two men took to one another. In a letter to Rousseau, the Frenchman declared he had "conceived for Boswell an immediate and lasting affection," while Boswell confided to his journal that the "genteel amiable" Deleyre had won him over by his "simplicity of manners."[12] He observes that they spoke with "unreserved gaiety," but one wonders if the conversation ever touched on religion. Deleyre happened to be an atheist—indeed, in his skepticism he was not alone at the royal court. His most celebrated colleague at Parma was the French thinker, the Abbé Etienne de Condillac, who served as preceptor to the duke's children, but was also the author of the celebrated *Traité des systèmes,* a powerful series of arguments on behalf of philosophical materialism. It happened that Boswell had certain spiritual concerns in common with Condillac: like his hero John Locke, the Frenchman, while insisting upon the sensationalist and materialist basis of human nature, also insisted upon the immateriality of the soul. Yet the conversation between the two men, brought together by Deleyre, remained superficial. After chatting briefly about metaphysics, Boswell records he jokingly told the "composed, sensible" Frenchman: "If I have gloomy chimeras, I also have agreeable ones. When I lie down at night I think that perhaps I shall wake up a Locke. You cannot demonstrate the contrary to me."[13] Perhaps the *plaisanterie* was funnier in French, but in any case Boswell does not record whether Condillac laughed.

Soon after Boswell took leave of Deleyre, the latter wrote to Rousseau about the visit. Though he had spent just two days in the Scot's company, Deleyre was sorry to see him go for reasons that are remarkably trenchant: "His oddness, his youth, and his melancholy [are] likely to keep him from gathering from his tour the fruits which he promises himself and which he badly needs." Worried that Boswell was too impressionable, Deleyre wondered if he would fall in with the wrong sort of people who would give him "pernicious views on religion"—by which he meant not skeptics, but sectarians. "He has already experienced many changes under that head, because he is seeking for the truth—a thing extremely difficult to discover in that heap of error in which the sects have buried it."[14]

Upon leaving Parma, however, Boswell did fall in with an Englishman, John Wilkes, who held pernicious views on not just religion, but also on morality and monarchy. And, indeed, on the Scots. Boswell had first been introduced to Wilkes in mid-May 1763 at Tom Davies's bookshop, shortly after his initial meeting with Johnson. By then, he was well aware of Wilkes's anti-Scottish broadsides in the *North Briton,* but given the vivacity of Wilkes's writing, and his blistering attacks at the government, Boswell could not but overlook the journalist's jibes at the Scots. Indeed, an impatient Boswell bought each issue when it was "fresh from the press."[15]

It was shortly after his election to Parliament that Wilkes launched the *North Briton,* little more than a cudgel to pound the government of Lord Bute. George III had named Bute, his former tutor, to lead the government, an ill-considered move given the man's lack of qualities for the post—few shared his own high opinion of his intellectual and political abilities—as well as widespread anti-Scottish prejudice among the English. In an issue of the *North Briton*, Wilkes not only attacked Bute's stewardship, but also questioned the truthfulness of the government's official speech that, according to tradition, was pronounced by the king. An outraged government arrested the rabble-rouser and marched him off to the Tower (where Wilkes demanded that he not be put in a cell once occupied by a Scot, for fear of catching smallpox).[16] The consequences, at least in hindsight, were predictable: when his parliamentary immunity led to his release a few days later, Wilkes discovered he had become a hero. In fact, Boswell had himself gone to the Tower that day with the intention to join the crowd gathered to cheer Wilkes as he walked out a free man, but had arrived too late.[17]

He was a hero of a particular stamp, however: Wilkes's indifference to the rules of parliamentary politics was matched by his scorn for the rules of sexual politics. A notorious libertine, Wilkes belonged to the "Medmenham Monks," a shadowy club of well-born men and influential figures led by the wealthy aristocrat Sir Francis Dashwood. Art and literature, as well as erotica and sex, were not only the subjects of the club's conversations, but its chief occupations as well. Debauchery with courtesans and drinking in epic proportions were commonplace; as one contemporary noted, the "nominal qualification" for membership "is having been in Italy, and the real one is being drunk."[18] Yet, the relationship between being a libertine and a proponent of liberty, between sexual practices and political principles, was quite intimate in the eighteenth century. Radical thought inevitably challenged not just political principles, but sexual mores as well; while philosophy was a public activity, it was just as easily pursued in the boudoir, as the Marquis de Sade's life and writings remind us.

In fact, it was the publication of Wilkes's obscene parody of Alexander Pope's *Essay on Man* that gave the government a second chance to lock him away. The irony that the charge was brought by Lord Sandwich, who had also belonged to the Medmenham Monks, was lost on few observers. But the government's determination to do whatever was necessary to imprison their tormentor was clear. Shortly after London workers, rallying to "Wilkes and Liberty," stormed London's Royal Exchange in November 1763 to prevent the government's official burning of an issue of the *North Briton,* Wilkes himself quit England for the Continent. Though he was physically courageous—a trait attested to by the several men who had fought him in duels—Wilkes thought a short exile from England would help to cool the government's anger. Instead, he presented Bute what seemed a golden opportunity and the latter stripped Wilkes of his immunity and declared him an outlaw. In effect, Wilkes lost all his rights and protections under British law. For nearly two and a half years, he was a man without a country, unable to return to England yet unwilling to surrender his attachment to individual liberties.

The status of outlaw became Wilkes. A physically ugly man, he was also quite witty and charming: "I need only half an hour to talk away my face," he once quipped.[19] Even Johnson, whose own physical presence was so disturbing to newcomers, lost sight of Wilkes's deformities—like a riptide pulling at a sandcastle, the grotesque jutting of his lower jaw distorted his entire face and seemed to pull at his (severely crossed) eyes—and after a few minutes of conversation concluded that Wilkes had a "cheerful countenance."[20] Twenty years before Boswell packed his bags for Holland, Wilkes had made the same trip for the same reasons. Rather than Utrecht, however, he settled in Leiden—the same city where Lord Auchinleck had studied—and became fast friends with a fellow student, Paul-Henri Thiry d'Holbach. Shortly after, d'Holbach moved to Paris, joined the circle of philosophes and hosted a literary salon well known for its hostility to religion. Even David Hume, the "great infidel," was shocked by the candor of the other habitués. Living in Paris while Boswell was touring the Continent, Hume was frequently a guest at d'Holbach's table. One evening, in his thickly accented French, the Scottish skeptic declared he did not believe in atheists since he had never met one. In reply, his host asked him to look around the table at the eighteen fellow guests: "I can show you fifteen atheists right off. The others haven't made up their minds."[21]

While we do not know what these young friends discussed during their time in Leiden, religion and faith must surely have been a favorite subject. No less surely, the conversations sharpened Wilkes's religious doubts, but like the handful of fence sitters at d'Holbach's salon, he too had not yet made up his mind. Wilkes, like Hume, was a fiercely mordant critic of established religions; but also like Hume, he refused the absolute certainties espoused by atheists. Unlike Hume, however, Wilkes was not a deep or systematic thinker; instead, he was a journalist and politician as skillful with a sword as with a pen. As he would tell Boswell, he wrote best while in bed with women—writings on behalf of individual liberties as forthright and radical as were the author's character and private life.

Soon after having arrived in Turin, Boswell learned that Wilkes was in the same city. The Englishman, still in exile, had settled there shortly before with Gertrude Corradini, a beautiful Italian courtesan he had met in London. What to do? Not only was it risky to associate with a man on the English Crown's most wanted list, but it was simply incongruous to do so when, like Boswell, one was a

Scot and monarchist. At the same time, Boswell was drawn to the man; that Wilkes was an outlaw played no small role in his attraction: "I was very curious," he wrote in his journal, "to see him in his misfortune." In an invitation to dinner, Boswell displayed his gift of warm-hearted candor: "I am told that Mr. Wilkes is now in Turin. As a politician, my monarchical soul abhors him. As a Scotsman I smile at him. As a friend I know him not. As a companion I love him. I believe it is not decent for me to wait upon him. Yet I wish much to see him . . . If Mr. Wilkes chooses to be my guest, I shall by no means oppose it."[22]

Wilkes failed to get the invitation before retiring for the evening, so Boswell renewed the offer the following day. He explained that as "an old laird and a steady royalist," he could not possibly call on Wilkes, but he was nevertheless very eager to meet with him. Would he not dine at Boswell's inn? "To men of philosophical minds there are surely moments when they set aside their nation, their rank, their character, all that they have done and all that they have suffered in his jumbling world. Such moments may be most philosophical, as they are clear of all prejudices, good as well as bad."[23] Yet, once again, the invitation arrived too late and Wilkes left Turin for Rome the following day.

But the invitations had impressed Wilkes. His exile had begun to weigh on him, as did the death of a close friend and collaborator, Charles Churchill, who had died in his arms in France. Moreover, Wilkes was still spurned by most English travelers, was increasingly beset by financial difficulties, and desperately missed his daughter, still in London. In the midst of these travails, Boswell burst with his ebullience and persistence. Consequently, when by chance they happened to meet a couple of weeks later at Rome's customs office, they fell into each other's arms—a fortuitous meeting that marked the beginning of an enduring friendship. During their stays in Rome, the two men saw a great deal of one another. Wilkes urged Boswell to keep up his journal: "You must go on. Publish what you have by you." Long separated from Johnson, long criticized by his father, Boswell was dazzled by Wilkes's encouragement: "*Such* compliments," he scribbled in one of his memoranda.[24] (Ironically, at this point in his Italian tour, Boswell broke off his journal, while keeping up his daily memoranda.)

At the same time, Wilkes's political pronouncements also dazzled, but for different reasons. When in one of their conversations Boswell insisted on George III's virtuous character, Wilkes agreed the king had all the right private virtues. The problem, however, was that the king "wants to encroach on our liberties. He is laying the foundation of the ruin of his family." When Wilkes declared that George was no better than the Stuarts, Boswell took up the challenge with Jacobite élan: "Then I fall down and worship the image that he has set up. I reason not.'Tis my taste."[25]

Despite the political chasm gaping between them, it was to Boswell's taste to ignore it. When the Englishman quit Rome for Naples on February 18, with Corradini and her mother in tow, Boswell soon followed. But not before he had whored to a Wilkesian degree. His memoranda record the buying of services from a "charming" girl whose mother served as her procurer: "Much enjoyment," Boswell noted. No doubt under the influence of Wilkes, he added: "Nothing debases mind like narrowness ... Be Spaniard: girl every day."[26] At the cost of thirteen shillings, Boswell kept his vow until, in a rather haggard state, he set out for Naples along the Appian Way on February 25.

———————

Naples was the furthest south most British tourists traveled, and even then mostly in winter. They were attracted to a city steeped in ancient history—Virgil's tomb was thought to be in Naples, and the theater at Herculaneum had been excavated shortly before Boswell's visit—but were often repelled by the torrid summers and a local population reputed to be thieves and savages. While a growing number of travelers went to Naples for reasons of health—the warm winters became a popular remedy for various illnesses during the second half of the century—others came to damage their health. When not enervated by the heat or wine, male tourists in particular were frequently floored by venereal disease.

As a result, for northerners who ventured this deep into Italy's boot, a strong constitution was a necessity. Having toured Italy shortly before Boswell, Edward Gibbon declared that the ideal tourist must meet a certain number of physical qualifications: "He should be endowed with an active, indefatigable vigour of mind and body, which can seize every mode of conveyance, and support with a careless smile every hardship of the road."[27] While Boswell more than met these requirements apart from repeated bouts of gonorrhea, he boasted a solid physical constitution—the Appian Way nevertheless took its toll on him. Soon after arriving in Naples, he wrote to Wilkes, observing that his "bones [were] almost broken by that rough Appian Way, although I travelled at the slowest of rates, in almost snake-like fashion."[28]

In a nod to Wilkes, reputed for his fluency in Latin and familiarity with classical sources, Boswell wrote his letter in Latin. He also tossed aside his earlier fears about associating with an outlaw—perhaps he felt at greater liberty in Naples, where the distance and exotic character of the city played a role—telling Wilkes that wherever they met "we shall have wine and laughter" and recalling the promise made in Rome that "we should be much together in Naples."[29] Wilkes was delighted to make good on the promise: the memoranda Boswell wrote while in Naples bulge with the excursions and conversations he had with Wilkes. Perched on donkeys, the friends one day ascended a mountain to visit a villa Wilkes had thought to rent; two days later, they traveled to Vesuvius, climbed to the summit, and lay on their bellies at the edge of the crater to gaze inside it until forced away by billows of ash and smoke.

These sights served, however, mostly as dramatic backdrops to conversations between the two men. Wilkes impressed Boswell as deeply as had Rousseau, even Johnson. There was, of course, the Englishman's notoriety as a journalist and politician that had initially attracted Boswell, but he found Wilkes's intelligence and character equally compelling. The ease with which he wore his radical ideas, close-fit between his values and actions, and his steady refusal of cant and scorn for pieties were striking. "I always tell the truth," he told Boswell—a claim he fell short of, one suspects, less often than most men.[30] Wilkes's graceful integrity and great learning, however, dovetailed with an affable and warm personality, one that prized good company as much as good laws. In a letter to Rousseau, Boswell hit upon these rarely paired qualities: Wilkes, he wrote, "is a man who has thought much without being gloomy, a man who has done much evil without being a scoundrel."[31]

Most crucially, when it came to mortal questions that drove Boswell to quiz other great men, questions that weighed on Johnson and exasperated Voltaire, Wilkes responded in a very different fashion. As they prepared for their ascent of Vesuvius, the ancient volcano that in AD 79 had buried the Roman cities of Pompeii and Herculaneum under molten rock and still belched smoke into the sky, Boswell's thoughts turned toward the subjects of death and eternity. Climbing a mountain slope deep in ash, Boswell asked Wilkes for his thoughts about the afterlife and salvation. The Englishman laughed, his jaw sawing back and forth: "I never think on futurity, as there is not data enough." As for the nature and destination of the soul, Wilkes allowed that he had read on the subject when he was in Holland, but never since gave it a thought. When Boswell insisted on discussing the problems of fate and free will, Wilkes would have none of it: "Let'em alone!" Boswell could not let it alone, however, telling his companion that the very thought of the Kirk made him tremble. Wilkes replied it had nothing to do with a vengeful God; instead, he assured Boswell, "That's the strength of your imagination."[32]

What Wilkes would not let alone, to Boswell's embarrassment, were women. During their climb at Vomero, the libertine justified the life he had lived: "A man who has not money to gratify his passions does right to govern them." But as he had always had the means, Wilkes continued, he also had the good sense to indulge. "Thank heaven for having given me the love of women. To many she gives not the noble passion of lust."[33] In an earlier conversation, Wilkes revealed that his student days in Holland had been very different from Boswell's: "I was always among women at Leiden. My father gave me as much money as I pleased. I'd have three or four whores and was drunk every night." Yet, Wilkes added, he always took the sacrament at church.[34] Not surprisingly, when Boswell told him about Zélide, Wilkes's advice was straightforward: "Go home by Holland and roger her. You might be in her . . ."[35]

On March 20, a little more than two weeks since he had arrived in Naples, Boswell was ready to return to Rome. By then, he had rogered several prostitutes, a few of whom also plied a living as singers, and drunk in excess with Wilkes and contracted scurvy, which he attributed to "vicious humours from my blood" having been extracted by the warm air. Whether it was due to the climate, or the lack of vitamin C, the disease blistered Boswell's chin and neck so severely that, as he wrote to John Johnston, it was "almost certain that no Woman under fifty would give me a kiss without being paid for it."[36]

Indeed. Upon returning to Rome, Boswell discovered that along with scurvy, he had also caught yet another case of gonorrhea.

———

Boswell had knotted a friendship with Wilkes in Italy that would last long after both men returned to Great Britain and their lives took different paths. The Englishman's radical politics clashed with the Scot's romantic attachment to monarchy, and for a short time while pursuing his own ultimately futile political ambitions, Boswell thought it prudent to avoid his controversial friend. Yet their mutual affection abided these occasional jolts. In jest, Wilkes assured Boswell that "Rousseau and other champions of liberty will in time pluck out of your lairdish breast the black seeds of Stuartism with which you are now so strongly impregnated."[37] As Boswell once told Wilkes, "Though we differ widely in politics and religion, *il y a des points où nos ames sont unies* [there are points where our souls are one]."[38] A member of Boswell's London "gang," Wilkes would meet with Boswell during the latter's periodic escapes from Scotland. At the London tavern, one of their favorite haunts, Boswell recalled: "When Wilkes and I sat together, each glass of wine produced a flash of wit, like gunpowder thrown into the fire. Puff! Puff!"[39]

Those puffs reveal something that Wilkes alone seemed to offer Boswell. Long after his return to Great Britain, when the luster of the continental tour had faded and the corrosion of self-doubt had again set in, Boswell was always buoyed by his visits with Wilkes: "I was in excellent spirits and a pretty good match for him," he exclaimed after one meeting, "better than I remember myself."[40] Life always seemed more joyous when he was in Wilkes's company, and not simply because the company was so unapologetically raffish. In fact, Wilkes glimpsed a certain reserve with Boswell when he recounted his sexual adventures: "You too like the thing almost as well as I do, but you dislike the talk and laugh about it, of which I am perhaps too fond."[41]

But when Wilkes turned his eye to matters of greater moment, the Scot found little to dislike. Boswell tried on several occasions to make the case for Christianity to Wilkes, urging his friend "to seek consolation from the immortality of the soul." There are powerful arguments to believe in its immortality, Boswell insists, but then almost immediately seems to have second thoughts: "It depends on ourselves to cultivate elevating hope."[42] The older man waved off Boswell's pleading with good humor: "*Hope* shall always be my motto, and I continue to look forwards, though not quite so far as so good a Christian as Mr. Boswell."[43]

For Boswell, the candor and cheerfulness with which the unbelieving Wilkes approached sacred matters guaranteed the existence of a benign God. Far from disabusing the younger man of his faith, Wilkes' bon mots instead comforted his need to believe in a good and great God. How else to explain this singular man's existence? Wilkes's constant felicity, Boswell marveled, "shakes my solid speculations on human woe."[44] In a letter to Rousseau, Boswell captured this galvanizing aspect to Wilkes's character: "His lively and energetic sallies on moral questions gave to my spirit a not unpleasant agitation, and enlarged the scope of my views by convincing me that God could create a soul completely serene and gay notwithstanding the alarming reflection that we all must die."[45]

———

Once returned to Rome and far from Wilkes, who had remained in Naples, Boswell again battled these alarming reflections. To

Rousseau he confessed that his conduct had not been what he had expected when he left Môtiers. But now, he added, "the fever is past. I am as you would wish to see me."[46] Except, that is, when he wasn't as he wished Rousseau to see him. The "fever" never subsided entirely, flaring up especially at night with the persistence and violence of Vesuvius. Boswell punctuates his journal during this period with telegraphic yet desperate notes about nocturnal visits to brothels, followed by earnest resolutions to never visit them again. During the day, however, he was a model student of antiquity. He hired a Scottish antiquary, Colin Morison, as his personal guide to the city's ruins and ancient sites. So intent to steep in the city's past, Boswell insisted on conversing in Latin with his fellow Scot; within days, they "harangued on Roman antiquities in the language of the Romans themselves."[47] Moreover, he visited J. J. Wincklemann—calling on the celebrated German classicist was de rigueur for all serious tourists—and took copious notes of his museum visits. Just outside the city, decaying ruins and well-tended land transported Boswell into the distant past: at Tusculum, where Cicero had had his summer villa, the Scot immersed himself in "the genius of the place, and was supremely happy."[48]

The experience at Tusculum prompted Boswell to sketch an essay on happiness, modeled on Cicero's *Tusculan Questions,* in which he muses on religion. Assuming a "perfectly impartial" perspective, he realized "how much more clear light has been imparted to the world during the eighteen hundred years that have rolled on since Cicero."[49] Of course, the perfectly partial Scot also meant "since Christ"—less the historical figure, however, than the lead actor in the stupendous theatrical production of the Roman Catholic Church. When not visiting ruins and galleries, or brothels and bawdy houses, Boswell gravitated to the churches and cathedrals. While this itinerary was not unusual for British tourists, Boswell's particular reasons and responses were, on the contrary, out of the ordinary. Popery and papists were the era's great bugbears in Great Britain. The great majority of English and Boswell's fellow Scottish travelers shuddered at the imagined dark powers and great reach of the Roman Catholic Church—the source, in their eyes, of superstition and obscurantism, political repression and clerical autocracy. Great Britain's traditional enemies, France and Spain, were Catholic, while the Jacobite rebellions were fueled, in part, by attachment to the Catholic Church. The cult of relics, the places of reputed miracles, the pomp of holidays and pilgrimages both appalled and attracted British voyagers. As one visitor, Charles Hotham, exclaimed after his stay in Rome during Holy Week: "Without having been in Rome one can't imagine the Pageantry and outward show of religion one sees here at the same time that in reality there is nowhere less. They carry things here to so great a height that I have seen Roman Catholics themselves ashamed of them; and of all the places I have seen I know none so fit to convince a man of the absurdity of Popery as Rome itself."[50]

Far from convinced of Catholicism's absurdity, Boswell was overcome by its power and beauty. The "heights" of Rome's religious pageantry left him dizzy, but also reassured him. The same rituals and liturgical elements he found so compelling during his clandestine stay in London a few years earlier were again present, but with far greater flash and flame, especially during the Easter holidays. On Good Friday, Boswell joined a great crowd for Pope Clement XIII's benediction and, the following day, joined an immense crowd at St. Peter's to observe high mass; the experience, marked by "universal silence; universal devotion," made him "quite sure there must be some truth beyond the skies." Having received the pope's blessing, this child of Scottish Calvinism found himself "quite in frame." With his peculiar brand of latitudinarianism taking flight under Michelangelo's great dome, Boswell was certain that Roman Catholicism was "*one* way of adoring the Father of the universe," a legitimate path to faith and one that persuaded him there was "no hell for ever."[51] He was particularly impressed by the pope's "modesty": while serving dinner to the priests whose feet he had previously bathed, the pontiff "looked like a jolly landlord and smiled when he gave to drink."[52]

Whether he knew that Clement's modesty reached as far as the Vatican's nude statues—the pope ordered fig leaves for their private parts—Boswell does not say. What he does record, however, is that he bedded another prostitute just one day after his near-epiphany at St. Peter's. No doubt the light-filled nave of the basilica and masses gathered below lifted Boswell's faith; but it seems equally certain that the promise of forgiveness pulled at him after a night on the town. Just days after Easter mass, "Signor Gonorrhea" again paid Boswell a visit: "resign [yourself] to punishment," he writes, "but be calm."[53] It is not clear if, by "punishment," Boswell meant the usual syringe filled with mercury shot into his penis, or being forced to the sidelines for an extended period.

As his carriage left Rome on June 14 for Tuscany, Boswell opened a copy of *Persian Letters*.[54] While he does not comment in his journal on Montesquieu's remarkable tale of two Persian men, Uzbek and Rica, who travel to Paris to broaden their world, the story does seem to have left a deep impression on him. The genius of Montesquieu's epistolary novel is in its narrative sleight of hand. Rather than having Westerners observe the foreign ways of other peoples, the author has Uzbek and Rica offer a series of disorienting reflections on the foreignness of *French* morality, politics, society, and religion. No doubt Boswell was taken by the erotic elements in the novel—the further Uzbek travels from Persia, the less control he has over the sulfurous activities in his harem—but the character of Rica must have particularly struck him. Much younger than Uzbek, and much more open to the new ways of the old world, Rica overhears a conversation at a Parisian literary salon in which the subject happens to be him. "How can one be Persian?" asked a bemused woman.

The question makes Rica smile, and makes the reader think. Of course, the real question is "How can one be any one thing at all?" Persian or French, British or Italian, Catholic or Protestant: How do we take for granted that our particular view of the world is the right one, the good one, and the universal one? Boswell's travels had begun to impress this same lesson on him. Like Rica, the young Scot's curiosity and tolerance, eagerness to question, and desire to experience were irrepressible and influenced his attitude toward other political and religious systems. Or, indeed, to systems—if that is the word—which denied the reasonability and necessity of religion.

Such was the case with Alexandre Deleyre, Rousseau's friend and correspondent whom Boswell had met shortly after arriving in Italy. As he traveled north, Boswell was determined to call again on Deleyre, who had shown him such warmth and sympathy during their earlier meeting. In mid-July, he sent a letter to the Frenchman, warning him that he would visit him "in hopes of being consoled and strengthened." The reason, as Boswell had already confessed to several others, was his many sexual transgressions in Rome and Naples. "Sir, I do not deserve your good opinion of me, since I have plunged into gross libertinism. Do not expect me to talk in sanctimonious fashion about repentance, but is it not humiliating to find myself a slave to sensual pleasures, and convinced that my love of virtue is no more than a visionary admiration which one ardent desire or flash of ridicule can destroy?" With a Rica-like insight into the relativity of customs and beliefs that reigns among the world's nations, Boswell then adds: "Leave others to live in peace according to their fancies and let us live according to ours, happy if we can find ways to pass without boredom or sadness this earthly existence of which we understand nothing."[55]

Entering Parma on August 1, Boswell was keen to see his "accomplished and amiable friend." His eagerness was matched by Deleyre's, who called at Boswell's inn upon learning the Scot had arrived. Following emotional embraces, they walked to a nearby garden and soon found themselves launched into a conversation on God and immortality. Boswell's hazy deism dictated the necessity of a divine architect or artisan, one who had created the world and, moreover, waited for us with open arms when our visas for this world expire. In his melancholy and gentle fashion, Deleyre upended Boswell's perspective. As they sauntered in the garden, Deleyre told Boswell that he found it no more improbable that the world exists through "a fortuitous concourse of material substances in continual motion from all eternity" than that it was made by a divine being. Looking back on their conversation the next day, Boswell marveled: "I paused and thought with wonder, here is an atheist, the most virtuous and amiable of men. An atheist, whom I have always regarded with horror which the multitude impute to that character. And have I an atheist for my friend?" How could that be? Had he not been "taught to think an atheist the most wicked of beings, a daring rebel against the Lord of the Universe"? Yet Deleyre was neither wicked nor rebellious—on the contrary, he was a "candid philosopher whose mind is not convinced of the one eternal cause."

Boswell then admits to a remarkable feeling: "I felt a strange sensation of doubt by no means unpleasing, as it filled me with a suite of ideas totally new to me." But rather like Uzbek in the *Persian Letters*, who momentarily entertains the possibility that no eternal standard of justice exists before recoiling at the consequences, Boswell adds that he "soon returned from this unbounded wandering. I thought that a bad education had given M. Deleyre so hideous a view of God that it was his interest to think there was none; and I am convinced that the inclination of philosophers for or against any truth makes the same arguments seem as different to them as the same colours seem to different eyes."[56] Clearly, Boswell fails here to recall that he, too, had a "bad education [that] had given him a hideous view of God." Yet, no less clearly, he accepts that Deleyre's argument is as telling as his own. How can one be Persian? For Boswell, the question is instead, "How can one be atheist?" And the answer nearly becomes for Boswell as it was for Montesquieu: it is a matter of education, and not absolute truth.

———

On August 5, Boswell took leave of the "consolatory refuge" that Deleyre had provided in Parma. He remained in Italy for six more weeks, during which he found a different kind of "consolatory refuge" in Siena, having seduced Girolama Piccolomini, the wife of the mayor and mother of four children. After several weeks the relationship had run its course. Though he cared for Piccolomini, Boswell was emotionally incapable of the commitment she demanded. (More than a dozen years older than her lover, Piccolomini understood him all too well; long after he had returned to Great Britain, she wrote: "The good in you amazes me as much as the bad."[57])

More important, Boswell's thoughts had by then already fastened on a very different kind of conquest: Corsica. The island had been on Boswell's mind ever since his visit to Rousseau the preceding December. It was at Môtiers, during the dinner at Rousseau's cottage, that Boswell learned that his host had recently been asked to write a constitution for an independent Corsica. To be sure, a few weeks earlier, Rousseau had received a letter from Matteo Butta-foco, a Corsican officer serving in the French army, who, in reading *The Social Contract,* came upon the passage in which the philoso-pher declared that Corsica was the one country still worthy of a republican constitution: "The valor and constancy with which that brave people has been able to recover and defend its freedom would amply deserve having some wise man teach it how to preserve it. I rather suspect that one day this small island will astonish Europe."[58] Rousseau might just as well have placed a classified offering his ser-vices as Corsica's wise man. Buttafoco wrote to Rousseau, mislead-ingly declared he represented the Corsican freedom fighters, and asked Rousseau to write such a constitution. The offer was too tempting to turn down: Rousseau could shape the world while re-maining in Môtiers. Warning Buttafoco that he could not travel to Corsica in person, Rousseau asked for Corsica to come to him in the guise of documents and books.

Rousseau had, in fact, told Boswell during their first conversa-tion, when they paced the cottage floor together, that he had been asked by Corsican representatives to write a constitution for their country. Boswell did not at first react to the news, but it clearly struck a romantic chord in the young Scot. No doubt thinking, or dreaming much about it over the next several days, Boswell re-turned to the subject during his last conversation with Rousseau over dinner. Fixing Rousseau's gaze, Boswell asked: "Would you do me the favor of making me your ambassador to Corsica? Do you need an ambassador? I offer you my services. Monsieur Bos-well, ambassador extraordinaire to the Island of Corsica on behalf of Monsieur Rousseau!" Uncertain whether his guest was sincere or insane, Rousseau laughed: "Why not be crowned as King of

Corsica?" With a wide smile, Boswell replied: "Ah, that is beyond my means. But at least I can now say that I refused to become king!" Rousseau, for once, was at a loss for words. After a pause, he asked Boswell if he liked cats.[59]

While Boswell did not like cats—they were, he told Rousseau, ungrateful and disloyal—he did like the idea of traveling to Corsica. The prospect of such a trip must have often returned to his thoughts during the spring, and he seems to have come to a decision in May. In a letter he wrote to Rousseau in that month, Boswell revealed his plans: "I cannot restrain myself from paying a visit to those brave islanders who have done so much for their independence, and who have chosen M. Rousseau as their legislator." He asked Rousseau for a letter of recommendation to Pasquale Paoli, the leader who personified liberty for his fellow Corsicans, but bravely announced that even without such a letter, he would sail for the island.

Rousseau eventually provided the letter, recognizing the extraordinary nature of Boswell's decision. Extraordinary insofar as Corsica was no more on the itinerary of British tourists than were the Shetland Islands. No Englishman—or Scot, for that matter—had traveled into the jagged interior of Corsica, where some forty mountains climb on one another's backs at least 6,000 feet above the Mediterranean. Even the *Encyclopédie,* that massive compendium of all that was known under the Enlightenment sun, managed to offer just a few lines on the island when volume "C" appeared shortly before Boswell's voyage. When Boswell published his account of Corsica a few years later, he was quite right to assert that it "is indeed amazing that an island so considerable, and in which such notable things have been doing, should be so imperfectly known."[60]

Corsica had indeed long been a stage for notable things. Since 500 BCE, when the Phoenicians disembarked on the eastern coast of the island, Corsica had been the unwilling host to a series of foreign invaders. By the mid-eighteenth century, the latest in this long line of rulers, the city-state of Genoa, was at its wits' end with a rebellious peasantry spurred to resistance by their rulers' feckless and greedy ways. A series of revolts had convulsed the island, climaxing with the tragicomic episode of King Theodore. A minor German prince who, much like Boswell three decades later, was in search of a cause and vocation, Theodore landed on the coast in 1736, promising to free the islanders from the grip of Genoese oppression if they would crown him king of Corsica. A charismatic aristocrat, Theodore seduced the Corsicans, then left the island as suddenly as he came to it once the Genoese put a price on his head. King Theodore, as Boswell later remarked, gave up "his views of ambition for safety."[61] Safety, perhaps, but not security: twenty years later, Theodore died in a debtor's prison in London.

Unable to tame the islanders, the Genoese had decided, shortly before Boswell embarked for the island, to outsource their problem to the French army. The results were mixed. Each time the French army pushed toward the interior and turned affairs back to Genoa, the Corsican rebels then pushed the Genoese back to the beaches and cliffs. The tango's climax occurred in 1764, when the Genoese republic forgave its outstanding loans to the spendthrift Bourbon monarchy in return for stationing French soldiers in Corsica's coastal cities. The four-year rental codified the evolving reality on the island's rocky soil: the coasts belonged to the Continent, while the core belonged to the Corsicans.

While Corsica had been subject to a long history of invasions, travelers rarely if ever set foot on the mountainous island. It was reputed to be a wild place peopled by barbarous tribes who, when not battling invaders, were battling one another; a world where vendettas and violence were endemic, and passable roads and decent inns were rare. In fact, the British government, also responding to the Genoese government's request for help in suppressing the rebels, issued a warning to British nationals to avoid Corsica. British subjects guilty of corresponding with Paoli's men would face the legal consequences, including imprisonment, of "his majesty's high displeasure."[62]

Predictably, the many perils associated with visiting the island—from its rugged topography and revolutionary inhabitants to its diplomatic isolation and his own king's warnings—magnified Corsica's allure for Boswell. Moreover, he would view at firsthand the making of history—or, more accurately, the remaking of ancient history. Like the republican heroes of the ancient Roman republic, the Corsicans were fighting for their liberty. And liberty was certainly in the air of Georgian England. As the historian Linda Colley argues, Great Britain in the mid-eighteenth century simmered with debates over the nature and extent of liberty, a national conversation to which Boswell was no stranger.

This backdrop explains Boswell's fascination not only with Wilkes who, as Colley observes, had become the era's great "personification of liberty," but also with Paoli.[63] As Boswell would later explain, he wished to go to Corsica in order to "find what was to be seen no where else, a people actually fighting for liberty, and forming themselves from a poor, inconsiderable, oppressed nation into a flourishing and independent state."[64] Though a monarchist and traditionalist, Boswell also had a deep attachment to liberty as a Scot, the son of an overbearing father, and a romantic. Wilkes saw this last trait clearly: just as Boswell was an "enthusiast" for the king and religion according to Wilkes, he was also an enthusiast for liberty. "We have both the *vivida vis* [lively force], which marks us."[65]

This quality also drove the man Boswell was determined to meet, General Pasquale Paoli. The son of Giacinto Paoli, a powerful chief who, having given his support to Theodore, followed the king into exile, Pasquale had returned to become leader of Corsica's rebels in 1755. A man of massive build and supple mind, Paoli was educated in Naples and, like Boswell, was steeped in the literature and history of ancient Rome. Unlike Boswell, the young Corsican had also read with purpose, and now applied to the present the lessons he had learned from the past. When the island's general council elected him their general, Paoli first succeeded in pushing the Genoese troops back to a handful of towns, then pushed his island's fractious families to agree to significant political and social reforms. Enthused by the writings of Tacitus and Plutarch and inspired by the example of the Roman republic, Paoli set about founding a new republic on Corsica—even if that meant hammering into being a citizenry worthy of the responsibility. From the capital of Corte, he abolished feudal customs and traditions, founded a university and printing press, and suppressed the tradition of the vendetta. Corsica appeared on the verge of truly notable things, and Europe was divided on whether to applaud or lament them.[66]

As he prepared to embark from Leghorn for Corsica, the great fear that crowded Boswell's mind was that pirates would prevent him from applauding Paoli. Anxious that Barbary corsairs would seize the bark and chain him forever to their galleys, Boswell had gone to the local British envoy at Leghorn to obtain a special passport to serve as a diplomatic shield. (Handing the document to Boswell, the official told him he hoped it would be of no use to him.) He found cause to worry, as well, about the crew of the bark on which he found passage to the Corsican port of Centuri. It was as if Boswell's libertine reputation had preceded him: soon after the bark left Leghorn, the sailors, speaking in Italian, warned him that, should he try to debauch a Corsican woman, he should "expect instant death."[67]

Yet neither this warning, nor lack of wind on the first day, dimmed for long Boswell's spirits. Moved by the crew's singing of an Ave Maria as the sun sank below the horizon, and revived by a night's sleep under the stars, Boswell lent an eager hand at the oars the next day. When the green and rugged island finally hove into view on October 13, Boswell could scarcely contain himself: "As long as I can remember anything, I have heard of 'The Malcontents of Corsica, with Paoli at their head.' It was a curious thought that I was just going to see them."[68]

Seeing Paoli turned out to be an arduous affair once the bark docked at Centuri. As a paler than usual Boswell was led to the house of Paoli's local representative, he recalled the warnings he heard in Leghorn that assassins lurked in the shadow of every house and rock on Corsica. Though a tall tale, it did seem every house harbored armed men. As Boswell and his escort, armed with a gun, passed along the streets, men carrying muskets and swords sallied out from gardens and alleys. Boswell was at first alarmed by the sight, even though he was prepared to "see everything in Corsica totally different from what I had seen in any other country." But he comforted himself by reciting a couple of lines from Ariosto: "Together through dark woods and winding ways / They walk, nor on their hearts suspicion preys."[69]

Centuri clings to the rocky northwestern coast of Cap Corse, a stubby finger of land sticking out from the island's northern rim. To reach Corte, the rebel's seat of government, required a grueling journey to the center of the island. There were no easily traveled roads from the northern coast to Corte, but instead a web of narrow paths trodden by mules and villagers that threaded through deep valleys and along precipitous mountain slopes. Remarkably, Boswell clambered his way along these trails ablaze in his scarlet and green suit and shod in shoes better suited for London's streets than Corsica's mule paths. Impatient with the slow progress of the mule that carried his baggage over a narrow path overlooking the sea, Boswell persuaded the animal's owner to himself shoulder the portmanteau containing his full wardrobe, including formal attire, so they could make better time.[70] At times, rather than mules, local women carried his bags balanced on their heads; at night, given the absence of inns, he would stay in private houses or convents.

When Boswell reached Corte, six days had passed since his arrival in Centuri, but in Boswell's imagination more than two millennia had transpired. As he followed his guides, engaging them in conversation and listening to them sing, Boswell passed not just into another world, but into another age that was shaped and colored in his imagination by his classical education, but also by the sentimental education Rousseau had provided. In a scene that echoes the *Second Discourse*'s dithyrambs on man in his natural state, Boswell got down from his horse and walked along with his guides, "doing just what I saw them do." When they were hungry, they "threw stones among the thick branches of the chestnut trees which overshadowed" them and ate until they were full. When they were thirsty, they "lay down by the side of the first brook, put [their] mouths to the stream, and drank sufficiently." Entering a small village to water the mules, Boswell found himself surrounded by the inhabitants, all of whom were "brave and rude," a "stately and spirited race" not yet corrupted by civilization, even though they were armed to the teeth thanks to the technological prowess of that same civilization. Their warlike dances, legs pounding the ground as they circled a fire, seemed to come straight from a distant age still untainted by civilization—despite the muskets that the Corsicans were thrusting high above their heads.[71]

When he reached Corte, Boswell discovered that Paoli was not at home. He had left a few days before for Sollacaro, a town even deeper south, in order to preside at a local court. Exhilarated by his trek, but also exhausted, Boswell decided to rest for two days before pushing on. Touring the city with the mayor's son, the Scot met members of the Supreme Council—"solid and sagacious" one and all—visited the university—"a pretty large collection of books"—and climbed to the city's castle that also served as prison. His morbid interest in public executions again surfacing, he asked the commandant's permission to interview both the castle's prisoners and the hangman. The latter, made a pariah by his profession and exiled to a small room in one of the castle's turrets, fascinated Boswell. "I never beheld," Boswell recounts, "a more dirty rueful spectacle. He seemed sensible of his situation, and held down his head like an abhorred outcast." According to his guide, the hangman was Sicilian, not Corsican, for the good reason that no Corsican would ever descend to such depths: "Not the greatest criminals, who might have had their lives upon that condition."[72] Whether this was true hardly matters, for Boswell believed it was true: yet one more sign of the innate nobility of the Corsican people.

The moral distance between the castle's turret and Paoli's residence in Sollacaro was as great as the physical distance between the earth's two poles. Hence the deepening sense of awe Boswell felt when he left Corte to meet the general. At each village the visitor passed through, "brave rude men" welcomed him with simple meals and miraculous tales about their leader. The general, it seemed, was a man unlike others—indeed, he was something more than a mere mortal. "Questo grand'homo mandato per Dio a liberare la patria!" they declared time and again, lifting one hand toward the sky, the other grasping the barrel of a musket.

If Paoli was, in fact, a godsend for the liberation of Corsica, Boswell was ready to broadcast the gospel—that is, if he had the wherewithal to rise to the occasion. At first, he doubted he had: "When I at last came within sight of Sollacaro, where Paoli was, I could not help being under considerable anxiety." Clearly, this encounter was of a different magnitude from those with Rousseau and Voltaire, perhaps of even greater magnitude for Boswell than the introduction manqué with Frederick the Great. The great physical effort he made in order to reach this place accounts for his unease, but only in part. There was, as well, Boswell's sharpening sense of history, of its salutary as well as dramatic possibilities. He was transfixed now not by the future of his soul, but instead by the future of a noble and worthy past that Paoli seemed to embody.

Brought to the general's residence, Boswell's confidence nearly crumbled: "I feared that I should be unable to give a proper account why I had presumed to trouble him with a visit, and that I should sink to nothing before him."[73] Walking through the house's antechamber, Boswell was wracked by spasms of insecurity as intense as those he felt at Davies's bookshop when Johnson rolled into view. And while wit was not part of Paoli's heroic arsenal, he was at first as dreadful as the Englishman. When Boswell entered the general's room, he confronted a tall man whose massive body was clothed in a gold and green uniform. Taking from Boswell the letter written by Rousseau, Paoli understandably said little. He had never authorized Buttafoco to approach the philosopher, and while he welcomed the celebrity that Rousseau's support brought to his cause, Paoli rightly saw himself as his nation's lawgiver. Setting down the letter, Paoli slowly paced the floor for several minutes, saying

scarcely a word while staring hard at Boswell "as if he searched my
very soul." Paoli, Boswell learned, was a great reader of faces—
though one certainly did not require an advance degree in physi-
ognomy to perceive the Scot's great admiration and goodwill. But
the ice finally melted only when Boswell declared: "Sir, I am upon
my travels, and have lately visited Rome. I am coming from seeing
the ruins of one brave and free people: I now see the rise of another."[74] Paoli thanked, but also corrected his guest: the Corsicans
had no wish to become like the ancient Romans. Instead, all they
sought was their independence and happiness.

From that moment, the relationship between the two men
warmed. During the six days Boswell spent in Sollacaro, Paoli
treated him not just as a visiting dignitary, but increasingly like a
son. "Every day," Boswell realized, "I felt myself happier." Boswell
would dine with Paoli and his fellow officers, engaging them in conversations about the island's future. When the *ambasciadore ing-
lese,* as Boswell was called, stepped out, Paoli's handpicked guards
stepped out with him. They even marched alongside Boswell when,
one day, he rode Paoli's horse. With the eyes of Sollacaro fixed on
him astride that magnificent animal draped in red velvet and gold
lace, the Scot understood "the pleasure of state and distinction with
which mankind are so strangely intoxicated."[75]

Boswell's account—whether he was commenting on the food
served at table, recording remarks made by his Corsican hosts, or
rendering descriptions of buildings and landscapes—reflects his
sustained fascination with Paoli. Long before he became the biographer of Johnson, the Scot was already rehearsing the role in his
meetings with Paoli. At night, Boswell retired to his room where
he transcribed his conversations with Paoli, at times listing his many
observations, at other times creating vignettes. He confesses he had
"presumed upon [Paoli's] goodness to me" by peppering him with

hundreds of questions on even the most private circumstances of his life. Yet Paoli enjoyed the attention even when Boswell burst into his bedchamber one morning when he was still getting dressed.[76]

Regardless of the context, the Corsican leader never failed to impress his visitor. At one moment, Paoli is unleashing lightning bolts at a Corsican who, having fought for Genoa, had returned to Corsica to seek pardon. Paoli granted it, but warned: "I shall have a strict eye upon you; and if ever you make the least attempt to return to your traitorous practices, you know I can be avenged of you."[77] At the next moment, Paoli quotes from Virgil's *Aeneid* when Boswell asks what forces him to remain on Corsica: "A patriot's love wins out, and boundless lust for praise."[78]

When Paoli recited that line, spoken by Anchises to Aeneas in the underworld, Boswell told himself: "I wish to have a statue of him taken." No matter that he lacked a sculptor: Boswell had his pen to carve Paoli's statue. Paoli was, of course, aware that Boswell's frantic note-taking was the raw material for a written portrait of the Corsican leader. But Paoli was not pretending to be someone he was not; instead, he was striving to be what he was meant to be or what his people held him to be. It is telling that while Boswell was strolling through Paoli's library in Sollacaro, he came across a handful of English books. Along with Pope's *Essay on Man* and Jonathan Swift's *Gulliver's Travels,* there were a few tattered volumes of Joseph Addison and Richard Steele's *Spectator.* On the distant and rustic character of the stage in Sollacaro Paoli's self-presentation was all the more powerful and convincing—indeed, *sincere* as Addison, Steele, and Adam Smith understood the word. It is, perhaps, also telling that soon after his return to Great Britain, Boswell sent Paoli the complete editions of the *Spectator* and *Tatler.*

No less tellingly, Boswell discovered that Paoli was an avid reader of the *North Briton.*[79] What Paoli thought about Wilkes, Boswell does not say, and he refrained from sharing his own thoughts on the matter. But the Corsican must have admired the Englishman's battle on behalf of liberty—it was, after all, the same battle he was waging in Corsica. Like Wilkes, Paoli was fighting on behalf of his people: "I am desirous," he told Boswell, "that the Corsicans should be taught to walk of themselves."[80] But when an astonished Boswell asked how he could be so "superior to [personal] interest," Paoli told him he was mistaken: "It is not superior; my interest is to gain a name. I know very well that he who does good to his country will gain that: and I expect it."[81] As Boswell understood, this seemingly paradoxical claim would have made perfect sense to either Virgil or to Smith.

Paoli and Wilkes shared another trait that, for Boswell, was essential to greatness: heroism. This was an especially crucial quality in an age like his, of philosophical and religious doubt— an era that led Johnson to declare: "I have lived to see things all as bad as they can be." A time, according to the nineteenth-century historian and moralist Thomas Carlyle, of skepticism—a "little word [in which] there is a whole Pandora's Box of miseries." For Carlyle, as for Johnson and Boswell, skepticism meant not just intellectual doubt, but also moral doubt: "All sorts of infidelity, insincerity, spiritual paralysis." As Carlyle lamented: "The very possibility of Heroism had been, as it were, formally abnegated in the minds of all. Heroism was gone forever."

Yet while Carlyle seems to have overlooked the likes of Wilkes and Paoli, Boswell did not. "Never was I," Boswell declared, "so thoroughly sensible of my own defects as while I was in Corsica."[82] For the young Scot, the Corsican leader revealed that heroism was still alive—a discovery of immense importance. Heroism not only rebuked a world domesticated by politics and technology, but also represented a different path to immortality. For the six days

Boswell stayed in Sollacaro, everything he saw and heard was filtered through his great desire for certainty in both this world and in the next. "The contemplation of such a character really existing was of more service to me," he announced, "than all I have been able to draw from books, from conversation, or from the exertions of my own mind."[83]

Inevitably, Boswell spoke to Paoli about his chronic bouts of melancholy, attributing them to his "metaphysical researches" and efforts to "reason beyond my depth." Like Wilkes, but with greater gravitas, Paoli dismissed such investigations as worse than pointless. He had read the same thinkers Boswell had, but concluded they had little to say of importance: "Let us leave these disputes to the idle. I always hold firm one great object. I never feel a moment of despondency."[84] Paoli's great object, of course, was to secure his fame by winning Corsica's independence. Boswell, too, needed a worthy object, one that would secure him a kind of immortality as well. "From having known intimately so exalted a character, my sentiments of human nature were raised, while, by a sort of contagion, I felt an honest ardour to distinguish myself, and be useful, as far as my situation and abilities would allow."[85]

Like Sallust, the failed Roman politician and general who turned historian in order to achieve glory, Boswell concluded he could not make history. But he could do something equally important: write history. In his preface to his published account of his tour of Corsica, he declared: "For my part, I should be proud to be known as an author; and I have an ardent ambition for literary fame; for of all possessions I should imagine literary fame to be the most valuable." But Boswell knew himself too well. Literary fame is lasting, he added, because a book's greatness would never be "lessened by the observation of [the author's] weaknesses."[86]

Upon his return to Great Britain, Boswell did secure his literary fame. As he recalled much later in life, "It was wonderful how much Corsica had done for me, how far I had got in the world by having been there. I had got upon a rock in Corsica and jumped into the middle of life." Jump he did, but leave behind on that rock his "weaknesses" he did not.

— 10 —

AFTER CORSICA, BEFORE FUTURITY

If I were you, I should regret annihilation.

LEAVING BEHIND CORSICA, Boswell lingered in Italy till mid-December to recover from a bout of malaria and a crippling in-grown toenail, the price of his recent adventure. With his health on the mend, he took a series of carriages along the coastal road, arriving in Marseilles on December 21, 1765. He remained long enough to attend a performance at the new opera house and damn it for not being Italian: "The French squeaking and grimaces were insufferable to a man just come from the operas of Italy. O Italy! Land of felicity!"[1]

But it was less the felicity of Italy than the sublimity of Pasquale Paoli that filled Boswell's imagination. In a letter to Rousseau written from Lyons on January 4, 1766, Boswell exclaimed: "I am bound to the Corsicans heart and soul."[2] The young Scot, still under the influence of the Corsican leader, believed himself transformed. He had become a new man, having undergone a profound change that neither visits to cathedrals nor philosophers had succeeded to effect. Looking down on the French from the heights of Corte, he sighed: "I viewed with pity the irregularities of humanity."[3] But Boswell could not breathe for long in the rarefied atmosphere of Corsica. While insisting that it is only "merit which engages me, be it in myself or in others," Boswell broke the vow he took upon leaving Paoli never again to whore when a "tall and decent pimp" in Marseilles introduced him to a certain Mademoiselle Susette. As if he was excusing himself to the absent Paoli, Boswell found that the woman had "hardly any of the vile cant of prostitutes."[4]

Boswell managed to overlook such lapses. In his letter to Rousseau, he exclaimed that the voyage to Corsica had affected him "in the same way that Plutarch's *Lives* would if they were fused in my mind. Paoli has given a temper to my soul which it will never lose. I am no longer the tender, anxious being who complained to you in your Val de Travers. I am a man. I think for myself."[5] Even Paris failed to seduce this newly hardened and self-elected representative of the Corsican nation. Entering the city in mid January, Boswell notes that he was "not affected much." The following day, upon awakening in his rented chambers, he felt "no change of ideas from being in Paris," as if he were astonished this was so.[6]

There was little reason, though, for such astonishment: the sameness Boswell felt was largely because he frequented the homes of mostly British and Scottish residents in Paris. He called on Horace Walpole, who thought as little of Boswell—he is the "quintessence of busybodies"—as he did most everything and everyone else.[7] But Walpole nevertheless encouraged Boswell to write up his tour of Corsica, for which "there are no authentic accounts."[8] More important was the renewed friendship with John Wilkes. During the summer, political changes in Britain had fueled Wilkes's hopes that this "most brave and most generous nation" would soon pardon him. As a result, he left Italy—and Signora Corradini, pregnant with someone else's child—for Paris in order to be closer to London. As he made his way north, Wilkes stopped at Ferney to pay the by-now requisite call on Voltaire. The two men bantered freely, with the lord of Ferney insisting that his guest must "live in London, or Paris, or Heaven—or Hell." Laughing, Wilkes chose the last option, since Voltaire had in a poem "put there the very best company: most of the popes, many cardinals, almost all kings."[9] Upon arriving in Paris toward the end of September, Wilkes took up his old friendship with Baron d'Holbach, with whom he was "more intimate than ever."[10] Intimacies of a different variety were also reported in the Parisian *libelles,* or scandal sheets, which hinted broadly that Wilkes had set up shop with a variety of courtesans.

When Boswell learned that Wilkes was in Paris, he quickly drove to his residence and, finding he was out, left his card. When Wilkes returned the visit, the two men embraced one another and almost immediately fell to discussing Corsica. "I wonder you could leave it," Wilkes declared. Indeed, as he passed the island on his small sailing ship on his way to Marseilles, Wilkes had pulled off his hat and, though Boswell would not set foot on Corsica for another three months, raised a glass to drink to his Scottish friend's health.[11] He also pulled at Boswell's leg, telling him that Paoli had asked him to command a regiment on the island. Wounded that anyone other than he should have Paoli's favor, Boswell hurriedly pointed out that the rebels were not organized according to regiments. But Wilkes would not cede his ground, shrugging: "Oh, the equivalent of a regiment."[12]

Several days later, on January 27, Wilkes was called on not for his good humor, but instead for his sympathy. Sitting in Wilkes's parlor, Boswell picked up a copy of the *St James Chronicle* and was shocked to read his mother's obituary. Euphemia had died a week earlier and though his father had sent him the news that same day, the letter had not yet reached Boswell. "Quite stunned," Boswell stumbled through the day and spent the night in feverish agitation.

Lord Auchinleck's letter arrived the following day, detailing his wife's final days and his own despair: "It will occur to you how much I need your assistance . . . and expect you home with all speed." Upon reading the letter, Boswell burst into tears, praying to his mother "like most solemn Catholic to saint."[13]

Yet it was Wilkes who provided the greatest comfort. It was not that the freethinker had changed: a few days earlier, during an exchange with a Catholic priest and Boswell, Wilkes declared that the only advantage to Christian faith is its affirmation of bodily resurrection. And as for that, Wilkes scoffed, "I care no more to be raised in the same body than in the same coat, waistcoat and breeches."[14] But when Boswell opened his heart to Wilkes, confusedly expressing the guilt he felt not to have been at his mother's bedside when she died, his friend was visibly moved. Wilkes urged him to return quickly to Scotland: "Consider how you have avoided the pain of seeing mother dying," he said, "and how you'll go back and comfort father, and amuse him by telling him of all you've seen."[15]

Boswell did set about to make plans for his return, but they included a twist straight from the book Johnson damned as that "corrupt work" by a "barren rascal," Henry Fielding's *Tom Jones*.[16] While Boswell was touring Italy, Rousseau had been forced into exile yet again, thanks to Voltaire's anonymous pamphlet discussed in Chapter 8, which revealed Rousseau's fathering of five children. The news rocked not just the Republic of Letters, but quite literally also Rousseau. One night in early September, the good citizens of Môtiers, outraged that they were harboring such a miscreant, stoned Rousseau's cottage. He and Thérèse were forced to flee the village, but were unable to turn to either Geneva or Paris as a home.

At that moment, like a vast deus ex machina, David Hume descended on the scene. Preparing to return to Scotland after having served as private secretary to the British ambassador to France, Hume wrote to Rousseau, offering to accompany him to Great Britain, where the great philosophe might live in peace. Hume's gesture thrilled the Republic of Letters, and touched Rousseau, who gladly accepted the invitation. But there was a hitch. When he left for his Parisian rendezvous with Hume, Rousseau had left behind Thérèse, tasked with packing up their belongings. When she finally arrived in Paris several weeks later, Rousseau had already crossed the Channel. Given a hero's welcome in London, an uneasy Rousseau prevailed upon Hume to find him respite from the maddening crowd of onlookers. It was thus in Chiswick, a village on London's outskirts, that that caftan-garbed exile, renting a room above a green grocer, waited impatiently for Thérèse's arrival.

His impatience deepened as Thérèse, worried by her ignorance of England and English, delayed her crossing. It was in the midst of her hesitations that Boswell appeared in Paris—a providential event for Rousseau's companion. Calling on Thérèse, Boswell discovered he had suddenly been cast in the role of savior: "Mon Dieu, Monsieur," Thérèse exclaimed, "if we could go [to England] together!" Dazzled by the prospect of assisting Rousseau, Boswell immediately agreed to do so. Yet, when the day came to leave, Boswell found himself momentarily paralyzed. While his carriage waited on the frigid morning of January 31, Boswell paced in his room, finally crying aloud: "Is it possible that my mother is dead?"[17] Receiving no answer, he climbed into his carriage, collected Thérèse at the Hôtel de Luxembourg, and in a somber frame of mind left Paris.

Busy watching over Rousseau in England, Hume sighed when he learned about the travel arrangements. Boswell was "very agreeable," he explained to a Parisian friend, but he was also "very mad": a "young gentleman in search of adventures" who had gone to Corsica on Rousseau's recommendation. As for this newly hatched adventure of accompanying Madame Levasseur, Hume was skeptical. The young Scot, he warned, "has such a rage for literature that I dread some event fatal to our friend's honour."[18] The philosopher proved prescient: by the second night of their eleven-day trip from Paris to Dover—their packet boat at Calais was delayed several days—Boswell and Thérèse found themselves sharing the same bed. Inevitably, Boswell recounted his sexual prowess in his journal: "My powers were excited and I felt myself vigorous." No less inevitably, he also recorded Thérèse's more nuanced response: "I allow that you are a hardy and vigorous lover, but you have no art."[19] It was Boswell's artlessness, however, that is most telling. When his first attempt at lovemaking had failed miserably, Boswell burst into tears. Was his distress due to his poor performance? Or, instead, to the sorrow and guilt he carried over his mother's death? He does not say, but does note that Thérèse took pains to comfort him—a gesture perhaps expressing her maternal concern as much as her amorous solicitude. Euphemia was dead, but the religious fears and anxieties she had planted in her son were, and would remain, very much alive.

By February 13, when he arrived in Chiswick with Thérèse, Boswell seemed more disappointed in Rousseau's reaction than in his own actions. While the exile covered Thérèse with kisses, Boswell marveled that the "illustrious" Rousseau now "seemed so oldish and weak." Cruelly, Boswell discovered he "had no longer enthusiasm for him."[20] The two men discussed Corsica, but Boswell was loath to linger. Guilt over his seduction of Thérèse might have been at play: the dimming of admiration for someone you have just cuckolded comes easily. Boswell might also have been disoriented to find his former confessor living above an English greengrocer rather than below the Jura summits. While quaint, Chiswick was hardly sublime, and Rousseau now struck Boswell as a sad, if not tragic figure.

More important, Boswell had fallen into the orbit of two individuals who would dominate his thoughts for the remainder of his life: Johnson and Paoli. As soon as he took leave of Rousseau and Thérèse, Boswell cantered back to London. One and a half years had passed since he had watched Johnson lurch from the dock at Harwich, and while their correspondence had been irregular, their attachment to one another never wavered. In a letter waiting in Paris for Boswell, Johnson acknowledged, though did not apologize for, his anemic correspondence: what now counted was Boswell's imminent return to London. "I long to see you, and to hear you; and hope that we shall not be so long separated again. Come home, and expect such a welcome as is due to him whom a wise and noble curiosity has led, where perhaps no native of this country ever was before."[21]

Boswell was not disappointed by Johnson's welcome. When the carriage pulled in front of Johnson's Fleet Street lodgings, the Scot flew past the door and into the huge man's arms. Then, with a gesture as spontaneous as it was theatrical, Boswell kneeled and asked Johnson's blessing.[22] After a long visit, Johnson hugged his young friend "like a sack" and muttered: "I hope we shall pass many years of regard."[23] Neither man then knew that their lives would be forever attached by the many years of conversations and clashes, collaborations and irritations that led to the writing of *The Life of Samuel Johnson*.

Not surprisingly, during Boswell's short stay in London, he spent much of his time at the Mitre with Johnson. Their conversations, when not touching on Boswell's past travels, took up Boswell's im-

mediate future. They jousted about Boswell's meetings with Rousseau and Wilkes: "It seems," Johnson tartly observed, "you have
kept very good company abroad!" Turning their talk to Voltaire
hardly mollified Johnson, who reminded Boswell that while Rousseau was "a very bad man," Voltaire was hardly better: "Why, Sir,
it is difficult to settle the proportion of iniquity between them."[24]
What was less difficult to settle, in Boswell's eyes, was Johnson's
undiminished greatness compared to his European peers. It was
as if he had traveled eighteen months and met his age's most celebrated figures, only to return home and know Johnson for the first
time. "I felt my veneration for him in no degree lessened," Boswell
realized, by all that he had seen and heard. "On the contrary, by
having it in my power to compare him with many of the most celebrated persons of other countries, my admiration of his extraordinary mind was increased and confirmed."[25] Boswell had again
found the moral and intellectual rock left behind when he climbed
aboard his packet boat in 1763.

Most critically, Johnson encouraged Boswell to pursue his idea,
still loose and undefined, to write about Corsica. What was called
for, Johnson declared, was something other than a long and scholarly work: "You cannot get to the bottom of the subject." In fact,
there was no need even to try: any account of Corsica would capture the attention of a reading public wholly ignorant of the island
and its history. "All you tell us," observed the great man, "is what
we don't know." No less important, he added, was the nature of the
telling: casually, conversationally tell us what we don't know. In a
word, "Give us as many anecdotes as you can"—advice Boswell
would take to heart, of course, not just for his account of Corsica,
but subsequently for his life of Johnson.[26]

It turned out, however, that Boswell had already begun writing,
if not *on* Corsica, than *for* Corsica more than a month before he

stepped again on British soil. In early January, while still in France, he launched the first of several salvos of "paragraphs," or short dispatches, to the *London Chronicle* on the political and diplomatic situation in Corsica. The paragraphs, which purported to relate actual events and conversations concerning Corsica, were instead what Boswell, with his habitual candor, later described as a blend of fact and invention. In a word, the paragraphs were outright propaganda on behalf of Paoli's struggle. Framed as reports written by an anonymous English observer, they trace with mounting suspense a visit paid to the island by a mysterious "Scots gentleman." It turns out the stranger is none other than Boswell himself of course, who in turn is quoted on his encounter and conversations with the brave and doughty Corsican rebels. Boswell intended the paragraphs to spur public sympathy for the Corsica cause, as well as prod the government to throw its support behind Paoli. What did factual truth matter, he seemed to say, when the historical and moral claims of the Corsicans were at stake?

That James Boswell starred in this particular series of paragraphs was, no doubt, an attractive fillip. But his was nevertheless a supporting role in this journalistic ruse for the story's true hero, General Paoli. In fact, Boswell saw himself as fulfilling a pledge he had made his host at Sollacaro. Toward the end of Boswell's stay on Corsica, Paoli had asked him to make the case for the island's independence with the English government: "Only undeceive your court. Tell them what you have seen here. They will be curious to ask you. A man come from Corsica will be like a man from the Antipodes."[27] Once back in London, Boswell stole valuable time from Johnson to carry out Paoli's request. Most important was his effort to meet the man Johnson had considered a dictator while in office, the remarkable orator and former prime minister, William Pitt.[28]

Despite being a Whig, Pitt had won wide respect in his crusade against government corruption; under his leadership during the Seven Years War, he had established Britain's global supremacy, and because of his support of the increasingly restless American colonists, no one seemed better suited to take up the Corsicans' cause. Upon receiving a carefully crafted letter from Boswell, a preoccupied and gouty Pitt nevertheless agreed, though somewhat ambiguously, to meet with the Scot. At 9:00 a.m. on February 23, Boswell rang at Pitt's residence, only to be told that his host was still in bed. Promising to call ten more times that same day if need be, Boswell was again at the door an hour later, and Pitt realized he had no choice but to receive him. With his leg propped on a stand, the statesman welcomed Boswell and warned his guest that they had to limit the conversation to allusions: as a privy councilor, he was obliged to report to the king any direct communications with foreign political figures. Pitt nevertheless made clear his admiration for the Corsican cause, as well as his regret that Paoli thought Pitt had ignored the island: "I should be sorry that in any corner of the world, however distant or however small, it should be suspected that I could ever be indifferent to the cause of liberty."[29] Indeed, such indifference toward Corsica, and more particularly toward a man of Paoli's moral stature was unthinkable: "He is one of those men," he told Boswell, "who are no longer to be found but in the *Lives* of Plutarch."[30]

Boswell's journalism and meetings failed to galvanize either the government or public opinion, but rather than giving up, he simply changed tactics. Upon his return to Auchinleck, when not occupied with his father and completing his qualifications for the Scottish bar, he continued to manufacture "firsthand" accounts of events in Corsica. More importantly, Boswell also began to gather material for the book he now planned to write on his tour of the island.

Paoli sent him a package of documents and observations from
Corte, while Sir John Dick, the British consul at Leghorn whom
Boswell had befriended, supplied him with information on the
island's history. Piling these and other sources in the family library,
Boswell did what he so rarely did: work with unbroken concentra-
tion, great fluidity, and high spirits. He completed most of the man-
uscript by late spring, and the book was in press by autumn.

Johnson was of two minds about his young friend's project. He
thought, rightly, that Boswell should play to his literary strength.
Rather than offering a history of the island, he should instead re-
create, with ample anecdotes, his own tour. But Boswell's preoccupation with Corsica also increasingly irritated Johnson: "I wish
you would empty your head of Corsica, which I think has filled it
rather too long." But Boswell, refusing to cede, shot back: "My noble-
minded friend, do you not feel for an oppressed nation bravely
struggling to be free? . . . Empty my head of Corsica! Empty it of
honour, empty it of humanity, empty it of friendship, empty it of
piety. No! While I live, Corsica and the cause of the brave islanders
shall ever employ much of my attention, shall ever interest me in
the sincerest manner."[31] Had he not written to Johnson about Paoli
while still in Corsica? Did not his letter, describing his meetings
with the Corsican leader, conclude with a Boswellian flourish: "I
dare to challenge your approbation"?[32]

In February 1768, when the *Account of Corsica* was published,
Boswell did receive Johnson's approbation (predictably, though, for
the journal of his tour, and not the historical account). No less importantly, he also won public acclaim. The book's first printing of
3,500 copies sold out quickly, as did the second run. A stunned Boswell noted that the book's success "has exceeded my warmest
hopes."[33] Translated into five languages and read on both sides of
the Atlantic—American revolutionaries quickly embraced Paoli as

one of their own—"Corisca Boswell," as he was dubbed, quite suddenly became, at the age of twenty-seven, an international celebrity. The Scot's identification with his cause climaxed in August 1769 at the Stratford-on-Avon Jubilee. Boswell appeared in a costume meant to resemble a Corsican rebel, including a pistol strapped to a belt and a musket slung over his shoulder.

Boswell's success on the stage of Stratford—"I was as much a favourite as I could desire," he declared—was not matched by Corsica's efforts on the stage of history.[34] Three months earlier, in early May, French forces decisively defeated Paoli's rebels at the Battle of Ponte Novo, an event cementing France's control of the island that persists to the present day. Rather than surrender, Paoli managed to escape to a waiting British warship and sailed to England, where he would live, apart from a short-lived return to Corsica under English protection, the reminder of his days. When Boswell learned Paoli had arrived in London, he rushed to the Corsican's apartment on Old Bond Street, where Boswell was first embraced by the overjoyed valet and then ushered into the general's bedroom. Though still in his nightclothes, Paoli gave a shout when he heard Boswell's voice and took his visitor, who had burst through the door, "all in his arms, and held [him] there for some time."[35]

Almost immediately, Boswell began plans to introduce the two hulking heroes of his life, Paoli and Johnson, to one another. In early October, the much anticipated meeting took place: "They met with a manly ease, mutually conscious of their own abilities, and of the abilities of each other." Paoli spoke Italian, Johnson spoke English, and Boswell interpreted, seeing himself as "an isthmus which joins two great continents." Intriguingly, the evening's great subject of conversation was the question of infidelity, whose spirit, Paoli sighed, "was so prevalent." Johnson agreed, but added the hope that like a cloud, the "gloom of infidelity" would soon dissipate as "the sun broke forth with his usual splendor." Paoli suggested that "fashionable infidelity" was the product of the age's desire to display courage: "Men who have no opportunities of showing it as to things in this life, take death and futurity as objects on which to display it." The Corsican's observation dovetailed neatly with Johnson's worldview: "Fear is one of the passions of human nature, of which it is impossible to divest it."[36] Boswell did not offer his own reflections on the exchange—indeed, what could he add to so obvious a truth?

The evening was a great success. Paoli found he had been right to hold Johnson in "great veneration," while Johnson affirmed that the Corsican had "the loftiest port of any man he had ever seen."[37] The two continents, rather than colliding, aligned with scarcely a tremor. How could they not? The two men embodied those ancient values that Boswell most admired, though frequently failed to practice: personal integrity and public authority, intellectual lucidity and stoic responsibility. What Boswell wrote about Johnson toward the end of his own life in 1793 applied equally to Paoli: his friend's life was "an effectual antidote to that detestable sophistry which has lately been imported from France, under the false name of Philosophy."[38] While Boswell was taking specific aim at revolutionary events in France—the Terror was just then unfurling—he was equally hostile to the blistering effect of untrammeled rationalism on faith, tradition, and virtue. Johnson and Paoli were, for Boswell, what Thomas Carlyle would later call "superior natures" and what we might simply call heroes. Vulnerable to the fears, anxieties, and doubts that are our common lot, these individuals reveal themselves to be wholly uncommon in their capacity to confront and overcome them. Their fidelity to ideals, religious or political, though scarred by personal and historical failures, remained fast. This quality was crucial for Boswell: time spent in the company of these men was time spent without fear—or, at least without fear that paralyzed. "I looked at him," he wrote about Johnson, "as a man whose head is turned giddy at sea looks at a rock, or any fixed object."[39] What Johnson said of Francis Bacon applied as well to both him and Paoli: they were strong minds operating upon life.

———

Like most of us, Boswell was not this sort of hero. He could not prevent life from operating, in often punishing ways, on his mind. This was, in particular, the case with his fears over what would follow his life—fears that were both cause and consequence of his chronic bouts of melancholy. As he confessed to John Johnston, though he could drive away the "black dog" of melancholy, he could "never promise [himself] any long continuance of felicity."[40] The thrill of striding across the stage of history, and the public renown (but also ridicule) that followed, could not last. As Corsica's hopes for independence faded, so too did Boswell's élan.

The demands of Boswell's law practice were great, as were the expectations of his demanding father. In 1769, he married, against his father's wishes, his cousin Margaret Montgomerie, a remarkably patient and caring woman who bore him five children. Though incorrigibly unfaithful as a husband—his journal, which he shared with Margaret, records several more instances of gonorrhea—Boswell nevertheless was deeply attached to her, as he was to his three daughters and two sons. Torn between his professional and family duties in Edinburgh and his literary aspirations, which revolved around Johnson and his London circle, he failed to satisfy fully either one. By the early 1770s, the project to write Johnson's biography was gathering force, furthered by the tour of the Hebrides undertaken by the two friends in 1774. But these extended moments of engagement and frequent contentment would, as they had to, end, leaving Boswell in despair. "After every enjoyment comes weariness and disgust," he told his friend Andrew Erskine. "We never have a large lawn of agreeable life. It is cut to pieces with sunk fences . . . even where it is smoothest."[41]

Of course, so many of the fences were thrown up by Boswell's weaknesses. He continued to trawl the seedier districts of London and Edinburgh, drinking and whoring till early morning. Admonished by Johnson and Paoli—and, increasingly, Margaret—Boswell would swear repentance and *retenu*. Yet his vows to change were, sooner or later, disavowed by his recidivist ways, leaving him in an even bleaker state of mind. "While affected with melancholy, all the doubts which have ever disturbed thinking men, come upon me," he confided to his oldest and best friend, William Temple. "I awake at night dreading annihilation," "or being thrown into some horrible state of being. We must own, my friend, that moral and religious truths are not such as that we can contemplate them by reason with a constant certainty. The disposition of our tempers, of our spirits influences our persuasion; though we know that we may help it in part."[42]

Or not help, of course. Grimly scoring the pages of his journal are references to his faltering faith and anxieties plaguing him in his waking and sleeping hours. He often seemed a man flayed alive: "I exist in misery," he moaned one night.[43] After an evening devoted to a forceful conversation over whether the universe was governed by necessity, Boswell was so overwhelmed by melancholy that he "went out to the wood and groaned."[44] Johnston and Temple were not the only ones made privy to their friend's tormented thoughts, and remarkably so too were his children. One morning Boswell joined his eldest daughter Veronica in bed, then still a child, and told her "how pretty angels would come and carry her from the kirk hole [the grave] to Heaven, where she would be with GOD and fine things."[45] Though he meant to reassure his child, Boswell instead terrified her. But he could not help himself: "I saw death," he wrote, "waiting for all the human race, and had such a cloudy and dark prospect beyond it, that I was miserable as far as I had animation." He loved his family, he murmured, "but I had distinctly before me the time which must come when we shall be separated by death."[46]

By 1776, most of Boswell's earthly ambitions had been shattered. His repeated assaults on the world of patronage and politics had all ended in routs, while his financial affairs, never good, had worsened considerably as he grew estranged from his father, who had remarried following the death of Boswell's mother. The sense of failure at times weighed so heavily that Boswell even considered destroying his journal. "I had lately a thought that appeared new to me, that by burning all my journal and all my written traces of my former life, I should be like a new being."[47] Could any reflection have driven closer to the bone? Such an act, given how closely his sense of self was bound to the journal, was closer to suicide than rebirth.

It was during this bleak period of life that, on July 7, 1776, Boswell knocked at the door of David Hume's house in Edinburgh. Both his friends and enemies had recently discovered that the "great infidel" was dying of cancer—an event that spurred morbid curiosity. William Temple voiced the questions many wondered to themselves when he asked Boswell how Hume carried himself "in the near approach of dissolution? Had he no apprehensions, no misgivings? Did he neither fear nor desire a futurity?" Temple, for one, was certain that Hume had abjured his pagan ways: "The concurrent belief of barbarous as well as civilized mankind, the justice of the Deity, the frequent impunity of the wicked in this present life, must have risen, crowding and shouldering him in his thoughts, and insinuating that his discernment and penetration were not so superior as he once fondly persuaded himself, to that of men full as wise and full as enlightened."[48]

Notwithstanding Temple's disdain, Hume's discernment and penetration remained superior even as death approached, while his sense of humor continued unabated. Shortly before Boswell's visit, another friend called on Hume. When his doctor asked if he should tell the visitor that his health was improving, Hume smiled: "Doctor, as I believe you would not choose to tell anything but the truth, you had better tell him that I am dying as fast as my enemies, if I have any, could wish, and as easily and cheerfully as my best friends could desire."[49]

Boswell counted himself a friend, and no doubt wanted Hume's death to be as easy as possible. But he could have done with a bit less cheerfulness. In calling upon Hume, Boswell wanted to pay his respects, but as Temple revealed, also wished to see a man who, having spent his life as a skeptic, was now preparing for his death as a believer. Yet he was shocked by what he did see: Hume's once great bulk punctured by the cancer, his gaunt frame was reclining in the study, a book of philosophy propped in his bony hands. Yet, Boswell marveled, the dying man "seemed to be placid and even cheerful. He said he was just approaching his end. I think these were his words."[50]

Though shaken, Boswell did not lose sight of the reason for his visit. Insisting he knew not how he "contrived to get the subject of Immortality introduced," Boswell turned the conversation toward those matters with which he had wrestled for most of his life. Was he not, he asked Hume, religious when he was young? Yes, of course, Hume replied. Like Boswell and nearly every other Scot, he had read

The Whole Duty of Man when he was a boy. But this turned out to be his undoing. "He made an abstract from the catalogue of vices at the end of it," Boswell reported, "and examined himself by this, leaving out murder and theft and such vices as he had no chance of committing, having no inclination to commit them. This, he said, was strange work; for instance, to try if, notwithstanding his excelling his schoolfellows, he had no pride or vanity. He smiled in ridicule of this as absurd and contrary to fixed principles and necessary consequences."[51]

Boswell protested, but the old skeptic was enjoying himself too much. "The morality of every religion was bad," Hume announced. And when he hears a man is religious, Hume added, he must be a rascal, though he did generously acknowledge he knew of some very good men being religious. Uncertain whether his host was making sport of him, Boswell guided the conversation to the nature of the soul: Would Hume persist, he wondered, "in disbelieving a future state even when he had death before his eyes"? When Hume calmly persisted, an increasingly desperate Boswell insisted it was at least *possible* for such a future state to exist. As possible, Hume answered, as a piece of coal not catching flame when placed on a fire. Was it not, he added, a "most unreasonable fancy that we should exist forever?"

Reason, of course, was the last thing Boswell could exercise on this subject. Did not the thought of annihilation, he demanded, make Hume uneasy? Taking a leaf from the Epicureans, Hume responded it made him no less easy than the thought that he had not been. Once again, Boswell sought to hear the cry of anguish and declaration of faith, but he instead heard only the urbane reassurance that neither was necessary. He was torn: How could he not laugh at Hume's brilliant sallies? But how could they, as well as the sound of his own laughter, not appall him? As he later reflected,

"I felt a degree of horror, mixed with a sort of wild, strange, hurrying recollection of my excellent mother's pious instructions, of Dr. Johnson's noble lessons, and of my religious sentiments and affections during the course of my life. I was like a man in sudden danger eagerly seeking his defensive arms; and I could not but be assailed by momentary doubts while I had actually before me a man of such strong abilities and extensive inquiry dying in the persuasion of being annihilated."

Rummaging through his remaining store of arguments, Boswell declared he believed the Christian religion with the same certainty he believed history. Hume parried this last effort with ease—"You do not believe it as you do the Revolution"—gently noting that belief in something that had no historical, logical, or experiential grounding is only that, a belief. At that moment, Boswell recalled a meeting that took place years before with Hume when the philosopher exclaimed he had no wish to be immortal. To an astonished Boswell, the younger and healthier Hume explained that since his current state was quite satisfactory, why risk finding himself in a different state that, in all probability, would be worse than better? Boswell now reminded the dying Hume of this conversation, and asked if the prospect of seeing his friends again in eternity did not please him. Hume smiled—eternity was large enough for his many enemies, too—and dismissed such a notion as absurd.

By now, even Boswell understood he could take no more time from a man with so little time left. How surprising, he thought, to find this man "talking of different matters with a tranquility of mind and a clearness of head that few men possess at any time." As he prepared to take his leave, however, Boswell blurted: "If I were you, I should regret annihilation. Had I written such an admirable history, I should be sorry to leave it." "I shall leave that history, of which you are pleased to speak so favorably," Hume replied, "as perfect as I can." Hume's surgeon had entered the room and Boswell said his goodbyes, leaving the scene "with impressions that disturbed [me] for some time."

Hume died the following month, on August 25, but even in death he still had to contend with Boswell. Upon learning the news, Boswell drank himself nearly blind and with the little sight left him, took a prostitute to the north slope of Castle Hill—hard by West Bow, the street whose witches and ghosts so haunted him as a child. Four days later, with his friend John Johnston, a sobered and somber Boswell braved a violent rainfall and visited the empty grave where Hume's coffin would be lowered later that day. Retreating behind a wall for shelter, the two friends fell in with the rain-drenched procession as it passed on its way to the cemetery. It was reported that as Hume's coffin was taken from his house, someone in the gathered crowd cried out, "Ah, he was an atheist," to which another voice responded, "No matter, he was an honest man."[52]

Had he overheard them, no doubt Boswell would have agreed with both men. But not Johnson. Taking tea with his great friend in London several months later, Boswell described the shock he experienced when Hume persisted "in his infidelity when he was dying." And yet, Boswell continued, the prospect of annihilation did not terrify the bedridden skeptic. Galvanized by his companion's remark, Johnson was abrupt and unforgiving: "It was not so, Sir. He had a vanity in being thought easy." As Johnson warmed to his harangue, Boswell could not help but reflect on his friend's sudden passion: "The horror of death which I had always observed in Dr. Johnson, appeared strong tonight." Both because he wished to provoke Johnson, and because he shared the same sense of horror, Boswell remarked that he had known moments in his life when he had not been afraid of death: Was it so inconceivable that, for a man like Hume, these moments could be longer and deeper? Swatting away any such possibility—it was Hume's pride, the older man bellowed, that made him act unconcerned—Johnson affirmed the impotence of reason in the face of such mysteries: "Ah! We must wait till we are in another state of being, to have many things explained to us." Even Johnson's superior mind, Boswell concluded, "seemed foiled by futurity."[53]

Less than a year after Hume's death, Boswell began an ambitious, yet often overlooked, literary project. In October 1777, he published in *London Magazine* the first of seventy monthly essays, a series he entitled *The Hypochondriack*. In the inaugural essay, the author, who maintained his anonymity, announces what appears to be the modest goal of his work: "To divert Hypochondriacks of every degree from dwelling on their uneasiness [and] communicate to them that good humour, which if it does not make life rise to felicity, at least preserves it from wretchedness." Few were better qualified than the author to write such essays, since he was "so well acquainted with the Distemper of Hypochondria," but was now cured and eager to help "some of my unhappy companions, who are now groaning under it."[54]

While Boswell insisted the essays were written with others in mind, reading them reveals his greatest subject remained James Boswell. During the six years in which the essays appeared without a break, Boswell touched—at times lightly, at times pedantically, but most often sincerely—subjects as varied as love and war, luxury and diversion. Just a handful of topics, however, were essayed more than once; tellingly, religion had a three-month run, as did death—the same concerns that course through his continental travels.[55] In writing these particular essays, Boswell was attempting to essay his own life, surveying the weaknesses, fears, and hopes that had scored it. His attitude toward death, the centrality it held in his life, had not changed. Boswell was no less afflicted by these thoughts than he had been during his tour. But he had gained greater insight into his condition, the way in which his melancholy was so intimately tied to his anxieties over death and his inability to reason himself free of them: "A Hypochondriack fancies himself at different times suffering death in all the various ways in which it has been observed; and thus he dies many times before his death. I myself have been frequently terrified, and dismally afflicted in this way; nor can I yet secure my mind against it at gloomy seasons of dejection."[56]

It was impossible, Boswell noted, to dismiss the question's magnitude. "The thought of being at once and forever deprived of everything that is agreeable and dear to us must doubtless be very distressing." Perhaps thinking back to his last conversation with Hume, Boswell continues: "It is in vain for the sophist to argue, that upon the supposition of our being annihilated, we shall have no affliction as we can have no consciousness. For all but very dull men will confess, that though we may be insensible of the reality when it takes place, the *thought* of it is dismal."[57] For Boswell, reason was not equal to the task of absorbing the reality of our end, this thought of our death. Instead, religion alone offered respite. "Religious Exercise of all the Faculties and Affections," he declares, "is the only way which a wise man would wish to follow."[58]

This declaration will strike many readers, then as now, as neither very surprising nor very original. They are right on both counts, but perhaps because they are asking the wrong question about these writings and about Boswell at his stage in his life. His essays were only in part lessons in how to master melancholy: reason, he understood, was not equal to the task, and religion alone was our one solace. Rather than essays in self-mastery, which is what we find in Johnson's work; instead of efforts at undeception, which is what we find in Hume's writings; in place of exercises of wit, which is what we find in Voltaire's flourishes, we find in these essays a mixture of Rousseauian self-exploration and thoroughly Boswellian candor. Frederick Pottle writes of the "invincible mediocrity" of Boswell's mind—by which he meant the Scot had an unparalleled gift of portraying his life in terms of normal experience.[59] Though he sought out and surrounded himself with men and women who were larger than life, Boswell is like us, but only more so. In his great swings of exuberance and enervation, his moments of great insight and great weakness, Boswell not only embodied the enduring doubts and hopes that mark the modern age, but also expressed them with an intellectual honesty and spare artistry no less enduring. He wished that his journal be nothing more than the "faithful register of the variations of [his] mind."[60] He succeeded beyond his wildest wishes. In his account of his Grand Tour and the grand questions of life, Boswell also registers our own variations of mind.

NOTES
ACKNOWLEDGMENTS
INDEX

NOTES

Prologue

1. Daniel Defoe, *A Tour Thro' The Whole Island of Great Britain* (New York: Garland, 1975), vol. 4, 116.
2. Tobias Smollett, *The Expedition of Humphrey Clinker*, ed. James Thorson (New York: Norton, 1983), 203.
3. Donald Campbell, *Edinburgh: A Cultural History* (Northampton, MA: Interlink Books, 2003), 42–43.
4. Quoted in Arthur Herman, *How the Scots Invented the Modern World* (New York: Three Rivers Press, 2001), 17.
5. Little more than a decade ago, the cultural historian Robert Darnton was still claiming that the Enlightenment was heaved into the world from Paris. See his article "George Washington's False Teeth," *New York Review of Books,* March 27, 1997.
6. Peter Gay, *The Enlightenment: The Rise of Modern Paganism* (New York: Norton, 1966), 3.
7. Most recent are the works of Jonathan Israel: *Radical Enlightenment* (New York: Oxford University Press, 2001) and *Enlightenment Contested* (New York: Oxford University Press, 2006).
8. The intellectual historian J. G. A. Pocock has most forcefully made this case; see Roy Porter's survey in *The Creation of the Modern World* (New York: Norton, 2000).
9. The standard work in this field is Roy Porter and Mikulas Teich, eds., *The Enlightenment in National Context* (Cambridge: Cambridge University Press, 1981).

10. Quoted in Charles Withers, "Toward a Historiographical Geography of Enlightenment in Scotland," in *The Scottish Enlightenment: Essays in Reinterpretation,* ed. Paul Wood (Rochester, NY: University of Rochester Press, 2000), 81 (italics in original).

11. Charles W. J. Withers, *Placing the Enlightenment: Thinking Geographically about the Age of Reason* (Chicago: University of Chicago Press, 2007), 7.

12. Israel, *Radical Enlightenment,* 3–4.

13. Ibid., 5.

14. In particular see Robert Darnton's *The Literary Underground of the Old Regime* (Cambridge, MA: Harvard University Press, 1985).

15. Quoted in Roy Porter, *Flesh in the Age of the Enlightenment* (New York: W. W. Norton, 2003), 117.

16. Charles Taylor, *A Secular Age* (Cambridge, MA: Harvard University Press, 2007), 14.

17. Ibid., 149.

18. Quoted in Erich Heller, *The Importance of Nietzsche* (Chicago: University of Chicago Press, 1988), 7.

19. Charles Taylor, *Sources of the Self* (Cambridge, MA: Harvard University Press, 1989), 512.

20. Ibid., 520.

21. William Robert Scott first used the phrase in his book *Francis Hutcheson: His Life, Teaching and Position in the History of Philosophy* (Cambridge: Cambridge University Press, 1900), 265.

22. Richard Sher, *Church and University in the Scottish Enlightenment* (Princeton: Princeton University Press, 1985), 4.

23. Michel Malherbe, "The Impact on Europe," in *The Cambridge Companion to the Scottish Enlightenment,* ed. Alexander Broadie (Cambridge: Cambridge University Press, 2003), 299.

24. See Herman, *How the Scots.*

25. Hugh Trevor-Roper, *History and the Enlightenment* (New Haven: Yale University Press, 2010).

26. Quoted in E. C. Mossner, *The Life of David Hume* (Oxford: Oxford University Press, 1980), 371.

27. Quoted in Sher, *Church and University,* 3.

28. James Boswell, *The Correspondence of James Boswell and William Johnson Temple,* vol. 1, ed. Thomas Crawford (Edinburgh: Edinburgh University Press and Yale University Press, 1997), 6.

29. James Boswell, *Boswell in Holland, 1763–1764,* ed. Frederick Pottle (New York: McGraw-Hill, 1956), 281.

30. James Boswell, *The Life of Samuel Johnson,* ed. David Womersley (New York: Penguin, 2008), 247.

31. See, in particular, Pierre Hadot, *Philosophy as a Way of Life,* trans. Michael Chase (Blackwell: Oxford University Press, 1995), and *What Is Ancient Philosophy?,* trans. Michael Chase (Cambridge, MA: Harvard University Press, 2002).

32. Alexander Nehemas, *The Art of Living: Socratic Reflections from Socrates to Foucault* (Berkeley: University of California Press, 1998), 1.

1. In the Kirk's Shadow

1. Quoted in Peter Martin, *A Life of James Boswell* (New Haven: Yale University Press, 2000), 35.

2. Walter Scott, *Minstrelsy of the Scottish Border,* in *Complete Works of Sir Walter Scott* (New York: Connor and Cooke, 1833), 2:115.

3. James Boswell, "Sketch of the Early Life of James Boswell, Written by Himself for Jean-Jacques Rousseau," in Frederick Pottle, *James Boswell: The Earlier Years, 1740–1769* (New York: McGraw Hill, 1966), 2.

4. Ibid.

5. Henry Graham, *The Social Life of Scotland in the Eighteenth Century* (London: Adam and Charles Black, 1900), 317.

6. Ibid., 318.

7. Ibid., 297.

8. Ibid., 399.

9. James Boswell, *Boswell, Laird of Auchinleck 1778–1782,* ed. Joseph Reed and Frederick Pottle (Edinburgh: University of Edinburgh Press, 1993), 200.

10. Quoted in Martin, *Life of James Boswell,* 36.

11. Boswell, "Sketch," 2.

12. James Boswell, *Correspondence of James Boswell and John Johnston of Grange,* ed. Ralph Walker (London: Heinemann, 1966), 3.

13. Boswell, "Sketch," 3.

14. James Boswell, *London Journal 1762–1763,* ed. Frederick Pottle (New Haven: Yale University Press, 1950), 274.

15. Quoted in Ian Simpson Ross, *Lord Kames and the Scotland of His Day* (Oxford: Oxford University Press, 1972), 21.

16. Boswell, *Correspondence of James Boswell and John Johnston of Grange,* 84.
17. Ibid., 78.
18. Boswell, *London Journal,* 274.
19. *Correspondence of James Boswell and John Johnston of Grange,* 78.
20. In March 1763, John Johnston wrote to Boswell that a package containing several pages of his journal—which Boswell had asked his friend Johnston to read—had been opened, presumably by Lord Auchinleck, who had been kept in the dark about Boswell's enterprise (Boswell, *Correspondence of James Boswell and John Johnston of Grange,* 58–60). As Boswell blurted out in a subsequent letter to Johnston: "I would willingly impute all that my parents do, to a real tho' mistaken concern about me: But this was really so very ungenteel and really so very hard that it pains me exceedingly. It was doing what no Parent has the right to do, in the case of a Son who is a Man, and therefore an independent individual."
21. Roy Porter, *The Creation of the Modern World: The Untold Story of the British Enlightenment* (New York: Norton, 2000), 68.
22. Quoted in Martin, *Life of James Boswell,* 46.
23. James Boswell, *Correspondence of James Boswell and William Johnson Temple 1756–1795,* ed. Thomas Crawford (New Haven: Yale University Press 1997), 1:161.
24. Ibid., 1:17.
25. The phrase is taken from Boswell's letter to Temple dated July 29, 1758, in Boswell, *Correspondence of James Boswell and William Johnson Temple,* 1:8.
26. Ibid., 1:6.
27. Ibid., 1:7.
28. Ibid., 1:25.
29. John Lockhart, *Memoirs of the Life of Sir Walter Scott,* quoted in Ross, *Lord Kames,* 258. In this passage, Auchinleck is referring to his son's stay with the Corsican revolutionary Pasquale di Paoli, but this could not have been the first time his son's antics drove him to such thoughts.
30. Boswell, *London Journal,* 85.
31. Quoted in John Brewer, *The Pleasures of the Imagination: English Culture in the Eighteenth Century* (London: Routledge, 1997), 94.

32. Quoted in Richard Sher, "Scotland Transformed," in *Scotland: A History*, ed. Jenny Wormald (Oxford: Oxford University Press, 2005), 206.

33. Daniel Defoe, *A Tour Thro' The Whole Island of Great Britain* (New York: Garland, 1975), 4:116.

34. Nicholas Phillipson, *Adam Smith: An Enlightened Life* (New Haven: Yale University Press, 2010), 28.

35. Brewer, *Pleasures of the Imagination*, 333.

36. Graham, *Social Life of Scotland*, 137.

37. Quoted in Phillipson, *Adam Smith*, 31.

38. Boswell, *Correspondence of James Boswell and John Johnston of Grange*, 10.

39. Quoted in Phillipson, *Adam Smith*, 134.

40. Ibid., 135.

41. Ibid.

42. Boswell, *Correspondence of James Boswell and John Johnston of Grange*, 7.

43. Quoted in E. C. Mossner, *The Life of David Hume* (Oxford: Oxford University Press, 1980), 400.

44. Boswell, *Correspondence of James Boswell and William Johnson Temple*, 1:29.

45. Adam Smith, *The Theory of Moral Sentiments*, ed. D. D. Raphael (Indianapolis: Liberty Fund, 1982), 9.

46. Ibid., 46.

47. Ibid., 146–147.

48. Ibid., 153–154.

49. Keith Brown, "Reformation to Union, 1560–1707," in *The New Penguin History of Scotland*, ed. R. A Houston and W. W. J. Knox (London: Penguin Press, 2001), 189.

50. In his *Statistical Account of Scotland* (1792), John Sinclair underscores the stunning diversity of religious practice in late eighteenth-century Scotland. For a summary, see Sher, "Scotland Transformed," 180.

51. Graham, *Social Life of Scotland*, 491.

52. Sher, "Scotland Transformed," 181.

53. Brewer, *Pleasures of the Imagination*, 333.

54. This, at least, is Pottle's observation, though he offers no textual evidence on its behalf. See Pottle, *James Boswell*, 46.

55. Jacques Bossuet, *An Exposition on the Doctrines of the Catholic Church in Matters of Controversy* (London: Keating, Brown and Co., 1813), 37.

56. Ibid., 38.
57. Quoted in Martin, *Life of James Boswell,* 68.
58. Pottle, *James Boswell,* 46.
59. Ibid., 48.

2. At Home with Home

1. Quoted in Ian Simpson Ross, *Lord Kames and the Scotland of His Day* (Oxford, Oxford University Press, 1972), 324.
2. David Hume, "Of Refinement in the Arts," in *Essays Moral, Political and Literary,* ed. Eugene Miller (Indianapolis: Liberty Fund Press, 1985), 270–271.
3. Quoted in Ross, *Lord Kames,* 206.
4. Quoted in Luigi Turco, "Moral Sense and the Foundations of Morals," in *The Cambridge Companion to the Scottish Enlightenment,* ed. Alexander Broadie (Cambridge: Cambridge University Press, 2003), 137.
5. Quoted in T. D. Campbell, "Francis Hutcheson: 'Father' of the Scottish Enlightenment," in *The Origins and Nature of the Scottish Enlightenment,* ed. R. H. Campbell and Andrew S. Skinner (Edinburgh: John Donald Publishers, 1982), 173.
6. See Arthur Herman, *How the Scots Invented the Modern World* (New York: Three Rivers Press, 2001), 70–71.
7. Quoted in James Buchan, *Crowded with Genius: The Scottish Enlightenment: Edinburgh's Moment of the Mind* (New York: HarperCollins, 2003), 70.
8. Quoted in Herman, *How the Scots Invented,* 82.
9. James Boswell, *The Life of Samuel Johnson,* ed. David Womersley (New York: Penguin, 2008), 545.
10. Lord Kames, *Essays on the Principles of Morality and Natural Religion,* ed. Mary Moran (Indianapolis: Liberty Fund Press, 2005), 24.
11. Ibid., 29.
12. Ibid., 64.
13. Ibid., 69.
14. Ross, *Lord Kames,* 248.
15. Quoted in ibid., 38–39.
16. Quoted in Frederick Pottle, *James Boswell: The Earlier Years, 1740–1769* (New York: McGraw-Hill, 1966), 94.

17. Quoted in Richard B. Sher, "'Something That Put Me in Mind of My Father:' Boswell and Lord Kames," in *Boswell: Citizen of the World, Man of Letters,* ed. Irma Lustig (Lexington: University of Press of Kentucky, 1995), 68.

18. Ibid., 70.

19. Ibid.

20. James Boswell, "Sketch of the Early Life of James Boswell, Written by Himself for Jean-Jacques Rousseau," in Pottle, *James Boswell,* 5.

21. Ibid., 6.

22. Peter Martin, *A Life of James Boswell* (New Haven: Yale University Press, 2000), 92.

23. Adam Sisman writes that McQuhae was meant to be a reader of the journal Boswell kept once he went to London in November 1763. But Mc-Quhae was involved only in the inception and reading of the Harvest Jaunt journal. See *Boswell's Presumptuous Task: The Making of the Life of Dr. Johnson* (New York: Penguin, 2000), 29.

24. Ross, *Lord Kames,* 367.

25. See ibid., pp. 309–314, for a discussion of this aspect to his legal career.

26. Ibid., 311. Herman (*How the Scots Invented the Modern World,* 106) is more severe on Kames than Ross. He discusses the same episode but mis-identifies the condemned man as Thomas.

27. Ross, *Lord Kames,* 315.

28. Sher, "Boswell and Lord Kames," 70.

3. A Journal Is Born

1. James Boswell, *London Journal 1762–1763,* ed. Frederick Pottle (New Haven: Yale University Press, 1950), 39.

2. Lawrence Stone, *The Family, Sex and Marriage in England, 1500–1800* (New York: Harper and Row, 1977), 228.

3. Quoted in Adam Sisman, *Boswell's Presumptuous Task: The Making of the Life of Dr. Johnson* (New York: Penguin, 2000), 29.

4. David Hume, "The Rise of the Arts and Sciences," in *Essays Moral, Political and Literary,* ed. Eugene Miller (Indianapolis: Liberty Fund Press, 1985), 132.

5. John Brewer, *The Pleasures of the Imagination: English Culture in the Eighteenth Century* (London: Routledge, 1997), 106.

252 NOTES TO PAGES 57–69

6. Ibid., 109.
7. Quoted in ibid., 31.
8. Daniel Defoe, *A Tour Thro' The Whole Island of Great Britain* (New York: Garland, 1975), 2:325.
9. Tobias Smollett, *The Expedition of Humphrey Clinker,* ed. James Thorson (New York: Norton, 1983), 84.
10. Boswell, *London Journal,* 44.
11. Ibid., 47.
12. The phrase "genteel lodging" is found in Boswell's "Scheme of Living," a document he wrote shortly after his arrival in London. See appendix I in Boswell, *London Journal,* 335.
13. Boswell, *London Journal,* 67, 113.
14. See Frederick Pottle, *James Boswell: The Earlier Years, 1740–1769* (New York: McGraw-Hill, 1966), 97.
15. Quoted in Brewer, *Pleasures of the Imagination,* 106.
16. Ibid., 112.
17. Boswell, *London Journal,* 62.
18. Ibid., 62.
19. Ibid., 68–69.
20. Ibid., 182.
21. Ibid., 98.
22. Ibid., 288.
23. Ibid., 206.
24. See Pottle, *James Boswell,* 92.
25. Quoted in E. C. Mossner, *The Life of David Hume* (Oxford: Oxford University Press, 1980), 223.
26. David Hume, *A Treatise of Human Nature,* ed. L.A. Selby-Bigge (Oxford: Oxford University Press, 1975), 253.
27. Ibid., 260.
28. Boswell, *London Journal,* 173 and 181.
29. David Hume, *The History of England* (New York: Harper, 1876), 5:256.
30. Ibid., 3:303.
31. Ibid., 5:294.
32. Boswell, *London Journal,* 139 and 155.
33. Ibid., 166.
34. Ibid., 179.
35. Ibid., 192.
36. Pottle, *James Boswell,* 109.
37. Ibid., appendix II, 341–342.

38. James Boswell, *Correspondence of James Boswell and John Johnston of Grange*, ed. Ralph Walker (London: Heinemann, 1966), 81.

4. Enter Johnson

1. James Boswell, *The Life of Samuel Johnson*, ed. David Womersley (New York: Penguin, 2008), 2.
2. Samuel Johnson, *Selected Essays*, ed. David Womersley (New York: Penguin, 2003), 20.
3. Ibid., 11.
4. Ibid., 28.
5. Ibid., 17.
6. Ibid., 27.
7. Roy Porter, *Flesh in the Age of the Enlightenment* (New York: W. W. Norton, 2003), 168–169.
8. Quoted in W. Jackson Bate, *Samuel Johnson* (New York: Harcourt Brace, 1975), 313.
9. Ibid., 312.
10. Johnson, *Selected Essays*, 515.
11. Porter, *Flesh in the Age of Reason*, 174.
12. Boswell, *Life of Samuel Johnson*, 437.
13. Hume to Gibbon, March 18, 1776, in *The Letters of David Hume*, ed. J. Y. T. Grieg (Oxford: Clarendon Press, 1932), 2:68. Hume is making reference to the great Ossian debate: after initial hesitation, he concluded that the cycle of poems by a Gaelic bard named Ossian, held by its "discoverer" James Macpherson to be authentic, was in fact a fraud. But his remark has equal relevance for the controversy over miracles.
14. Boswell, *Life of Samuel Johnson*, 234.
15. James Boswell, *London Journal 1762–1763*, ed. Frederick Pottle (New Haven: Yale University Press, 1950), 283.
16. Quoted in Bate, *Samuel Johnson*, 351.
17. Quoted in Frederick Pottle, *James Boswell: The Earlier Years, 1740–1769* (New York: McGraw-Hill, 1966), 121.
18. Quoted in Bate, *Samuel Johnson*, 391.
19. Peter Martin, *A Life of James Boswell* (New Haven: Yale University Press, 2000), 532.
20. Quoted in Margery Bailey, "Introduction," in James Boswell, *The Hypochondriack*, ed. Margery Bailey (Palo Alto: Stanford University Press, 1928), 1:77.

21. Quoted in Porter, *Flesh in the Age of Reason*, 309.
22. Quoted in Bate, *Samuel Johnson*, 371. As Bate notes, toward the end of his life Johnson burned the near entirety of his journal entries and papers written between 1762 and 1768. It may well be that he feared posterity's judgment on this period of his life.
23. Ibid., 372.
24. Boswell, *Life of Samuel Johnson*, 500.
25. Johnson, *Selected Essays*, 431.
26. Boswell, *London Journal*, 211.
27. Ibid., 161.
28. Ibid., 254
29. Ibid., 254.
30. Boswell, *Life of Samuel Johnson*, 868.
31. See Frank McLynn, *Crime and Punishment in Eighteenth Century England* (London: Routledge, 1989) and Kirstin Olsen, *Daily Life in Eighteenth Century England* (London: Greenwood, 1999).
32. Pottle (*James Boswell*, 15–16) discusses this possibility.
33. Boswell, *London Journal*, 252.
34. Ibid., 194.
35. James Boswell, *Correspondence of James Boswell and John Johnston of Grange*, ed. Ralph Walker (London: Heinemann, 1966), 75.
36. Boswell, *Life of Samuel Johnson*, 117.
37. Ibid., 244.
38. Ibid., 235.
39. Ibid., 229.
40. Ibid., 217.
41. Ibid., 242.
42. Ibid., 228.
43. Ibid., 647.
44. Ibid., 375.
45. Boswell, *London Journal*, 101.
46. Shortly after his visit to Tyburn, Boswell, too terrified to return to his own lodgings, crept into the bed of his friend Andrew Erskine (*London Journal*, 253).
47. Quoted in Bate, *Samuel Johnson*, 452.
48. Boswell, *Life of Samuel Johnson*, 683.
49. Ibid., 427–428.
50. Ibid., 218.
51. Ibid., 1003.

52. Ibid., 222–223.

53. Ibid., 246.

54. Ibid., 226.

55. Ibid., 25.

56. Ibid., 971.

57. Johnson, *Selected Essays*, 130.

58. Boswell, *Life of Samuel Johnson*, 229.

59. Ibid., 1000 and 1005.

60. Ibid., 245.

61. Daniel Defoe, *A Tour Thro' the Whole Island of Great Britain* (New York: Garland, 1975), 1:46.

62. Boswell, *Life of Samuel Johnson*, 248.

63. Quoted in Bate, *Samuel Johnson*, 316.

64. Boswell, *Life of Samuel Johnson*, 330.

65. Ibid., 234.

66. Ibid., 226.

67. Ibid., 248.

5. *Derelict in Utrecht*

1. James Boswell, *Boswell in Holland, 1763–1764*, ed. Frederick Pottle (New York: McGraw-Hill, 1956), 4.

2. James Boswell, *Correspondence of James Boswell and John Johnston of Grange*, ed. Ralph Walker (London: Heinemann, 1966), 111.

3. Ibid., 112.

4. James Boswell, *Correspondence of James Boswell and William Johnson Temple, 1756–1795*, ed. Thomas Crawford (New Haven: Yale University Press, 1997), 1:61.

5. Boswell, *Boswell in Holland*, 11.

6. Ibid., 12.

7. Boswell, *Correspondence of James Boswell and William Temple*, 1:63.

8. Samuel Johnson, *Selected Essays*, ed. David Womersley (New York: Penguin, 2003), 90–92.

9. James Boswell, *The Life of Samuel Johnson*, ed. David Womersley (New York: Penguin, 2008), 120.

10. Boswell, *Correspondence of James Boswell and John Johnston of Grange*, 117.

11. Boswell, *Correspondence of James Boswell and William Temple*, 1:73.

12. Boswell, *Boswell in Holland*, 49.

13. Ibid., 49 and 56.
14. Ibid., 68.
15. Ibid., 45.
16. Ibid., 388–390.
17. Ibid., 135–136.
18. Ibid., 76.
19. Charles Pierce, *The Religious Life of Samuel Johnson* (New York: Archon Books, 1983), 78.
20. Quoted in ibid., 79.
21. Boswell, *Boswell in Holland*, 260.
22. Ibid., 89.
23. Ibid., 92.
24. Ibid., 36.
25. Quoted in W. Jackson Bate, *Samuel Johnson* (New York: Harcourt Brace, 1975), 372.
26. Quoted in ibid., 373.
27. Pierce, *Religious Life of Samuel Johnson*, 133.
28. Boswell, *Life of Samuel Johnson*, 315.
29. Pierce, *Religious Life of Samuel Johnson*, 51.
30. Boswell, *Life of Samuel Johnson*, 694.
31. Quoted in Roy Porter, *The Creation of the Modern World* (New York: Norton, 2000), 104.
32. Samuel Clarke, *The Works of Samuel Clarke* (London: Knapton, 1757), 1:257.
33. Porter, *Creation of the Modern World*, 104.
34. Ibid., 98.
35. Quoted in Peter Gay, *The Enlightenment: The Rise of Modern Paganism* (New York: Norton, 1966), 2:384.
36. Boswell, *Correspondence of James Boswell and William Temple*, 1:81.
37. Ibid., 78.
38. Ibid., 81.
39. Ibid., 72.
40. Ibid., 67.
41. Boswell, *Boswell in Holland*, 19.
42. Ibid., 41.
43. Ibid., 52.
44. See Frederick Pottle's account in *James Boswell: The Earlier Years, 1740–1769* (New York: McGraw-Hill, 1966), 80–84.

45. Boswell, *Boswell in Holland*, 179 (italics in original).
46. Ibid., 181.
47. Quoted in Pierce, *Religious Life of Samuel Johnson*, 38.
48. Boswell, *Boswell in Holland*, 183.
49. Ibid., 189.
50. Ibid., 198.
51. Ibid., 193.
52. Ibid., 194–195.
53. Ibid., 196 and 217.
54. Ibid., 211.
55. Ibid., 252.
56. Ibid., 282.
57. Pottle, *James Boswell*, 106.
58. Ibid., 105.
59. Quoted in E. C. Mossner, *The Life of David Hume* (Oxford: Oxford University Press, 1980), 275.
60. Boswell, *Life of Samuel Johnson*, 571.
61. Quoted in Thomas Ahnert, "The Moral Education of Mankind: Character and Religious Moderatism in the Sermons of Hugh Blair," in *Character, Self, and Sociability in the Scottish Enlightenment*, ed. Thomas Ahnert and Susan Manning (New York: Palgrave Macmillan, 2011), 68.
62. Quoted in ibid., 71.
63. Quoted in ibid., 75.
64. Quoted in ibid., 77.
65. Boswell, *Boswell in Holland*, 140–141.
66. Ibid., 246.
67. Ibid., 224–226.
68. Ibid., 221.

6. Belle de Zuylen

1. James Boswell, *Boswell in Holland, 1763–1764*, ed. Frederick Pottle (New York: McGraw-Hill, 1956), 374.
2. The date of publication remains in dispute and Frederick Pottle speculates that the book was, in fact, published *after* Boswell had arrived in Utrecht. See ibid., 293–294, n.1.
3. Ibid., 56.

4. Ibid., 64.
5. Ibid., 74.
6. Ibid., 259.
7. Ibid., 178.
8. Quoted in Mona Ozouf, *Les Mots des femmes* (Paris: Fayard, 1995), 67.
9. Ibid., 64. See also André Bandelier, "Des Gouverneurs et gouvernants suisses dans les Provinces-Unies au siècle des lumières," in *Belle de Zuylen/Isablle de Charrière: Education, Creation, Reception*, ed. Suzan de Dijk (Amsterdam: Rodopi, 2005), 103–123.
10. Isabelle de Charrière, *There Are No Letters Like Yours: The Correspondence of Isabelle de Charrière and Constant d'Hermenches*, trans. Janet and Malcolm Whately (Lincoln: University of Nebraska Press, 2000), 287.
11. Ozouf, *Mots des femmes,* 58.
12. "Portrait of Zélide," in Boswell, *Boswell in Holland,* 188.
13. See Raymond Trousson, *Isabelle de Charrière et Jean-Jacques Rousseau* (Brussels: ARLLFB, 1985), 3.
14. "Portrait of Zélide," in Boswell, *Boswell in Holland,* 184.
15. Ibid., 185.
16. Boswell, *Boswell in Holland,* 140–141 (italics in original).
17. Ibid., 147.
18. James Boswell, *Correspondence of James Boswell and William Johnson Temple, 1756–1795,* ed. Thomas Crawford (New Haven: Yale University Press, 1997), 1:94.
19. Boswell, *Boswell in Holland,* 200.
20. Ibid., 178.
21. Ibid., 138.
22. Ibid., 331.
23. Ibid., 380.
24. Ibid., 284–285. Richardson had also told Boswell that he thought too much when the latter complained about his "black ideas of religion."
25. Ibid., 306–307.
26. Ibid., 311.
27. Ibid.
28. Quoted in Silvia Sebastiani, *The Scottish Enlightenment: Race, Gender, and the Limits of Progress* (New York: Palgrave Macmillan, 2013), 138.
29. Boswell, *Boswell in Holland,* 320.

30. Ibid., 346. In the same letter, Boswell also tells de Zuylen that he is subject to "attacks of melancholy sometimes so strong that it is well nigh impossible to support them."
31. Ibid., 368.
32. Quoted in Jenene Allison, *Revealing Difference: The Fiction of Isabelle de Charrière* (Newark: University of Delaware Press, 1995), 146.
33. Quoted in Laurence Vandoflen, "Belle de Zuylen/Isabelle de Charrière et l'incrédulité," in *L'Atelier du Centre des recherches historiques* 4 (2009): 6.
34. de Charrière, *There Are No Letters*, 120.

7. Waiting for Frederick

1. James Boswell, *Boswell in Holland, 1763–1764*, ed. Frederick Pottle (New York: McGraw-Hill, 1956), 268.
2. Frederick Pottle, *James Boswell: The Earlier Years, 1740–1769* (New York: McGraw-Hill, 1966), 141–142.
3. James Boswell, *James Boswell: The Journal of His German and Swiss Travels, 1764*, ed. Marlies Danziger (New Haven: Yale University Press, 2008), 191.
4. Ibid., 179.
5. Jeremy Black, *The British Abroad: The Grand Tour in the Eighteenth Century* (New York: St. Martin's Press, 1992), 139.
6. Boswell, *James Boswell*, 179.
7. Black, *British Abroad*, 240.
8. Boswell, *James Boswell*, 11.
9. Ibid., 196.
10. Ibid., 205.
11. Ibid., 70.
12. Ibid., 19–20.
13. Quoted in Louis Dupré, *The Enlightenment and the Intellectual Foundations of Modern Culture* (New Haven: Yale University Press, 2004), 238.
14. Boswell, *James Boswell*, 76.
15. James Boswell, *Correspondence of James Boswell and William Johnson Temple, 1756–1795*, ed. Thomas Crawford (New Haven: Yale University Press, 1997), 108.
16. Boswell, *Boswell in Holland*, 311.
17. Boswell, *Correspondence*, 108.
18. Boswell, *James Boswell*, 52.

19. David Sorkin, *The Religious Enlightenment: Protestants, Jews and Catholics from London to Vienna* (Princeton: Princeton University Press, 2008), 161.

20. Boswell, *James Boswell*, 19.

21. Quoted in Michael Suarez, "Johnson's Christian Thought," in *The Cambridge Companion to Samuel Johnson*, ed. Greg Clingham (Cambridge: Cambridge University Press, 1997), 195.

22. Boswell, *James Boswell*, 78.

23. Ibid., 15–16.

24. Ibid., 22.

25. Ibid., 59–60.

26. Ibid., 42.

27. Boswell, *Correspondence*, 107.

28. James Buchan, *Crowded with Genius: The Scottish Enlightenment: Edinburgh's Moment of Mind* (New York: HarperCollins, 2003), 82.

29. Keith Lehrer, *Thomas Reid* (London: Routledge, 1989), 152.

30. Ibid., 168.

31. See Samuel Fleischacker, "The Impact on America: Scottish Philosophy and the American Founding," in *The Cambridge Companion to the Scottish Enlightenment,* ed. Alexander Broadie (Cambridge: Cambridge University Press, 2003), 331.

32. Arthur Herman, *How the Scots Invented the Modern World* (New York: Random House, 2001), 263.

33. Boswell, *James Boswell*, 42.

34. Boswell, *Correspondence*, 106.

35. Boswell, *James Boswell*, 65.

36. Nicholas Wolferstadt, *Thomas Reid and the Story of Epistemology* (Cambridge: Cambridge University Press, 2001), 254.

37. Boswell, *James Boswell*, 68.

38. Ibid., 72.

39. Ibid., 102.

40. Quoted in Alexandra Richie, *Faust's Metropolis: A History of Berlin* (New York: Carroll and Graf, 1998), 68.

41. Quoted in C. B. A. Behrens, *Society, Government and the Enlightenment* (New York: Harper and Row, 1985), 185.

42. Jonathan Israel, *Enlightenment Contested* (New York: Oxford University Press, 2006), 800.

43. Ibid., 805.
44. Peter Gay, *The Enlightenment: The Science of Freedom* (New York: W. W. Norton, 1969), 244.
45. Richie, *Faust's Metropolis*, 72.
46. Quoted in Behrens, *Society, Government and the Enlightenment*, 176.
47. The one reference Boswell makes to Berlin's Jews in his journals does not cast him in a kind light. Echoing the dismal stereotypes of his age, he wrote: "I was well jaded. I had a Jew and many other blackguards with me" (Boswell, *James Boswell*, 60).
48. Ibid., 28.
49. Ibid., 35.
50. Behrens, *Society, Government and the Enlightenment*, 180.
51. Pottle, *James Boswell*, 152.
52. Ibid.
53. Boswell, *James Boswell*, 116.

8. The Distance between Môtiers and Ferney

1. Jean-Jacques Rousseau, *Discourse on the Sciences and Arts*, in *The Major Political Writings of Jean-Jacques Rousseau*, trans. and ed. John Scott (Chicago: University of Chicago Press, 2012), 13.
2. Ibid., 88.
3. Ibid., 96.
4. Ibid., 101.
5. James Boswell, *James Boswell: The Journal of His German and Swiss Travels, 1764*, ed. Marlies Danziger (New Haven: Yale University Press, 2008), 174.
6. Ibid., 177.
7. Quoted in Leo Damrosch, *Jean-Jacques Rousseau* (New York: Houghton Mifflin, 2005), 393.
8. Robert Wokler, *Rousseau, the Age of the Enlightenment and Their Legacies* (Princeton: Princeton University Press, 2012), 80.
9. Roger Pearson, *Voltaire Almighty: A Life in Pursuit of Freedom* (London: Bloomsbury, 2005), 293.
10. Maurice Cranston, *The Noble Savage: Jean-Jacques Rousseau, 1712–1754* (Chicago: University of Chicago Press, 1991), 222.
11. Wokler, *Rousseau*, 81.

12. John Leigh, "Voltaire and the Myth of England," in *The Cambridge Companion to Voltaire*, ed. Nicholas Cronk (Cambridge: Cambridge University Press, 2009), 80.

13. Ibid., 83.

14. Robert Zaretsky and John Scott, *The Philosophers' Quarrel: Rousseau, Hume, and the Limits of Human Understanding* (New Haven: Yale University Press, 2009), 60.

15. The Voltaire Foundation is currently engaged in the Herculean effort to publish the entirety of Voltaire's corpus.

16. Pearson, *Voltaire Almighty*, 99.

17. Maurice Cranston, *Jean-Jacques: The Early Life and Work of Jean-Jacques Rousseau, 1712–1754* (Chicago: University of Chicago Press, 1982), 128.

18. Ibid., 202.

19. Pearson, *Voltaire Almighty*, 217.

20. Ibid., 222–223.

21. Jean Orieux, *Voltaire* (Paris: Flammarion, 1966), 210.

22. Quoted in Zaretsky and Scott, *Philosophers' Quarrel*, 26.

23. Ibid., 57.

24. Susan Neiman, *Evil in Modern Thought* (Princeton: Princeton University Press, 2002), 1.

25. Jonathan Israel, *Democratic Enlightenment: Philosophy, Revolution, and Human Rights 1750–1790* (Oxford: Oxford University Press, 2011), 54.

26. Voltaire, "Poem on the Lisbon Disaster," in *Toleration and Other Essays*, trans. Joseph McCabe (New York: G. P. Putnam's Sons, 1912).

27. Jean-Jacques Rousseau, *Correspondence complète*, ed. Ralph Leigh (Geneva: Voltaire Foundation, 1965–1995), 4:1060.

28. Jean-Jacques Rousseau, *The Reveries of the Solitary Walker*, trans. Charles Butterworth (Indianapolis: Hackett, 1992), 68.

29. John Scott, "Pride and Prejudice: Rousseau's Dialogue with Voltaire in the Lettre à Voltaire sur la providence," in *Rousseau and l'infâme*, ed. Ourida Mostefai and John Scott (New York: Rodopi, 2009).

30. Rousseau, *Correspondence complète*, 4:40.

31. Peter Gay, *The Enlightenment: The Rise of Modern Paganism* (New York: Norton, 1966), 435.

32. Pearson, *Voltaire Almighty*, 287.

33. See ibid., 301–303.
34. Peter Gay, *Voltaire's Politics: The Poet as Realist* (New Haven: Yale University Press, 1988), 278.
35. Pearson, *Voltaire Almighty*, 301.
36. James Boswell, *The Life of Samuel Johnson*, ed. David Womersley (New York: Penguin, 2008), 266.
37. Gavin de Beer and André-Michel Rousseau, "Voltaire's British Visitors," *Studies in Voltaire and the Eighteenth Century* 49 (1967): 99.
38. Ibid., 99–100.
39. Boswell, *James Boswell*, 309.
40. Ibid., 323.
41. Pearson, *Voltaire Almighty*, 274.
42. Ibid., 275.
43. Boswell, *James Boswell*, 309.
44. James Boswell, *Correspondence of James Boswell and William Johnson Temple, 1756–1795*, ed. Thomas Crawford (New Haven: Yale University Press, 1997), 124.
45. Boswell, *James Boswell*, 309.
46. Boswell, *Correspondence*, 124.
47. Ibid.
48. Ibid.
49. Boswell, *James Boswell*, 317.
50. Ibid., 318.
51. Boswell, *Correspondence*, 124.
52. Ibid.
53. Ibid., 124–125.
54. Ibid., 125.
55. See Zaretsky and Scott, *Philosophers' Quarrel*, 67–71.
56. See Frederick Pottle, *James Boswell: The Earlier Years, 1740–1769* (New York: McGraw-Hill, 1966), 190–191.
57. Voltaire, *Philosophical Dictionary* (New York: Carleton House, 1955), 286.
58. Pottle, *James Boswell*, 210.

9. On Libertines and Liberty

1. James Boswell, *The Life of Samuel Johnson*, ed. David Womersley (New York: Penguin, 2008), 537.

2. Edward Gibbon, *Memoirs of My Life* (New York: Funk & Wagnalls, 1969), 151.

3. James Boswell, *Boswell on the Grand Tour: Italy, Corsica, and France*, ed. Frank Brady and Frederick Pottle (New York: McGraw-Hill, 1955), 24.

4. Ibid., 40.

5. Quoted in Frederick Pottle, *James Boswell: The Earlier Years, 1740–1769* (New York: McGraw-Hill, 1966), 201.

6. Boswell, *Boswell on the Grand Tour*, 38.

7. Ibid., 30.

8. Ibid., 38.

9. Ibid., 4.

10. Ibid., 37 and 34.

11. Ibid., 41.

12. Ibid., 46.

13. Ibid., 47.

14. Ibid.

15. James Boswell, *London Journal 1762–1763*, ed. Frederick Pottle (New Haven: Yale University Press, 1950), 227–228.

16. Christopher Hibbert, *George III* (New York: Basic Books, 1998), 115.

17. Boswell, *London Journal*, 250.

18. Arthur Cash, *John Wilkes: The Scandalous Father of Civil Liberty* (New Haven: Yale University Press, 2006), 32.

19. Ibid., 1.

20. Boswell, *Life of Samuel Johnson*, 622.

21. Quoted in Robert Zaretsky and John Scott, *The Philosophers' Quarrel: Rousseau, Hume, and the Limits of Human Understanding* (New Haven: Yale University Press, 2009), 82.

22. Boswell, *on the Grand Tour*, 25.

23. Ibid., 27.

24. Ibid., 50.

25. Ibid., 51.

26. Ibid.

27. Edward Gibbon, *The Autobiography of Edward Gibbon* (London: Murray and Son, 1869), 79.

28. Boswell, *Boswell on the Grand Tour*, 53.

29. Ibid.

30. Ibid., 55.

31. Cash, *John Wilkes*, 186.

32. Boswell, *Boswell on the Grand Tour,* 57.
33. Ibid., 56–57. I have, at times, fleshed out Boswell's reports, which are short and sometimes cryptic in the memoranda.
34. Ibid., 54.
35. Ibid., 57.
36. James Boswell, *Correspondence of James Boswell and John Johnston of Grange,* ed. Ralph Walker (London: Heinemann, 1966), 160.
37. Boswell, *Boswell on the Grand Tour,* 73.
38. Quoted in Cash, *John Wilkes,* 314.
39. Quoted in ibid., 386.
40. James Boswell, *Boswell in Extremes: 1776–1778,* ed. Charles Weis and Frederick Pottle (New Haven: Yale University Press, 1970), 226.
41. Quoted in Pottle, *James Boswell,* 208.
42. Boswell, *Boswell on the Grand Tour,* 75.
43. Ibid., 96.
44. James Boswell, *Correspondence of James Boswell and William Johnson Temple, 1756–1795,* ed. Thomas Crawford (New Haven: Yale University Press, 1997), 1:133.
45. Boswell, *Boswell on the Grand Tour,* 5.
46. Ibid., 81.
47. Ibid., 62.
48. Boswell, *Correspondence of James Boswell and William Temple,* 1:133.
49. Ibid.
50. Quoted in Jeremy Black, *The British Abroad: The Grand Tour in the Eighteenth Century* (New York: St. Martin's Press, 1992), 241.
51. Boswell, *Boswell on the Grand Tour,* 65.
52. Ibid., 64.
53. Ibid., 71.
54. Ibid., 88.
55. Ibid., 105.
56. Ibid., 112–113.
57. Ibid., 313.
58. Jean-Jacques Rousseau, *The Social Contract,* in *The Major Political Writings of Jean-Jacques Rousseau,* trans. John Scott (Chicago: University of Chicago Press, 2012), 199.
59. James Boswell, *James Boswell: The Journal of His German and Swiss Travels, 1764,* ed. Marlies Danziger (New Haven: Yale University Press, 2008), 290.

60. James Boswell, *James Boswell: An Account of Corsica and The Journal of a Tour to that Island*, ed. James Boulton and T. O. McLoughlin (New York: Oxford University Press, 2006), 10.

61. Ibid., 6.

62. Ibid., xviii.

63. Linda Colley, *Britons: Forging the Nation 1707–1837* (New Haven: Yale University Press, 2009), 11.

64. Boswell, *James Boswell: An Account of Corsica*, 161.

65. Boswell, *Boswell on the Grand Tour*, 97.

66. For the standard biography in English, see Peter Thrasher, *Pasquale Paoli: An Enlightened Hero, 1725–1807* (Hampden, CT: Archon Books, 1970).

67. Boswell, *James Boswell: An Account of Corsica*, 165.

68. Ibid.

69. Ibid., 166.

70. Ibid., 167.

71. Ibid., 173.

72. Ibid., 172.

73. Ibid., 174.

74. Ibid., 175.

75. Ibid., 176.

76. Ibid., 193.

77. Ibid., 180.

78. Ibid., 177. Boswell translated the line as "Love of the native land will prevail and the immeasurable desire for peace," but I have instead used Robert Fagles's translation for reasons of clarity. See Virgil, *The Aeneid*, trans. Robert Fagles (New York: Viking, 2006), 209.

79. Boswell, *James Boswell: An Account of Corsica*, 178.

80. Ibid.

81. Ibid., 177.

82. Ibid., 203.

83. Ibid., 192.

84. Ibid.

85. Ibid., 204.

86. Boswell, *James Boswell: An Account of Corsica*, 14.

10. After Corsica, before Futurity

1. James Boswell, *Boswell on the Grand Tour: Italy, Corsica, and France,* ed. Frank Brady and Frederick Pottle (New York: McGraw-Hill, 1955), 240.
2. Ibid., 261.
3. Ibid., 241.
4. Ibid.
5. Ibid., 260.
6. Ibid., 266.
7. Peter Martin, *A Life of James Boswell* (New Haven: Yale University Press, 2000), 368.
8. Boswell, *Boswell on the Grand Tour,* 270.
9. Ibid., 269.
10. Arthur Cash, *John Wilkes: The Scandalous Father of Civil Liberty* (New Haven: Yale University Press, 2006), 191.
11. Boswell, *Boswell on the Grand Tour,* 269.
12. Ibid.
13. Ibid., 272.
14. Ibid., 275.
15. Ibid., 276.
16. James Boswell, *The Life of Samuel Johnson,* ed. David Womersley (New York: Penguin, 2008), 352–353.
17. Boswell, *Boswell on the Grand Tour,* 277.
18. David Hume, *Letters of David Hume,* ed. J. Y. T. Grieg (Oxford: Oxford University Press, 1932), 2:11.
19. Boswell, *Boswell on the Grand Tour,* 279. Boswell's heirs ripped from the journal several pages devoted to his ten-day adventure with Thérèse, but not before his first editor, Colonel Isham, read them. It is his summary we are dependent on.
20. Ibid., 281.
21. Boswell, *Life of Samuel Johnson,* 263.
22. Boswell, *Boswell on the Grand Tour,* 281.
23. Quoted in Frederick Pottle, *James Boswell: The Earlier Years, 1740–1769* (New York: McGraw-Hill, 1966), 282.
24. Boswell, *Life of Samuel Johnson,* 266.
25. Ibid., 267.
26. Boswell, *Boswell on the Grand Tour,* 283.

27. James Boswell, *James Boswell: An Account of Corsica and The Journal of a Tour to that Island,* ed. James Boulton and T. O. McLoughlin (New York: Oxford University Press, 2006), 189.

28. Boswell, *Life of Samuel Johnson,* 716.

29. Boswell, *Boswell on the Grand Tour,* 295.

30. Boswell, *James Boswell: An Account of Corsica,* 219.

31. Boswell, *Life of Samuel Johnson,* 293.

32. Ibid., 262.

33. Boswell, *James Boswell: An Account of Corsica,* 18.

34. Quoted in Pottle, *James Boswell,* 425.

35. Ibid., 428.

36. Boswell, *Life of Samuel Johnson,* 303.

37. Ibid., 302–303.

38. Ibid., 7.

39. Adam Sisman, *Boswell's Presumptuous Task: The Making of the Life of Dr. Johnson* (New York: Penguin, 2000), 57.

40. Boswell, *Boswell on the Grand Tour,* 76.

41. Quoted in Martin, *A Life of James Boswell,* 327.

42. James Boswell, *Correspondence of James Boswell and William Johnson Temple, 1756–1795,* ed. Thomas Crawford (New Haven: Yale University Press, 1997), 394.

43. Martin, *Life of James Boswell,* 421.

44. Ibid., 431.

45. Ibid., 382.

46. Ibid., 384.

47. Ibid., 378.

48. Boswell, *Correspondence,* 418–419.

49. E. C. Mossner, *The Life of David Hume* (Oxford: Oxford University Press, 1980), 599.

50. Ibid., 597.

51. All quotations taken from Boswell's "An Account of My Last Interview with David Hume, ESQ," in *Boswell in Extremes, 1776–1778,* ed. Charles Weis and Frederick A. Pottle (New York: McGraw-Hill, 1986), 11–15.

52. Mossner, *Life of David Hume,* 603.

53. Boswell, *Life of Samuel Johnson,* 605.

54. James Boswell, *The Hypochondriack,* ed. Margery Bailey (Palo Alto: Stanford University Press, 1928), 1:108–109.

55. Only one topic received four essays: drinking. Yet Boswell's alcoholism became a serious, at times crippling problem only after his return from the continent.
56. Ibid., 1:203.
57. Ibid., 1:201 (italics in original).
58. Ibid., 1:210.
59. Pottle, *James Boswell*, 89.
60. Martin, *A Life of James Boswell*, 166.

ACKNOWLEDGMENTS

Without the help of several people—friends, family, colleagues, and a few strangers—I could never have written this book. I wish to thank my editor and friend, John Kulka, for his intelligence, insight, and inspiration; his assistant at Harvard University Press, Heather Hughes, for her great patience and good cheer; and copyeditor Paul Vincent and production editor Melody Negron for their superb work. My thanks, as well, to Jennifer Johnston for her careful work on the text and index. I am grateful to Karen Valihora at York University as well as my three anonymous readers for their careful readings and critiques. William Monroe, Dean of the Honors College at the University of Houston, generously invited me to teach a summer course on Boswell's work, and the enthusiastic engagement of the students in that small class was a great boon. My love and thanks to my wonderful family—Julie, Louisa, and Ruben—who put up with my attention to Bozzy longer than any husband and father should rightly expect. Finally, my particular thanks to my friend John Scott: my debt to him is greater than he suspects.

INDEX

″ ″ 15
23
27
44–45 – law
49 Boswell on Boswell
83–84 – early J+B relationship
86 – what made J. different
134 neology
139 B's self-definition